D0227194

TACiTUS

TACITUS

RONALD MELLOR

Routledge
Taylor & Francis Group

NEW YORK AND LONDON

Published in 1993

Paperback edition published in 1994 by

Routledge
270 Madison Ave,
New York NY 10016

Published in Great Britain by

Routledge
2 Park Square, Milton Park,
Abingdon, Oxon, OX14 4RN

Transferred to Digital Printing 2009

Copyright © 1993 by Routledge

All rights reserved. No part of this book may be reprinted or reproduced
or utilized in any form or by any electronic, mechanical or other means,
now known or hereafter invented, including photocopying and
recording, or in any information storage or retrieval system, without
permission in writing from the publisher.

Library of Congress Cataloging-in-Publication Data

Mellor, Ronald.
Tacitus / Ronald Mellor.
p.   cm.
Includes bibliographical references and indexes.
ISBN 0-415-90665-2 (hb)—ISBN 0-415-91002-1 (pb)
1. Tacitus, Cornelius.   2. Rome—Histography.   I. Title.
[DG206.T32M45 1994]
937'.07'092—dc20   94-28753
                                                                CIP

British Library Cataloguing-in-Publication Data also available.

Publisher's Note

The publisher has gone to great lengths to ensure the quality of this reprint
but points out that some imperfections in the original may be apparent.

For Eleanor Mellor

and Blake Mellor

Think of your ancestors and your descendants.

Tacitus, *Agricola* 32

Contents

Preface

A few years ago, when I realized that I had been reading and talking about Tacitus for half my lifetime, it seemed time to commit some of those words to the printed page. As boy and man, with teachers, students, colleagues, my conversations about Tacitus have never been boring—at least to me. An animated discussion about Tacitus with Brooks Otis in the New York Port Authority bus terminal coffee shop got me my first academic position. In the late 1960s, the largest and most enthusiastic Latin courses I have ever taught found Tacitus to be a commentary on the lies and political doublespeak of the Vietnam era. No one needed to make Tacitus "relevant" to those Stanford students; his searing indictment of the political manipulation of language so impressed them that a cautious teacher had to point out the complexity and ambivalence of his political stance. For decades Tacitus has also engaged my ancient history students; even in translation, the historian's ironic temper and his moral and political ideas have tremendous appeal in the late twentieth century.

That appeal is unfortunately still largely unknown; even professional modern historians and political scientists know little (and have read less) of this seminal figure in the shaping of modern political attitudes. I came to the obvious conclusion that it was time to present Tacitus to non-specialist readers. Still, it is one thing to talk and teach, quite another to write. There one's ideas must confront the accumulated weight of classical scholarship which can transform the keenest enthusiasm into a beaver-like hunt through bibliographies and the drudgery of checking references. The scholarly baggage on Tacitus is truly massive. For four centuries, commentators have explained and assaulted his texts and, on the basis of recent bibliographies, I estimate that scholars have published over five thousand items on Tacitus in the past fifty years alone. The pace is accelerating. Just in the past two years, an encyclopedic collection of volumes on Roman civilization includes three thousand pages of articles on Tacitus! Scholarly writers have clearly outstripped scholarly readers; one can read only a small fraction of what is published each year. The volume and density of all this material induces timidity; it prompts prudent scholars to write carefully crafted papers on narrow topics.

My own goal was, and is, less prudent: to convey why Tacitus's histories exercised a powerful fascination over centuries of dramatists, philosophers, and even politicians. Through his histories of Tiberius, Claudius, and Nero, Tacitus provides a compelling political and moral vision, but one which has too often been lost amid the apparatus of scholarship. Therefore I have kept the documentation sparse; the footnotes are intended only to point the reader toward fuller discussions of a topic. I have rarely bothered to signal disagreements with other scholars, and have usually preferred to cite quite recent discussions which provide greater bibliographical assistance. Some references may mask profound debts. The greatest single influence on nearly all contemporary Tacitean scholarship is Sir Ronald Syme's two-volume *Tacitus* (1958); I could have cited it dozens of times. The translations are my own, though I have borrowed freely from those of others.

Research has been aided by sabbaticals from U.C.L.A. and supported by grants from the U.C.L.A. Academic Senate. Much work was done, appropriately enough, in Rome in the pleasant confines of the American Academy, whose librarian Lucilla Marini and her staff were, as always, kind and efficient. I revised the manuscript while a Visiting Fellow of the Humanities Research Centre of the Australian National University in Canberra. Not, perhaps a very Tacitean venue, but the directors Graeme Clarke and Ian Donaldson made the Centre a wonderful place to work. Michael Grant, John Herington, T.J. Luce, J.P. Sullivan, and Tony Woodman read the entire manuscript and I am grateful for their criticisms, suggestions, and encouragement; Carlo Ginzburg's comments on the final chapter were enormously helpful; and my former student Brent Maddox of the J. Paul Getty Center and Elizabeth McGrath of the Warburg Institute kindly helped track down seventeenth- and eighteenth-century images of Tacitus. Gregory Dundas kindly prepared the index. In 1990 I attended the excellent Princeton conference on *Tacitus and the Tacitean Tra-*

dition; I am grateful to the organizers Jim Luce and Tony Wood-man for the opportunity to see in manuscript (and thus cite) their edited volume of the papers delivered on that occasion. My wife Anne Mellor did yeo(wo)man service in bringing an English professor's expert editorial eye to an early draft; her love and support often gave me strength to continue with the book. I am enormously grateful for both.

For Tacitus, history is ever present; the past shapes the present and both will determine the future. Thus it seems appropriate to dedicate this book with love and admiration to my only surviving ancestor and my only descendant, my mother and my son.

Los Angeles   R.M.
March 1992

Chronological Note

Nearly all the dates in the book are from the period of Tacitus's histories: the first century of the Christian (or Common) era. I have therefore only specified those dates which occurred before the Christian era (B.C.).

EMPERORS OF THE FIRST CENTURY

Julio-Claudian Emperors

Augustus (27 B.C.–14)—Octavian, the heir of Julius Caesar, defeated Marc Antony at Actium in 31 B.C. and was in 27 B.C. proclaimed "Augustus" and "Princeps."

Tiberius (14–37)—Ti. Claudius Nero succeeded at the age of 55 on the death of his stepfather, Augustus.

Caligula (37–41)—Gaius, great-grandson of both Augustus and Marc Antony, succeeded at the age of 25 his great-uncle, Tiberius. "Caligula" was a childhood nickname.

Claudius (41–54)—Claudius, nephew of Tiberius and uncle of Gaius, was so sickly and peculiar as a youth that Augustus and Tiberius passed him over for high office. After the murder of Gaius, the praetorians (who wished to preserve the dynasty) proclaimed him emperor at the age of 50.

Nero (54–68)—A descendant of both Augustus and Antony, Nero was adopted by his stepfather (and great-uncle) Claudius and succeeded at the age of 16. After his legions and even the praetorians revolted, Nero committed suicide and ended the Julio-Claudian era.

Civil War of 69

GALBA (68–69), OTHO (69), and VITELLIUS (69) all briefly held the imperial throne before the victory of VESPASIAN.

Flavian Emperors

Vespasian   (69–79)—An Italian from an equestrian family, T. Flavius Vespasianus commanded the Roman troops in Judaea when he was acclaimed emperor at the age of 60.

Titus   (79–81)—Vespasian's popular son came to the throne at the age of 40. He soon died of natural causes.

Domitian   (81–96)—Vespasian's younger son came to the throne at the age of 29 on the death of his brother. His wife and the praetorian prefects joined to assassinate him.

The "Good Emperors"

Nerva   (96–98)—A respected and trusted senator, Nerva came to the throne at 66 and soon adopted a popular and experienced general, Trajan, as his heir and successor.

Trajan   (98–117)—Born in Spain of the Roman governor and a Spanish mother, Trajan ushered in a golden age of tolerance and effective administration.

*Tacitus I consider the first writer in the
world without a single exception. His
book is a compound of history and
morality of which we have no other
example.*

THOMAS JEFFERSON
*to his granddaughter**

I

Introduction

Almost nineteen hundred years ago the Roman senator Cornelius
Tacitus radically transformed himself from a successful politician
to a great, and enduring, historical genius. His monographs and
historical narratives constitute a powerful indictment of the Roman Empire, suffused with that passion and pervasive partisanship that politicians, fresh from the fray of public life, bring to
their books. A deeply engaged public man, Tacitus saw his work
as a continuation of his political life and, like Cicero, he believed

* Letter of December 8, 1808 to Anne Cary Bankhead, in *The Writings of
Thomas Jefferson*, ed. A. Lipscomb (Washington, 1905) xviii 255.

that history should be both useful and moral; the historian was both a teacher and a judge.

Centuries earlier Thucydides used the present as a guide to the future, and serious historians followed this example. The past determines the present and, unless the historian intervenes, the present will shape the future. All historians hope to teach how to avoid the errors of the past, and many even believe that history has predictive power. Similar aspirations motivate our most thoughtful political commentators who put Tiananmen Square, the fall of the Berlin Wall, or the breakup of the Soviet Union into an historical context and try to provide policy guidance for the future. Tacitus goes further; he attempts to control the present by the threat of the future:

> I consider it the chief function of history to ensure that virtue be remembered, and to terrify evil words and deeds with a fear of posterity's damnation.[1]

Tyrants may control the present, but they cannot determine how future generations will view them. The future is where historians exercise power, and Tacitus revels in it.

Tacitus is far from the dispassionate Herodotean witness who observes, queries, and records; he is rather an all-powerful, relentless judge who adjudicates morality and politics: "to distinguish right and wrong, the useful and the dangerous."[2] Romans regarded as impractical the detachment so prized by Greek thinkers; theirs is a subjective, confessional literature that culminates in the greatest of that genre, Augustine's *Confessions*. Tacitus consciously and unconsciously reconstitutes the past through a confessional history, recounting past events as though they impinged on his own life and, in his mind, they did. His emotional engagement with his material is paramount; as so often in Roman writing, the mind follows the heart. It is pointless to yearn for a chimerical "objective" history that Tacitus with his intellectual gifts might have written if he were not burdened with his personal anger and profound frustration; his hatred drove him to the archives, focused his mind and sharpened his pen.[3] We must be grateful that it burned so long and so deeply.

Modern scholarship has a more comprehensive view of the early

Roman Empire based on a wider range of source material and it examines the importance of different social classes, of provincials, of everyday life, and of Jews, Christians, and other religious groups—topics which Tacitus scorned or merely ignored.[4] Tacitus is invaluable as a source, a mine of information for the exacting task of historical reconstruction, but he would seem to have been superseded by more recent and more scholarly histories. Why should anyone but a professional Roman historian bother to read Tacitus today?

Our European and American forebears from the Renaissance through the American and French Revolutions accorded Tacitus a central role in shaping the Western intellectual tradition. They regarded his historical writings as the most probing discussion of public morality and the most self-conscious political texts written in ancient Rome—Rome, which had shaped political thought in the Italian communes and in the new Republics of the eighteenth century. Tacitus was a student of both the social contract and the human psyche, and he recognized the need to understand the relation of the individual to society.[5] It was a combination unique in ancient historical writing but later fruitfully linked by modern novelists and twentieth-century historians. His political acumen was admired by Montaigne and Gibbon, his psychological analysis imitated by Stendhal, and his moral instruction ranked above all other by Francis Bacon.[6] Tacitus was once the most politically and morally influential of all ancient historians.

Yet today Tacitus is ignored by most readers of history. His denseness of detail, the unremitting bleakness of his vision, and his seeming resistance to general theorizing make his work seem less immediately appealing than the anthropology of Herodotus or the compelling political philosophy of Thucydides. Though there is a uniformity of tone (dark) and attitude (pessimistic), Tacitus does not seem to offer a coherent theory of history and his own obvious passion undermines any claim to objectivity in our modern sense. When nineteenth-century scholars developed a scientistic, Comtean conception of truth, and a professional, academic approach to history, they swept aside earlier historians who could not meet this standard: Herodotus became the "Father of Lies" instead of the Father of History (though he was later rescued as the Father of Anthropology); Livy was too gullible and Tacitus too biased. Tacitus remained interesting merely as a literary stylist unworthy of serious consideration as an historical thinker. Distinguished scholars called him "hateful" and "a slanderer"—echoing the bitter judgment of Napoleon a century earlier.[7]

In that optimistic age imbued with the glorious image of human progress, Tacitus's bitter and ironic appraisal of man's political and moral fate in the greatest age of the Roman Empire marked him as an historian of the dark side of human nature in an era which wished to deny its existence. When he sought to understand the wise actions of his nemesis Tiberius, he explained them through the emperor's hypocrisy.[8] His nature led him to resolve contradictions by assuming the worst. Tacitus was a pessimist, one of the great pessimists in the Western tradition. He understood the inevitability of human suffering and the unlikelihood that virtue would prevail. But victory is not the sole outcome of a battle; even the defeated may retain their honor and achieve eternal glory. The Britons defeated by Agricola, like Vergil's Trojans and Italians, earn praise even in failure. It is with a Vergilian melancholy that Tacitus tells his story of the senatorial order doomed to defeat by lesser men. It is best not to hold out false hope. *Sunt lacrimae rerum*, as Vergil said: "There is pain in human affairs;"[9] the wise do not deny or bewail such truth but rather try to salvage honor and dignity from their pain. At his best Tacitus elevates mere pessimism to an intellectual grandeur that led Gibbon to call him the "most philosophical of historians." And though he often seems near despair, he was in fact sustained by the very real hope that the wicked would be punished—by history and the historians who construct it. In George Orwell's novel *1984*, the "Ministry of Truth" cast inconvenient histories into a "memory hole" for destruction; by the actual year 1984, official statements were merely declared "inoperative."[10] Tacitus understood the historian's paramount duty to preserve memory. Our own century has also turned to history to give meaning to man's ultimate inhumanity: to historicize genocide. We can think of Alexander Solzhenitsyn in the gulag, the historians of African enslavement and of the Holocaust. Tacitus is their precursor.

Recent decades have seen a revival of scholarly interest in Tacitus—Tacitus's pessimistic vision of man's capacity for evil has, especially since 1945, again found a sympathetic audience, and we are more sophisticated about the bias inherent in all historians. Proclamations of "Objective" history are distrusted, while literary and historical theorists have begun to analyze the ambiguities inherent in historical composition. If every narrative demands a moral point of view, positivist objects to Tacitean bias must fade in the face of our broader conception of the historian's task.[11] Much has been written on his life, his sources, his style, the structure of his books, and their accuracy. But this lively scholarly dialogue has rarely penetrated beyond the professional cloister. Yet Tacitus provides early and influential analyses of issues that remain high on our intellectual agenda: political paranoia, freedom of speech, and the corruption of power. His treatments have often defined (usually through intermediaries) the terms of subsequent discussions. There is much in Tacitus to instruct and move and even, in the perverse way of tragedy, to delight—if only we read him. My purpose in this book is to inspire and guide that reading.

*Tacitus summarized everything
because he saw everything.*
MONTESQUIEU*

II

The Historian and His Histories

Life and Career

It was probably soon after the accession of Nero in 54 that Cornelius Tacitus was born into a prominent family of southern Gaul—an area by then so romanized that a contemporary thought it to be "more truly Italy than a province."[1] His father, who seems to have served as a financial official in northern Gaul about the same time, was an equestrian, a member of the administrative class so important in the running of the Empire, but still a large social

* *The Spirit of the Laws*, Book 30, Chapter 2.

step below the senatorial order.[2] After the Civil War of 69, the Emperor Vespasian (69–79) enrolled many more Spaniards and Gauls in the Senate; provincials were streaming into the capital to guide the destiny of the Empire.[3] Thus, having observed the excesses of the Neronian court and the terrible traumas of civil war, the young Gaul began his ascent to high office. Tacitus would reach the Senate and the highest offices of the state, but he retained a pride in his origins among the virtuous and old-fashioned provincial elite when he excoriated the degenerate nobles of Julio-Claudian Rome. He likewise idealized his father-in-law, the Gallic senator Julius Agricola, as possessed of a genuine nobility no longer found in the capital itself.[4] At the same time, Tacitus's rise in social status was accompanied, as it has so often been in other societies, by a snobbish contempt for his perceived social inferiors: easterners, freedmen, and the Roman masses.[5]

Our information about Tacitus, like our information on so many other ancient writers, derives chiefly from his own books, especially his biography of Agricola. His other works provide scattered autobiographical details and the letters of his friend Pliny give a glimpse into their shared activities in the early years of the second century. Still, our evidence remains so slight that we do not know for certain Tacitus's first name (Gaius or Publius) or more than the approximate dates of his birth and death.

During his adolescence, while the Roman world was convulsed in civil war, Tacitus tells us he passionately pursued the traditional study of rhetoric and eagerly attached himself to the retinue of leading orators in court, on the streets, and even in their houses.[6] He regarded rhetorical training not merely as a bag of oratorical tricks but as the acquisition of a profound literary culture, and he became a remarkably gifted orator. One can well imagine the biting wit and sarcastic irony that he brought into the courts. There the young provincial first came to public notice, and his marriage to the daughter of Agricola in 77 furthered his rapid advancement. He attributes his first public honors to Vespasian who died in 79 when Tacitus was about 23, and in the brief reign of Titus he was elected quaestor, which brought him membership in the Senate.[7] Domitian made Tacitus praetor and admitted him to one of the elite priestly colleges. Now competition for advancement became more severe, since only half the praetors were appointed to a three-year term as legionary commander. From 89 to 93 Tacitus probably commanded a provincial legion, perhaps in Asia[8]— apparently Agricola's supposed disfavor at court did him little harm. We know nothing of Tacitus for the three years of Domitian's terror (93–96), but he survived to reach the consulship, Rome's highest office, in 97, perhaps even nominated by Domitian before his assassination.

It was an extraordinary career for a young Gallo-Roman of equestrian background, but more extraordinary is Tacitus's claim that fifteen years were blotted out of his life by the tyranny of Domitian.[9] He had served Domitian loyally and been rewarded generously, yet the scars of those years inform all his writing. We cannot tell whether he felt the guilt of an unwilling collaborator, or merely the shame of a survivor—both are all too familiar in our own century where even the survivors of Nazi death camps or of Vietnam can carry a terrible burden of shame. While we will never know what Tacitus actually did under Domitian, we cannot doubt the personal agony which he suffered. After the relatively benevolent reign of Vespasian, whose sporadic persecution of recalcitrant philosophers and despised astrologers was unlikely to displease Tacitus excessively, Domitian revived imperial tyranny and the prohibition of free speech. For Tacitus, Domitian was a microcosm of the century of Empire, and his own relation to Domitian becomes the model for the relations of the Senate with the emperors since the accession of Augustus: collaboration, resentment, hatred. Through his devastating portrait of Tiberius, Tacitus attempts to exorcize his own guilt. He hates tyrants, but he also condemns the ostentatious deaths of self-proclaimed martyrs who do the state no good. He gropes toward the vindication of a middle path, which he calls *moderatio,* the path followed by his hero Agricola and, Tacitus would like to pretend, by himself. (Even that "best of emperors" Trajan was publicly praised for *moderatio* by Pliny.[10]) But the historian is too intelligent and finally too honest not to recognize the terrible truth of the senators' complicity:

> Soon our hands dragged Helvidius to prison; the reproachful
> looks of Mauricus and Rusticus shamed us and we were
> stained with Senecio's innocent blood.[11]

Cowardice and complicity followed by guilt, rage, and self-justification; not an unfamiliar story but in its candor a very human one. For Tacitus himself teaches that the failure to take responsibility for one's mistakes or to feel guilty for one's crimes is the most terrible of human traits, and he here takes the collective guilt of the senatorial class on his shoulders. As we see him in his writings, Tacitus is evasive, ambiguous, tortured, obsessed, and defensive—not unlike his nemesis Tiberius with whom he perhaps had a certain affinity.[12]

On the death of Domitian in 96, the elderly, childless, senator Nerva ruled for two years and adopted the general Trajan (98–117) as his successor. Tacitus surely was alluding to this new precedent when he records the elderly emperor Galba speaking in 69 in favor of legitimate power and adoption as opposed to the despotism and hereditary rule of Caligula and Nero.[13] Galba's choice of Piso did not save him, nor did it keep Rome from civil war, but Nerva was shrewder or more fortunate. There must have been dangerous moments, both for Nerva himself and for the Roman state, in the anxious months of 96 and 97 though we know little of those intrigues. The historian's praise of Nerva for having brought freedom into the principate[14] shows his initial approval of the new era which Gibbon celebrated as mankind's happiest age. As consul in 97, Tacitus gave the funeral eulogy for the revered ex-consul Verginius Rufus and a few years later he and Pliny garnered praise for jointly prosecuting the former governor of Africa for corruption.[15] Perhaps it was prudence that led Tacitus, who once promised to continue his Flavian history to the reigns of Nerva and Trajan, to turn instead to the Julio-Claudians.[16] He surly understood that, behind the benevolent facade of the new regime, Trajan's power was no less absolute than that of Tiberius or Nero. His public career continued to be successful; he was awarded the prestigious governorship of Asia in 112.[17] The historian probably died about 117.[18]

Tacitus the Historian

The orator and senator first turned to history as an escape from the terrible last years of Domitian. He saw that oratory was inevitably corrupted under tyranny and, like Polybius, he believed that history should be written by experienced politicians. Tacitus certainly had the necessary qualifications as a historian: psychological insight, political acumen, access to sources, a command of a supple and subtle style, and a wide literary culture. In ancient Rome, as in our own day, history (or "memoirs") could be the vehicle for the rage and bitter wit of disappointed politicians who sought to continue their public life through their writings. In the two decades after his consulship, Tacitus produced five books which demonstrate his increasing historical sophistication and stylistic virtuosity. Despite his seeming traditionalism, his body of work shows Tacitus to be the most experimental and adventurous of all ancient historians.

LIFE OF JULIUS AGRICOLA

In 98 Tacitus published a brief, admiring biography of his father-in-law Cn. Julius Agricola, long-time governor of Britain and one of the most successful generals of the Flavian era. It had long been traditional for Roman aristocrats to deliver at the death of a distinguished relative a public speech (*laudatio*) which glorified the entire family through the deeds of their ancestors and praised the public achievements and the private character of the deceased. In the Empire such tributes necessarily had a political edge, and Tacitus tells us that the published eulogies of the victims of Nero and the Flavians

> were capital crimes, and cruel punishment fell not only on the authors but even on their books. The public executioners had the task of burning in the Forum those tributes to our noblest philosophers.[19]

Under tyranny, praise of virtue is itself subversive, and it was only the murder of Domitian in 96 that allowed Tacitus to pay proper respect to Agricola. The *Agricola* begins and ends as a eulogy, and it is a sincere and moving one. But it is much more; in 98 any eulogy for a public man such as Agricola must be deeply political, and Tacitus does not disappoint us.[20]

The *Agricola* is a far more ambitious book than might at first appear. It has sometimes baffled scholars since it goes well beyond the usual contents of an ancient biography; it contains geography and ethnography, as well as historical narrative and formal speeches.[21] While it is important to point out the various elements in this biographical essay, it is pointless to debate the question of genre. In the guise of biography, Tacitus has produced an embryonic version of his complex historical masterpieces: the political agenda, the humiliation and resentment, and the literary strategies are already apparent. Like the *Histories* and the *Annals,* it begins with a prologue linking the present with the past.[22] The *Agricola* is the literary genesis of his moral, political, and psychological ideas.

There was a long tradition among Greek and Roman historians of including ethnographic material in larger historical works, as in the cases of Herodotus on Egypt or Julius Caesar on Gaul. Within its biographical framework, the *Agricola* contains the basic elements of ancient ethnography: discussions of geography, local customs, and political institutions.[23] When Tacitus reaches Agricola's appointment as governor of Britain, he includes a brief geographical description of the province and soon turns to the customs, government, and occupations of the people.[24] To his mind the Scottish tribes resemble the Germans while the southern Britons are ethnically, culturally, and religiously closely related to the Gauls. His famous description of the climate remains apt today: "The sky is covered by clouds and frequent rain, but the cold is not severe."[25] He comments both on agriculture and the mining of precious metals, and he compares British pearl fishers with those of the Indian Ocean. While we must be grateful for what Tacitus provides, there is much—such as a discussion of the Druids or a description of Romano-British cities—that is missing. But it is unreasonable to expect that a few pages of ethnography would satisfy our curiosity about barbarian Britain. Tacitus would do better in the *Germania.*

As a preliminary study for his histories, the *Agricola* provided Tacitus with an opportunity to try his hand at narration and at speeches. The most elaborate narratives recount Agricola's campaigns on Anglesey and in Scotland, in which Tacitus subordinates precise details of tactics to the visual and psychological elements of the battle and its cinematic sweep. Greek and Roman historians regularly composed speeches for the characters in their histories, and Tacitus asserts the *Agricola*'s claim to be more than mere family biography by including extended speeches for the general and for his British antagonist. The rebel chieftain Calgacus is otherwise unknown but the historian has provided for him a wonderful oration to the 30,000 Britons gathered in Scotland before the battle at Mons Graupius.[26] It is a proper Roman declamation, and Tacitus projects Roman rhetoric into the mouth of a remote barbarian tribal leader and thereby elevates him into an opponent worthy of Agricola. The speech echoes the familiar accusations of Rome's greed, cruelty, and love of power which Sallust also recorded,[27] and goes on to the most famous denunciation of Roman imperialism:

> To robbery, to slaughter, and to theft, they give the false name of "Empire"; where they create desolation, they call it "peace."[28]

Agricola's speech is briefer and more restrained, though it too alludes to an earlier text: Livy's account of Hannibal and Scipio addressing their troops.[29] Tacitus the orator employed his rhetorical skill in the service of history in these first speeches he wrote for others' voices.

Though Agricola is not the most detailed character in Tacitus's writings, the historian provides a good balance between the public and the private man, a man who emerges as more creditable (and more normal) than the characters portrayed in the *Histories* and the *Annals*. Tacitus devotes scant attention to Agricola's physical appearance; it is always the inner man that interests him. We read of Agricola's Stoic endurance at the murder of his mother and the early death of his only son, of his continuing devotion to his wife and daughter. With the ring of authenticity, Tacitus emphasizes his father-in-law's amiability, openness, and modesty, and registers his annoyance at people's skepticism that such a modest man could be truly famous.[30] In a Roman public figure, Agricola's modesty seems more like excessive shyness—his arrival at Rome by night to avoid publicity and never meeting with more than one or two friends—but the loyal Tacitus represents it as the only way to combine achievement with survival under the rule of a tyrant. Agricola is the first of the Tacitean survivors, through whom the historian praises accommodation and justifies his own career.

Throughout the *Agricola* Tacitus maintains the serious tone that one expects in history. Casual conversations, trivial details, and coarse anecdotes are absent, and Tacitus avoids the jokes found in Plutarch's lives.[31] His severity is relieved only by the story of the Usipi who were sold as slaves and gained notoriety from the telling of their adventures,[32] and by the occasional ironic turns of phrase such as abound in his mature style. The elevated tone, the brevity, and the descriptive power of Tacitus's historical works can already be seen in this highly rhetorical biography.

The *Agricola* contains a number of the political themes which are developed in greater detail in Tacitus's mature histories: the connection of censorship with the loss of political freedom; the insidious workings of imperial freedmen; and the corruption of values under an autocratic regime so that a good reputation is more dangerous than a bad one. But the central theme is one that lies at the heart of Tacitus's political philosophy: that "even under bad emperors men can be great."[33] Tyranny even brought an opportunity to exhibit new virtues, since *moderatio* was not mere passive acceptance but a laudable action.[34] Like Agricola, one should avoid the inflammatory setting of the Senate House and fight for Rome in the provinces: there honor is still attainable. In Rome itself, the compromise (*moderatio*) of an Agricola or of a Tacitus serves Rome better than the dramatic resistance of a self-appointed martyr. It is an apologia, but for whom? A psychologist might see Tacitus's own guilt and self-justification in his obsession with distinguishing compromise from collaboration; whatever its origin, the theme recurs throughout his writings.

Although Domitian's despotism left Tacitus a bitter and angry man, he expresses much warmth and benevolence in this laudatory biography. Agricola is praised not only for his modesty and military skill, but for his genuine affection toward mother, wife, and daughter. In the concluding chapters Tacitus, in the formal conventions of the genre, directly addresses Agricola.[35] If Agricola was fortunate to die before the worst of Domitian's terror threatened his family and friends, his death was tarnished only by the absence abroad of his daughter and her husband Tacitus. The historian seems to express genuine pain at the loss.

The final paragraph abounds with the rhetorical commonplaces of a Roman funeral address: Great souls do not perish with the body; your spirit will live forever; what we loved and admired will never die.[36] Familiar phrases even today, yet Tacitus invests them with a sincerity that lifts the conclusion from cliché to a powerful, personal farewell. Then Tacitus asserts that the achievements of Agricola will live forever, he could not know the irony of his words. From the few skimpy texts that survive we would know almost nothing of Agricola were it not for Tacitus. His military achievements would indeed have been forgotten, had not an historian, as an act of piety, cloaked them in the immortality of his words.

GERMANIA

Soon after the *Agricola,* Tacitus produced in the *Origin and Land of the Germans* (*Germania*) the only purely ethnographic monograph that survives from antiquity.[37] For centuries historians had inserted into their books ethnographic material on geography, local customs, political organization, and religious beliefs, and there was also a tradition of fabulous tales about distant societies, from Homer's Lotus Eaters and Cyclops to the stories which abound in the histories of Alexander's conquests of the East. The appearance of such pseudoethnography in novels and romances shows a widespread interest in exotic peoples and their customs.[38]

The *Germania* briefly describes the geography of Germany and discusses the local customs at length before providing an historical account of the various German tribes. But there is little evidence that the historian undertook personal research among the natives. Unlike Herodotus or Polybius, Tacitus relied almost entirely on written material: the books of Poseidonius, Caesar, and especially the elder Pliny (his friend's uncle) who wrote a history of the German wars about forty years earlier.[39] Though Tacitus may have added some current material that he gleaned from soldiers and merchants, the bulk of the *Germania* describes the barbarians as they were before the Civil War of 69.

There was little in the climate or landscape of Germany to appeal to a Mediterranean like Tacitus:

> Who would leave Asia Minor, North Africa, or Italy to go to Germany with its wild landscape and harsh climate—a country depressing to inhabit or to look on—unless one were a native?[40]

He quickly passes over physical geography and turns to the customs of the German people. Like other ancient writers, Tacitus sometimes generalized about barbarian peoples and transferred characteristics from one to another.[41] But much in his book has been confirmed by archaeology, and there is no reason to doubt Tacitus merely because he diverges from Caesar's account: German society had changed in the 150 years of Roman influence since Caesar crossed the Rhine.[42] And Tacitus prudently says little about areas (like eastern Germany) for which there was scant information.

The *Germania* is more than an essay written to inform the Romans about the land and peoples of Germany. An important function of ancient ethnography was to provide a contrast with one's own society, another perspective from which the writer could consider his own state and its customs.[43] Hence even utopian or fictitious societies could provide interesting material for social and political speculation, as Lilliput did for Swift and science fiction does today. While Tacitus certainly wishes to alert the Romans to the threat to the Empire that the Germans would pose in the future, his central purpose is not to praise Germany so much as to criticize Roman morality and political life through the implied comparisons.

Tacitus's anger at the fashionable immorality of contemporary Rome leads him to idealize German life in a far more flattering description than his later treatment of the Germans in the *Histories*. Their avoidance of unnecessary display, as in the practicality of their wedding gifts, manifests a seriousness clearly opposed to the frivolity of Roman society. Marriage is taken seriously and "no one there laughs at vice."[44] Young Germans are eager to prove their valor in battle, not in seduction.

The *Germania* also emphasizes the political freedom of the Germans who, unlike the Romans, make all-important decisions collectively: the power of kings is neither absolute nor arbitrary.[45] It is a blunt suggestion that Rome, despite the ostensible trappings of a constitution, is a monarchy. Amidst his criticism of Rome's moral and political condition, Tacitus also delivers a forthright warning for the future: that "free" Germany poses a far greater threat to Rome than do the kingdoms of the East.[46] If the Germans would unite, Rome might not be able to resist them. This is not fatalism but a challenge to the new emperor Trajan who, in 98, had just become emperor but was still campaigning on the northern frontier. Fatalism would be premature; Tacitus is urging Trajan to return to Caesar's aggressively expansionist foreign policy and fulfill the destiny of the Empire.

Since its rediscovery in the fifteenth century, some Germans have viewed this essay as an affirmation of their noble past and (lost) national independence.[47] The propagandists of the Nazi era saw Tacitus's ancient and racially unmixed Germans and Wagner's Siegfried as chaste and heroic supermen—prototypes of the "master race." Looking back on World War II, the great Italian-Jewish historian Arnaldo Momigliano concluded that the *Germania* was among the "most dangerous books ever written."[48]

DIALOGUE ON ORATORS

Since earlier times abounded with famous orators of genius, why is our own age so barren and bereft of eloquence that it hardly retains the name of "orator," which we only apply to the ancients; today we call good speakers "pleaders," "advocates," "counsellors,"—anything rather than "orators."[49]

Thus Tacitus addresses his friend Fabius Justus on the state of contemporary oratory. The *Dialogue,* like the philosophical and rhetorical dialogues of Plato and Cicero, records an intellectual conversation that (supposedly) transpired at a specific time and place. The time was about A.D. 75; the setting the house of Curiatius Maternus, an orator who preferred the writing of poetic tragedies (*Cato*) to public life. The other leading characters were Marcus Aper, a Gaul who vehemently defends contemporary oratory, and Vipstanus Messala, who yearns for the orators of the golden age. While the actual meeting may never have occurred, Tacitus skillfully delineates the personalities and their ideas with wit and good humor. There is no straw man; each speaker makes his case well and Tacitus, once a passionate practitioner of oratory, sympathized with certain ideas of each of the speakers.[50]

Aper first reproaches Maternus for wasting his time on poetry, which is in his mind suitable only for those without oratorical skill: a pleasant avocation. When he hotly tells his friend that there is no money, little chance of fame, and a good deal of danger in the poetry business, Aper has the tone of a modern Babbitt exasperated by the ambitions of an idealistic "artistic" son: Why not defend a friend in court rather than write a poem to honor long-dead Cato?[51] Contemporary orators enjoy wealth, prestige, political connections and patronage through their legal practice. But if Tacitus does not sympathize with Aper's admiration for the political expediency and material success of lawyers, he had a certain sympathy for his literary taste. Aper regards Cicero as rather long-winded: "Would anyone sit through the five speeches against Verres?"[52] Despite his previous disdain for poets, Aper goes on to assert that everyone now demands more poetic adornment in oratory; we must use Horace, Vergil, and Lucan. Taste changes; orators must change with it.

Maternus is the most political of the interlocutors. He attributes the change in oratory to an empire where political tyranny demanded a perversion of rhetorical skills. Since true oratory can only prosper in a free state, Maternus professes to withdraw from society and rely on poetry for his reputation, far from the sordid struggle of the forum and the court.[53] But Maternus was hardly remote from the political fray; the plays he wrote attacking tyranny (*Cato* and *Thyestes*) were probably responsible for his execution not long after the dramatic date of the *Dialogue*.

The late arrival of Messala ignites the conversation. He argues that the lack of a sound liberal education is responsible for the technically accomplished contemporary orators who do not have the culture, learning, and moral values of a Cicero.[54] Rhetorical skill has been emphasized at the expense of reading and literary study. Arguments should be presented plainly rather than tarted up in the "colorful clothes of a whore."[55] This conforms to Quintilian's view that the decline of oratory in the first century A.D. was caused by a reliance on declamatory exercises. Messala links the decline of oratory to the moral decline of an educational system that now teaches technique rather than values.

The decline of oratory is only one aspect of a perception of artistic decline that was a persistent theme in the literature of the first century.[56] All the speakers in the *Dialogue* accept that, during the last century, the world had changed and literature had also changed (for better or worse) as a consequence. Aper boasts that successful orators are rewarded with wealth and the friendship of emperors while Maternus suggests that great oratory blossoms only in an age of license and political struggle as in Athens or Republican Rome. Neither Sparta nor Macedon produced great oratory, nor does the peaceful time of Vespasian; no one can enjoy renown in an age of repose.[57]

Though no single speaker serves as an alter ego for Tacitus, he certainly sympathizes with Maternus who forsook oratory for poetry. By the time he wrote the *Dialogue,* Tacitus had proudly rejected oratory for history and turned his back on the barren bombast of the silver age. Though he regarded the new oratory as barren when it lacked political substance and social purpose, he was sympathetic to its pungent, poetic, epigrammatic style, a style that characterizes his great histories. Tacitus would have sympathized with Aper's defense of the new Latinity against Quintilian's attempt at a Ciceronian revival.[58]

That new Latinity is nowhere in evidence in the *Dialogue* itself. Its leisurely Ciceronian amplitude led early scholars to refuse to accept it as Tacitean. But Tacitus was a highly trained rhetorician who could write Ciceronian Latin when he chose to do so.[59] And it is more genuinely lively than most of Cicero's own.[60] It was not his natural voice, not even a slightly ironic one, yet it was the only possible style for a literary dialogue.[61] Most scholars now date the *Dialogue* not long after Trajan's accession in 98, most likely in 102, the consulship of the dedicatee Fabius Justus.[62] Tacitus had published the *Agricola* and *Germania,* and he was already at work on the *Histories.* The aspiring orator of 75 had become an historian. And yet he turned his hand to a Ciceronian dialogue, evoking if not imitating the master himself. The *Dialogue* is not merely literary history or literary criticism; it places literature within the wider political context of the early Empire and becomes the most important work of social literary criticism of the Roman Empire. Tacitus incorporates into this literary essay his program of the historical analysis of the effects of tyranny. The lasting lesson of the *Dialogue* is that art and society are intertwined, and both depend on the structure of political life. It is a lesson that cultural critics have revived with great enthusiasm in our own time.

HISTORIES

During the decade after the appearance of his two monographs, Tacitus was hard at work on a major narrative history of the Flavian emperors. At last the truth could be told. The *Histories,* a name attached by an early modern editor, covered the period from 69 to the death of Domitian in 96.[63] But only four complete books and part of the fifth survive—about a third of the whole— in which Tacitus covers less than two of the twenty-eight years. (It survives in a mutilated manuscript that also contains *Annals* 11–16.) The complex events of 69 with its four emperors and continuous civil warfare take more than three books and constitute the most detailed narrative of any period we have in all of Greek and Roman historiography, and the first chapters announce an historian of remarkable range.

Even if Tacitus was only an adolescent during the Civil War of 69, he lived close to the corridors of power through most of the Flavian period. He had seen much and heard even more. He used the records of the Senate for detailed accounts of speeches and debates, and asked friends (like Pliny) for eyewitness accounts of other events.[64] He also used earlier historians, but he creates his own narrative structure; he does not slavishly follow, as some of his Roman predecessors did, the vagaries of his sources.[65]

Roman annalistic historians are so named because they structured their histories according to the consular year. Livy reported the inauguration of new magistrates and other public political events before reporting the foreign wars of the year. Tacitus was far less interested in the meaningless charades of public office than in the realities of imperial power. While only retaining a basic chronological framework, he emphasized thematic developments and used the traditional form of republican annals to tell a very different story in a very different way.[66]

Thus, after a personal prologue, a summary of the causes of the Civil War, and a description of the state of the Empire, Tacitus appropriately begins the *Histories* on January 1, 69 with the accession of Galba to the consulship. It was an excellent place to begin and the dark opening pages provided Tacitus with the frame and the tone for his entire work: the murder of Galba in January of 69 is complemented by that of Domitian in 96. He presents the ill-fated Galba, a man with considerable qualities, as simply the wrong man at the wrong time.[67] Though Galba's integrity was unquestionable, it manifested itself as an anachronistic, priggish rigidity unsuited to a corrupt and selfish age.[68] Even a small act of generosity might have won over the troops and thus prevented the horrors of Otho and Vitellius, but that was not to be. The praetorians turned to Otho, a hedonist of the Neronian court, but he was not the only pretender. The German legions had also rebelled against Galba and acclaimed their commander Vitellius as emperor.

Book II opens with a brief glance at Vespasian in the East. Tacitus's admiration for Vespasian becomes clear: of all the emperors, only he became better after assuming power,[69] and, says Tacitus immodestly, he promoted men of genuine merit.[70] But the major focus is the conflict between the forces of Otho and Vitellius. It was the first civil war since Augustus and Antony fought at Actium a century earlier; but the latter, like Caesar and Pompey before them, refrained from pitched battles on Italian soil. Otho and Vitellius felt no such scruple. Otho was no commander; neither he nor his generals had the competence to fight against the seasoned German legions. Vitellius, who was still slowly marching through Gaul while his troops triumphed at Cremona, receives no glory from his victory. Though popular with the troops for his generosity, Vitellius is portrayed as a lazy glutton of no military distinction.[71] Surrounded by a Neronian entourage of actors and eunuchs, he remained oblivious to the real dangers of Vespasian until it was far too late.

In the third book the Flavian legions invade Italy and deal a devastating defeat to the Vitellian forces.[72] To their shame, they burn and sack the ancient Italian city of Cremona. Tacitus rapidly paints the moods of the legions, praetorians, and civilians, and the episode culminates with the horror of Rome itself in flames. The anticlimactic murder of the pathetic Vitellius closes the most masterful book of the *Histories*. It is a book of epic scope with Vergil ever present in the reminiscence of burning Troy as both Cremona and Rome are put to the torch.[73] Tacitus here achieved the most poetic history yet written at Rome.

Book IV treats both the Flavian dominance in Rome and the revolt of the Batavians under Julius Civilis. This account of the rebellious Germans is considerably less romantic, and less favorable, than in the *Germania*. Vespasian and his son Titus remained in Judaea, and Tacitus begins Book V with his confused and hostile description of the Jewish people and their religion.[74] The errors, such as making the Jews natives of Crete, do not speak well of Tacitus's research, since the Jewish historian Josephus lived at the Flavian court and had written books in Greek on Jewish history and customs.[75] Tacitus's bias against Eastern religions got the better of his judgment. The *Histories* as we have it concludes in mid-sentence with the impending collapse of Civilis's rebellion.

The pace of the early books of the *Histories* is remarkable. Despite the detail and the shifting focus of the action, the narrative is rapid and tightly organized.[76] The compressed style contributes to the swift progress of the story, and many paragraphs conclude with a memorable epigram. Dramatic vignettes, character sketches, and literary digressions (on Venus of Paphos or the cult of Serapis)[77] enliven the inexorable march of armies. This is largely public history, with many crowd scenes of armies, mobs, and provincials being addressed by public speeches; only later would a more mature Tacitus turn to secret history in the *Annals*. Nonetheless the tone of the *Histories* remains somber, if often ironic, with the disasters of 69 blamed on gods and men alike. The occasional act of heroism or example of unexpected virtue barely relieves the prevailing gloom.

It is the Civil War that sets the tone. Despite his acknowledgment that some Flavians acted from noble motives in embarking on civil war, Tacitus more generally regards it as the result of an uncontrollable lust for power and the greatest evil to befall the Roman people.[78] The Civil War destroyed military discipline and allowed the natives to rebel; it ensured that scoundrels would come to power; and it resulted in the terrible sacrilege of the burning of the temple of Jupiter on the Capitol (which the Druids had foretold as the triumph of the Gallic peoples).[79] The Civil War of 69 casts its dark shadow over all that survives of the *Histories*.

The theme of moral decline is omnipresent, from the sexual license of Otho and Vitellius to the craven behavior of the Roman armies. Where they once showed courage, the legions now were cowardly, insubordinate, and coddled by their commanders.[80] The troops squabbled among themselves and blamed their leaders for their own failings. They wished to sack a Roman city, and for the first time in Roman history an army swore allegiance to a foreign rebel.[81] A once free people has been corrupted by tyranny and license. The senators were little better. They gave up their newly won freedom of speech as soon as it was challenged after the Flavian victory.[82] Only Helvidius Priscus spoke with courage and frankness—and he paid with his life.

In the *Histories* Tacitus shows for the first time his impressive command of political theory and political reality. Whether in epigrams or in more theoretical speeches, he displays his mastery of the "secrets of power" with which his name has been linked through the centuries. No constitution can ensure the peaceful transfer of power if the army chooses to ignore it. Tacitus, writing under Trajan who had been adopted by Nerva, sees the adoptive monarchy as a means of avoiding hereditary despots and he puts such ideas in the speech Galba delivered on his adoption of Piso. Despite the irony of Galba's own impending demise, the speech (which we presume is pure Tacitus) articulates well in the age of Trajan the new theory of succession by adoption.[83]

The *Histories*, completed about 108, is a masterpiece of a mature historian. Within the conventional structure of speeches and debates, Tacitus has forged a swift and powerful narrative as well as an individual style. But his contribution goes beyond style and structure. Tacitus here analyzes the political institutions of the Roman state and he first presents his own ideology of Empire. He had served his apprenticeship well and he had become a master of his craft. In the next decade he will go still farther; the path from the *Histories* to the *Annals* leads from the externals to the internal, from excellence to genius.

ANNALS

The *Annals* is Tacitus's crowning achievement and this penetrating exposé of imperial politics represents the pinnacle of Roman historical writing. It survives in two separate blocks due to two different manuscripts. The first six books begin with the death of Augustus and the accession of Tiberius in 14 and end with the death of Tiberius in 37. Most of the fifth book is lost so that the account of the years 29–31 is missing. The second block goes from the middle of Book 11 (47 in the reign of Claudius) to the middle of Book 16 (66 in the reign of Nero). Thus Tacitus's treatment of Caligula is unfortunately completely lost as is the fall of Nero. Tacitus probably intended to conclude the *Annals* in eighteen books at the end of 68, since his earlier *Histories* begins on January 1, 69, though we cannot be certain that the work was ever finished.[84]

Tacitus composed the *Annals* in three hexads which form the basic structure of the work.[85] The first six books cover the reign of Tiberius and this hexad is conveniently divided by the first appearance of his evil praetorian prefect Sejanus at the opening of Book 4. The opening of the second hexad is lost, but it too closes with the death of an emperor, Claudius. The third hexad begins with the accession of Nero (13, 1: "The first death of the new regime . . .") with Tacitus explicitly referring back to the accession of Tiberius (1, 6: "The first crime of the new regime was the murder of Postumus Agrippa"). The parallel between these reigns extends to the implied comparisons of the domineering imperial mothers, Livia and Agrippina. Tacitus clearly divides the reigns of Nero and Tiberius into positive and negative phases, and probably followed ancient convention in doing the same for Caligula. While this follows the customary biographical practice of the gradual revelation of character, it is an actual fact that many rulers in quite different societies come to power amidst high hopes and later crush those expectations. Tacitus's structure is not merely a literary conceit; it may reflect historical reality.[86]

The *Annals* does not begin with the formal, Greek-style historical prologue setting out the personal goals of the author such as we find in the *Agricola* and the *Histories*.[87] The dense first chapters instead sketch the decline of the Republic and the triumph of Augustus. After his comments on the inadequate historical treatment of the Julio-Claudian emperors and a brief assertion of his own impartiality, Tacitus eagerly embarks on his story. In fact, his first two words, *urbem Romam* ("the city of Rome"), already define his restricted theme: the city of Rome and its government. Foreign wars and military mutinies are recounted to shed light on the emperors and their court. In the fifth century St. Jerome, not surprisingly, referred to Tacitus's book as *The Lives of the Caesars*.[88] These are not biographies, but Jerome correctly saw that Tacitus's interest never wandered far from the imperial palace and Rome itself.

The *Annals* begins with a retrospective glance at the seductive appeal of the reign of Augustus where the Roman people truly lost their collective political innocence. From the outset Tacitus deploys all his literary skills to give an immediate impression of duplicity and dynastic intrigue. And yet, amidst the irony, scorn, and exaggeration, he admits that Augustus had restored peace after nearly a century of civil conflict and that the provincials were much better off than they had been under senatorial rule. At the funeral of Augustus Tacitus uses the rhetorical device of having groups of spectators speak for or against the public and private life of the dead emperor.[89] By adopting Tiberius as his successor, they conclude, Augustus hoped to ensure his own future glory by invidious comparison. In these few pages on Augustus, Tacitus provides a grim backdrop for Tiberius's entrance.

The gloomy, anti-social Tiberius is the most complex character in Tacitus, perhaps in all of Latin literature. His natural diffidence is presented as dissimulation, his shyness as haughtiness, and his acts of generosity as hypocrisy. Yet, despite Tacitus's innuendos, he does acknowledge that the Empire was well administered and the laws were duly enforced until the ascendency of Sejanus over Tiberius in 23.[90] A few years later the emperor retired from public view and withdrew to the lovely island of Capri for the final ten years of his life. Tacitus paints a picture of paranoid politics and moral depravity, but he also allows us to see Tiberius as a wounded husband, a bullied son, and a friendless and lonely old man. Tiberius gave his trust to his praetorian prefect Sejanus who had once saved his life in a cave-in. But Sejanus consolidated his power and had the emperor's son murdered to further his own imperial ambitions. Tiberius's pre-emptive strike against Sejanus in 31 falls in the missing section of Book 5 and we must reconstruct it from other sources, but Tacitus's account of the aftermath amply displays the increased bitterness and distrust of the aging emperor, and the brief obituary is a classic account of the corruption of power.[91]

After a lacuna of ten years, Books 11 and 12 treat the last seven years of the reign of Claudius (41–54). Perhaps Tacitus followed his usual practice and presented a more positive image of Claudius in the early years of his reign when he conquered Britain,[92] but by 47 the emperor is portrayed as controlled by his freedmen and his women.[93] In the Tiberian books Livia's formidable presence is often sensed in the background; in the Claudian books Messalina and the younger Agrippina step confidently into the imperial spotlight. Messalina treated imperial power as a toy to be used to satisfy her lust and her whims, but Agrippina was more dangerous: she used her sexuality to increase her power.[94] The traditionalist Tacitus certainly believes that a man must keep his wife under control, and his contempt for Claudius is withering.[95] There is little of the wit or charm of Suetonius's Claudius in Tacitus's pathetic account of his final years before his murder by his fourth wife.

The last four surviving books of the *Annals* cover the twelve years from the accession of Nero through the matricide of Agrippina, the great fire of Rome, and the conspiracy of Piso with the death of Seneca. The young emperor's accession was promising, as the philosopher Seneca guided his intellectual and political development. But Tacitus soon turns to tales of Nero's sexual abandon matched by the degradation of his performing on the stage,[96] and bloody cruelty soon follows: Book 14 begins with Nero murdering his mother and ends with the killing of his wife Octavia. His tutor Seneca prudently retires amid the emperor's kisses, but he is soon forced to commit suicide in a stirring and dramatic scene.[97] Our text ends with Nero's reign of terror against the Senate; we must regret that the missing books contained Tacitus's account of the emperor's ludicrous singing tour of Greek festivals, the revolts in Judaea and Gaul, the final pathetic death of Nero, and the outbreak of the Civil War.

The *Annals* is far more than mere narrative history; Tacitus provides an analytical framework through several central themes: the growth of tyranny; the decline of Roman morality; and the misuse of language. In the first paragraph Tacitus moves from the monarchy through military dictatorship in the late Republic to the victory of Augustus and the succession of the Julio-Claudians. A recurring pattern of imperial tyranny and senatorial cowardice is repeatedly contrasted with the courage of Rome's barbarian enemies who fight and die to preserve their freedom. The German commander Arminius, the Gallic leader Sacrovir, and the British queen Boudicca are all given defiant speeches against Roman tyranny. When Roman senators do plot against Nero, the results are hardly heroic since the captured conspirators quickly betray their family and friends. Tyranny is accompanied by informers, manipulative freedmen, treason trials, and universal paranoia: despotism, sycophancy, and treachery form the web that ties together the whole of the *Annals*.

Closely linked with the rise of tyranny is the moral decline that pervades the Senate, the armies, and the entire Roman people. Tiberius was initially austere in his personal life, and he inspired fear when he reproached luxury, but his later orgies at Capri set a standard for Messalina, Tigellinus, and Nero. Even without the explicit detail of Suetonius, Tacitus links sexual license with a general collapse of political morality:

> If the souls of tyrants were revealed, they would show bruises and wounds—for as the body is scourged by lashes, so is the spirit by cruelty, lust, and malice.[98]

Tacitus also saw moral weakness in Roman unwillingness to expand their imperial dominion. The unwillingness to fight abroad led in Tacitus's view to civil wars in which ambitious men fruitlessly wasted wealth and Roman lives, in contrast to republican generals who had achieved their reputations by bringing treasure to Rome. The passive policy recommended by Augustus to Tiberius is to Tacitus a signal indication of the moral weakness of the imperial system.

Tacitus is fascinated by language and is particularly sensitive to its misuse. Language creates illusions to conceal political realities and the historian is determined to expose the lies that form the basis of imperial rule. "The titles of officials remained the same," [99] but he makes it clear that their powers have changed. His concern with language explains his near obsession with the censorship of writers, the ultimate political attempt to control language and suppress free thought.[100] Tacitus knew as well as any Roman the connection between word, thought, and power, and those links lie at the heart of his masterpiece.

The *Annals* finds Tacitus at the acme of his stylistic powers. The force of the work lies in its compact style which has a jackhammer quality. It is less smooth and more concentrated than the *Histories;* even the speeches are shorter and more intense. Though the style is craggy, the narrative can sometimes be remarkably swift as he leads his reader with the intensity of a forced march. Tacitus is a master of epigram and he does not lack a sense of humor, though his jokes, as we shall see, are bitter and ironic. The historian has created a very personal style which delivers his message with great energy and precision. The *Annals* is a bold work, in which the abrasive style perfectly suits its unsettling content.

In the *Annals* Tacitus reflects more profoundly than before on his role as an historian, and he interjects his personality into his account.[101] He is scornful of historians who record banal facts, and he makes clear his belief in the moral function of history.[102] The recording of virtuous and evil acts will not only teach future generations; it will also reward and punish and thereby encourage the good and deter the bad.[103] With all that said, I am not certain that we can pretend to understand fully the motives or personality of Tacitus. His intentions in writing the *Annals* seem to be moral and political, but his passion must stem from a deeper psychological source, perhaps guilt and the need to vindicate himself and his friends.

The *Annals* must have been completed about 117—probably not long before the death of Trajan and the accession of Hadrian. Sir Ronald Syme's suggestion that the biting portrait of Tiberius is aimed at Hadrian is an interesting way to explain Tacitus's passionate hostility to a long-dead emperor, but it seems unlikely that Tacitus, so timid under Domitian, would so openly criticize the reigning emperor.[104] The *Annals* is a brilliant and creative expression of deep personal suffering and political frustration. The accession of an unsympathetic new emperor seems relatively unimportant, in contrast to Tacitus's entire political and literary life, which was the apprenticeship for writing this greatest of all Roman prose works.

After this sketch of Tacitus's life and works, we turn to an analysis of the content of the histories. Tacitus was an historian, and the ancient historian played many roles as he presented and interpretated his material: an historical methodologist, a moralist, a psychologist, a political analyst, and, far from least, a literary artist. But the guises are not disguises: Tacitus always remains an historian and his ideas are firmly embedded in his historical texts. Still, as we shall see in the final chapter on the impact of Tacitus, his achievement transcends his own purposes in the enormous influence he had on later writers, philosophers, and politicians.

Tacitus, the first of historians who
applied the science of philosophy to the
study of facts.
GIBBON,
Decline and Fall of the Roman
Empire, *chapter ix*

III

❖ ——————————————————— ❖

The Historian's Method

Serious books of history have never been intended merely as records of past events, for there have always been many ways to recover the past. Just as in 1989 the world learned of the French Revolution from novels and biographies, films and television specials, political extravaganzas and museum exhibitions, ancient men and women learned of their own past from poetry, myths, and oral traditions. Historians of every age have had motives that go beyond those of the mere chronicler: whether idealistic pursuit of truth or a political, religious, or moral crusade. In antiquity, all serious writers intended both to entertain and to teach, and history was a literary genre, not the scientific one that it became in modern times. And it must teach a worthy subject; it should not record trivial facts for their own sake. The historian was not an antiquarian but he sought the underlying causes which shed light on moral and political life.[1] Writing history was not, in the words of one ancient historian, merely "telling tales to children."[2] Other Roman historical works aimed at a larger readership: Nepos's popular capsule biographies of great men; Florus's outline of Roman history; and the dramatic and fanciful histories in the Hellenistic tradition.[3] As is the case today, popular history is more digestible, and more fun, than the austere analysis of a great historian writing for the intellectual elite. But Tacitus, like Polybius before him, scorned incredible tales and sordid personal gossip as unworthy of serious history. The historian records in order to explain; he explains in order to teach:

> Yet it is useful to examine those seemingly trivial incidents which often give rise to great historical events . . . Since few have the inborn ability to distinguish right from wrong or the useful from the dangerous, most learn from the experience of others.[4]

Modern historians are aware that Thucydides first used scientific terminology to describe causation, and Polybius propounded a cyclical view of history. Though Tacitus cannot lay claim to any such striking innovation in historical method,[5] he does follow a different course in seeking moral causes for political events. Though he repeatedly recognizes the power of Fortune in human affairs, he still believes that the past forms a comprehensible pattern. That seeming contradiction is addressed near the beginning of the *Histories* where Tacitus sets out his program:

> Before I begin my project, it seems best to consider the condition of Rome, the feelings of the army, the attitude of the provinces, and the strengths and weaknesses of the entire empire. Thus we can learn not only events and consequences (which are often determined by chance) but the underlying logic and causes as well.[6]

While an individual disaster may be attributed to chance, Tacitus believes that it was the Romans' own greed and ambition that brought what he calls "the anger of the gods" upon them. There is an "underlying logic" and the Romans are not mere playthings of divine powers; they were responsible for their own fate. Tacitus writes moral history and he thus seeks moral causes.

It was his conception of moral causation that kept Tacitus from wholly embracing a cyclical determinism in history, however much he was attracted to a Sallustian vision of Rome's inexorable moral decline.[7] In a discussion on the growth of luxurious living and extravagant expenditures during the Julio-Claudian era and their decline after the death of Nero, Tacitus directly addresses historical cycles:

> Or perhaps there is a certain cycle in human affairs, so that moral standards alternate like the seasons. Everything was not better in the past; our own age has also produced many examples of honor and artistry that deserve future imitation.[8]

He is clearly reluctant to attribute too much to impersonal forces. As a moral historian, Tacitus demands that individual responsibility and free will remain a central element in his narrative and in the destiny of the Roman people.

Tacitus and His Sources

Tacitus stood among those ancient historians who combined literary artistry, intellectual coherence, and research. Because the positivism of the nineteenth century defined research, in the human as well as in the physical sciences, as the discovery of new data, it is the research that we usually find least satisfactory in pre-modern historians. We wonder why they did not lavish the care on determining facts that they expended on dramatic scenes, elaborate (though fictitious) speeches, and stylistic nuance. Tacitus, like Livy, has re-used descriptions of battles or battlefields, even to the extent of direct self-imitation.[9] Ancient historians often seem satisfied with a general poetic truth rather than with factual accuracy. And Tacitus, whose literary allure is so powerful, is a particularly troublesome case: did he really do research? did he concern himself with the literal truth?

If research is the consultation and evaluation of sources, there can be little doubt that Tacitus engaged in serious research though it is not often apparent in the smooth flow of his narrative.[10] Unlike Livy, who restricted himself to a few sources and refused to bestir himself to consult other easily available documents,[11] Tacitus consulted both obvious and obscure sources. Like other Roman historians, Tacitus thought that personal research was more important for the history of recent times and he diligently sought eyewitness accounts of important events. He seems to have consulted his friends Verginius Rufus and Spurinna, both active figures in the Civil War of 69. He asked his friend Pliny for an eyewitness account of the eruption of Vesuvius which destroyed Pompeii and Herculaneum in 79 and which Pliny as a teenager had observed from across the Bay of Naples.[12] Pliny's lengthy report survives in a letter to Tacitus; it is unfortunate that Tacitus's own version was contained in the lost portion of the *Histories* so we cannot see what use he made of this primary document. And yet Tacitus's research efforts seem restricted to politics, civil wars, and domestic events. For a man who served as governor of Asia his knowledge of Jews and Christians is woefully (and unnecessarily) confused, since the Jewish historian Josephus lived in Rome and Tacitus's good friend Pliny knew something of the Christians.[13] But Tacitus is contemptuous of all easterners—Greeks, Jews, and Egyptians alike—and he clearly thought them unworthy of the curiosity and research he lavished on court intrigues.

Scholars have spilled ink for more than a century in their quixotic hunt for Tacitus's precise sources.[14] Much can be conjectured; little can be proven. Though Tacitus himself rarely mentions specific sources for particular events, at the beginning of his treatment of Nero he does assert his general reliance on Fabius Rusticus, Pliny the Elder, and Cluvius Rufus:

> When the sources are unanimous, I will follow them; when they provide different versions, I will record them with attribution.[15]

These authors lived through the reign of Nero and could write of it in the (relative) freedom of Vespasian's reign. Pliny's long history of the German wars is now lost but we can recognize it behind the account of the German mutiny in the *Annals* and in the

Germania. But these were hardly the limits of Tacitus's sources; much comes directly from personal contact with survivors. Many of his friends and colleagues had lived under Nero and their memories do much to shape his picture of that bizarre reign.

Two other accounts of the Julio-Claudian emperors survive: the racy biographies of emperors written by the imperial librarian Suetonius, and the vast history of Rome penned in Greek by the third-century consul Dio Cassius whose account of the period survives only in a lengthy abridgement. Neither Suetonius nor Dio directly follows Tacitus, yet all three provide a similar picture of the hypocritical Tiberius that probably originates in a hostile source written under Caligula, whose parents Germanicus and Agrippina were so badly treated by his predecessor.[16] Tacitus goes beyond this common source to provide a level of detail and an acuteness of political perception that is unique to his version. Likewise, though Tacitus knew the common sources which Suetonius, Dio, and Plutarch used in their accounts of the Civil War of 69, his result is so different that we must attribute the final product to his own craft and intelligence rather than to his raw material.

The intelligence is Tacitus's own, but much of the detail comes from his diligent research in reminiscences, biographies, autobiographies, letters, and speeches of the time, as well as in the Acts of the Senate—a Roman approximation of the Congressional Record. This archival research is especially notable in the early books of the *Annals* and it may well have been a significant innovation in the historical writing of the time.[17] The speeches of Tiberius clearly fascinated Tacitus and we can sometimes hear an echo of that emperor's enigmatic voice, as in the aphorism on the death of Germanicus.[18] Tacitus also mimicked the earnest but rambling Claudius in his speech on the admission of Gallic senators. The original of that speech, which survives on an inscription, shows how Tacitus improved the argument while retaining the noble ideals and slightly pedantic tone of the emperor himself.[19] Then as now, princes and politicians tried to control their future reputation through autobiographies and memoirs. Tacitus would surely have used the autobiographies of Tiberius and Claudius, but he refers specifically only to the memoirs of the general Corbulo and those of the empress Agrippina.[20] Despite the absence of specific references, it is evident that the Tiberian and Claudian books of the *Annals* rely on a wide range of primary and secondary sources.

For his account in the *Histories* of the Civil War of 69 and the Flavian dynasty, Tacitus had friends who were major protagonists in the period; moreover, he himself had entered public life by 77. He was well apprised of the political realities of the age and he was determined to correct the Flavian propaganda that was contained in the historians of the period.[21] He wrote of Caecina and others who deserted Vitellius for Vespasian:

> Historians who wrote accounts of this war while the Flavians still ruled flatteringly attributed to these men motives like "concern for peace" and "love of country." But I think that, in addition to a natural fickleness and loyalty diminished by their betrayal of Galba, there was a jealous rivalry that others might eclipse them at Vitellius's court . . . [22]

In short term, history is written by the victors. The Flavian interpretation of the Civil War had become the authorized version for a quarter century but the death of Domitian allowed Tacitus—he would say required him—to criticize the historians and rewrite their history. Here he is not concerned with primary documents; he knew the witnesses and was secure of his ground. He needed only common sense and his own integrity to produce a revisionist history of the Flavian era.

This direct criticism of the Flavian historians is atypical of Tacitus; he is more interested in writing history than in rebutting historians. He takes facts and even epigrams from a variety of unacknowledged sources. Ancient writers were not concerned about accusations of plagiarism; they cited sources only to add credibility to their own account. Tacitus would find our obsessive need to footnote sources tiresome; he judged them privately and freely reorganized their material without troubling his readers with such details. The ancient reader looked for political intelligence and stylistic polish in an historical text; he did not expect the writer to justify himself with evidence of research. Yet the absence of extended discussion of sources does not preclude careful collection and thoughtful analysis of them. Tacitus had done both. Despite some blind spots, he used the sources of political history well.

The Accuracy of Tacitus's History

In his essay *On the Orator*, Cicero criticized the obvious bias of family records and says the first law of history is

> that an author must not dare to tell anything but the truth. And the second that he must make bold to tell the whole truth.[23]

It is, as Cicero knew, an easier principle to pronounce than to practice. Tacitus repeatedly announced his devotion to accuracy in contexts where he called into question the reliability of his predecessors. Already in his first book he proclaimed himself ready to tell the truth after the bookburnings and universal terror under Domitian:

> We should also have lost our memory along with our voice, had it been as easy to forget as to keep silence.[24]

Repression induces fear and hatred; some flatter while others bide their time to enact vengeance on their oppressors:

> But while we find it easy to distrust the sycophantic historian, slander and spite find eager ears. Flattery is thought to show subservience while malice hides behind the false mask of independence . . . I do not deny that my career began under Vespasian, was advanced by Titus and still more by Domitian, but those who profess honesty must write without partiality or hatred.[25]

The idea that earlier writers were sycophantic or hostile recurs at the beginning of the *Annals* where Tacitus criticizes Julio-Claudian historians and concludes with his famous claim:

> I shall write without indignation or favor; I am far removed from the motives to do so.[26]

Such professions of impartiality were hardly original with Tacitus; Sallust claimed in his *Catiline* that he is "free from ambition, fear, or partisan politics."[27] These declarations had become so conventional in the early Empire that while Tacitus was still a boy Seneca produced a mocking parody at the beginning of his satire on the (safely dead) Claudius: "there will be no offence nor kindness."[28] Yet there is no reason to doubt Tacitus's sincerity. He was severe on his predecessors because he thought they were compromised by favors or injuries done them by the emperors. Fair enough. And if the modern reader is astonished by Tacitus's view that he could not be biased because none of the Julio-Claudians had harmed him, the historian was merely following the ancient view that one could not show bias against those long dead.[29] Merely because he had never lived under Tiberius, could the historian not have animosity toward him? Tacitus, like most ancients and many moderns, believed in the impartiality of posterity. Bias was a matter of personal grievance or fear or sycophancy—the ancients did not regard an ideological belief as bias. So, in ancient terms, Tacitus could not be biased against the institution of the principate (or against barbarians or the urban mob), but only against individuals. When personal connections were absent, impartiality would seem to be inevitable.

Of course we cannot accept this narrow definition of bias. The Catholic and Protestant historiography of the Reformation or the varying accounts of the Crusades show that temporal distance does not necessarily bring impartiality. We know full well that an historian's choice of subject is likely to signal an engagement that makes claims of disinterested objectivity naive.[30] Still, Tacitus's claims do make a certain sense in a highly personalized political system. But it is harder to accede to his assertion that, because he had profited from Domitian, he could not be biased against him. This lack of self-awareness in an historian seething with anger seems incredible to us, especially in one who can be so subtle in treating Tiberius's own resentment of the smallest slight. But Tacitus would see no contradiction. Any historian, any public man, was expected to have strong political views; that was not bias. Bias stemmed only from what we would call today a tangible conflict of interest. Tacitus is concerned to show that his obvious hatred of Domitian is not rooted in a personal affront; in fact, Domitian's promotion of his career would have made only a *favorable* history of that emperor suspect. It seems astoundingly ingenuous, but before we condemn his psychological naiveté, we should recall that congressional ethics committees apply a similarly restricted notion of conflict of interest to contemporary legislators.

Tacitus's deep skepticism served him especially well where his predecessors had been biased or gullible. But it was no easier for him to write the history of Tiberius than it will be for the new generation of Soviet historians to write the history of Stalin's purges of the 1930s. Sources had disappeared and rumors must be used in the place of better evidence. Tacitus may report rumors, if only to deny them, because they shed a light on the times. The story that Tiberius connived in the murder of his own son Drusus was "a contemporary rumor strong enough to remain current today." He goes on at some length to refute this account and he provides the true story which was only revealed eight years after Drusus's murder. Tacitus concludes

> My reason for reporting and refuting this story has been to discredit, by one striking instance, false rumors, and to urge my readers not to prefer incredible tales—however widely circulated and eagerly believed—to the truth unembellished by romance.[31]

But the rumor serves a historical purpose. That such a story became widespread provides a gauge of the hatred of Tiberius. Thus the historian has his cake and eats it: a lurid story, told to great rhetorical effect before being disavowed, which makes a serious point and in so doing alienates the reader still further from Tiberius.

There were other seemingly preposterous rumors that Tacitus actually managed to confirm. He found it incredible that the empress Messalina would have dared to conclude a formal marriage ceremony with a distinguished senator and to spend the night with him while the emperor Claudius was only fifteen miles away on a visit to Ostia, and this in Rome "where everything was known and there was no discretion."[32] He protests that he has not embellished the story; he had actually found documents and witnesses to satisfy him that what common sense told him was unbelievable had to be believed. Reporters of modern famines, natural disasters, and genocides have had the same experience.

Tacitus is not always sufficiently skeptical; he occasionally accepts dubious material, not merely as rumors, but for the fabric of his history. His negative view of the Jews indiscriminately blurs together a few facts (Moses and Egypt; dietary laws; monotheism), biblical myths (Sodom and Gomorrah), preposterous nonsense (Jews originated in Crete), and anti-Semitic clichés (their lasciviousness). Tacitus even condemns them for what we find admirable: "They consider it a crime to kill an unwanted child." [33] He has accepted a hodge podge of truth and falsehood with little critical analysis. He similarly accepts the negative account of Claudius despite that emperor's real administrative achievements and his conquest of Britain, spheres that Tacitus usually values highly. Here Tacitus reveals that his vaunted skepticism was erratic. He so distrusted emperors that he was perhaps too credulous of negative sources about them.

Though Tacitus towers above other Roman historians in his command of chronology, geography, and military strategy, he still made mistakes. He is strongest on chronology and rarely errs on matters of importance. [34] The complex events of the Civil War of 69 are handled with authority, but Tacitus found the year-by-year structure of annalistic history caused him difficulties in wars far from Rome. [35] He occasionally admits that he has related the events of two years together, and sometimes he seems to telescope events, as in Armenia, without any clear indication he is doing so. But his chronological confusions are relatively insignificant.

His geographical and military shortcomings are more serious, if no less innocent. The Romans were not brilliant geographers; it was the sort of research, requiring intense curiosity to no immediate purpose, at which the Greeks surpassed them. Tacitus knew the northern and eastern frontiers only from books; his ignorance is understandable. But his account of military affairs has been subjected to more severe criticism, though even his critics far prefer him to Livy. In the last century Theodor Mommsen called Tacitus the most unmilitary of historians—a comment that has been quoted with some frequency. [36] While Tacitus was admittedly more interested in the human passions and political implications of war than in battlefield topography and military tactics, modern historians and archaeologists have acquitted him of serious carelessness. He is most confused in his account of Germanicus's campaigns in Germany which had taken place a full century before he was writing.[37] There was no possibility of witnesses and he was at the mercy of idealizing sources. But in the *Histories* and *Agricola* where more complete records and surviving witnesses allowed for a critical analysis of the events, Tacitus provided excellent accounts of the battles of Cremona and the revolt of Civilis.[38] Despite minor errors, archaeology has usually buttressed the Tacitean version.[39] Even his laudatory, but suspect, comment "that no general ever exploited the advantages of a site more shrewdly than Agricola"[40] has been confirmed by the excavators of the Agricolan forts in Britain. If Tacitus did not master military strategy as well as a Caesar, both his facts and his interpretations of military history are generally reliable and his account of the human drama of civil war is unsurpassed.

Even historians who profess the value of truth, who conduct serious research, and who get their facts right, may still mislead their readers. There is a continuum from the innocent ambiguity and confusion inherent in all written texts—can "cause" for any historian mean what it does for a scientist?—through the shadings of interpretation to bare-faced lies. No text can fully represent reality; it must select certain details and in the selection itself lie interpretation and distortion. And we now know that the links between antecedent and consequent events are infinitely more complex than cause and effect. The ideas of Jesus Christ, Karl Marx, and Sigmund Freud have forever changed our ideas of human motivation and even historians who do not subscribe to their respective creeds are forever changed by them. Tacitus was untouched by these and other ideas, and thus lies on the far side of a vast gulf. We may scorn an explanatory model that relies so heavily on literary effect; he (if he had the opportunity) might scorn one that relies on the afterlife, economic determinism, or infantile sexuality. As we begin to analyze the distortions of Tacitus, we would do well to rein in our inclination to condemn the transparency of his political bias. All historians have prejudices and preconceptions; like a great forest or Mount Everest, it is simply easier to see them from afar.

Tacitus certainly held strong views on the personalities and policies of the imperial court, but there is no evidence that he invented or suppressed the facts. He explicitly tries to analyze what he reads and hears, and even warns against uncritical belief. But if the facts are as accurate as possible, we see the advocate's hand arranging the evidence or the prosecutor's voice urging the jury of posterity to find for conviction as any attorney might do today. Tacitus avoids direct accusation, but he convicts by hearsay and innuendo; he attributes thoughts and motives where he could not possibly have evidence for them; and he projects impressions which are contradicted by his own facts.[41] His powerful rhetorical skills used the facts to achieve a higher "truth." And though these unsubstantiated insinuations would be unacceptable in modern academic historical writings, they confirm Tacitus's basic honesty since he retains discordant facts which enable a perceptive reader to demystify that rhetorical "truth." We see Messalina and Agrippina as stereotypes of depravity, but the details show the enormous difference between the flighty, spoiled, and lascivious Messalina and the cold and cunning Agrippina. Even the skillful administrator can be found lurking in the details of the account of the bumbling Claudius. The first impression is uniformly bleak, but a more careful look at the text reveals illuminating refinements of detail. His passionate opinions should not obscure the fact that he is the most accurate of all the Roman historians.[42]

Fact and Impression

The third-century Christian apologist Tertullian called Tacitus "the most articulate of liars,"[43] presumably for his aspersions on Christians and Jews, but there are, in fact, few demonstrable direct lies in Tacitus. Still, scholars have long observed the contradictions between the facts reported and the impression given by the historian.[44] The flow of narration sometimes obscures contradictory material, as when Tacitus skates quickly over the fact that the brutal Agrippa was unsuitable for the throne,[45] or that the provincials were better off under the Empire than under the rapacious governors and tax collectors of the Republic.[46] These details are soon forgotten, while Tacitus's interjections create instead a prevailing impression of imperial tyranny and cruelty:

> I realize that most writers omit the trials and punishment of many men. They tire of the repetition, fearing what they found tedious and depressing would produce a similar revulsion in their readers. But I have found much worth knowing, even if unrecorded by others.[47]

All true, but the comment underlines the horror of what were relatively few trials. Executions make a greater emotional impact than acquittals; cruelty than kindness.[48] The psychology of the tabloid press is not far from Tacitus's manipulation of his readers' sensibilities. This ability to weave a false tapestry from accurate details reappears in our own time in yellow journalism and political campaigns.

This disjunction between facts and innuendo appeared for the first time in the *Agricola*. Tacitus knew Domitian well and hated him with every fiber of his being; he did not allow facts to stand in the way of his prejudices. Though it was after Agricola's death in 93 that Domitian's paranoia inspired a cruel reign of terror, Tacitus suggests earlier imperial machinations against his hero.[49] Some courtiers may well have intrigued against Agricola, but there is no evidence for Domitian's complicity; Tacitus himself specifically denies the rumors of poison.[50] Domitian is even shown as genuinely moved by Agricola's self-restraint. Despite all the secret plots and discreditable motives attributed to the emperor, Tacitus does not document a single hostile act against Agricola; in fact Domitian acts with appropriate concern and sorrow at the illness and death of his loyal general. The facts do not convict the emperor; only the drumbeat of Tacitean opinion casts him in the role of a monster. Perhaps there is a political reason for this portrait. Agricola, like Tacitus, had an exceptional career under Domitian, and the Stoic intellectuals who survived the reign might not think well of their success. Domitian's suspicion and intrigue rescue Agricola from the accusation of collaboration, and the portrait of the paranoid emperor was welcome in the influential circles of Tacitus's new friends.

Tacitus is a great reporter of rumors, unconfirmed stories that cast a bleak shadow over the emperors even though the historian is careful not to vouch for these tales. The *Annals* begins with the death of Augustus; at the funeral Tacitus has unnamed people speak favorably and unfavorably about his reign. Of course he gives a more detailed report of the latter group:

> Nor did he adopt Tiberius as his successor from personal fondness or from concern for the state; aware of his arrogance and cruelty, Augustus sought increased glory by the unfavorable comparison.[51]

Tacitus gives great prominence to such slurs on Tiberius to provide a dark backdrop to his succession. But he knew well that Augustus had no real alternative: his previous choices as heir were long dead and Tiberius had in the meantime become Rome's most successful general and most experienced administrator. Despite Tiberius's blameless early life, Tacitus still reports the rumors to defame Augustus and to add dramatic effect on the succession. The historian's integrity is barely preserved by the fig leaf of the unattributed source: "some people said."

From Tiberius's accession to his death, rumors and Tacitean innuendo swirl around him. Until the rise of Sejanus and the reign of terror, he was accused of few direct crimes, but Tacitus implies that the emperor was linked to the death of Germanicus and to the treason trials, despite the fact that the emperor sarcastically dismissed the earliest of such charges. Hearsay suggests that Tiberius hypocritically masked his secret hatreds. But how could Tacitus (or the rumor-mongers) penetrate the mind and heart of so enigmatic an emperor? Why does the skeptical historian recount at such length rumors which are clearly baseless? Tacitus's goal is to defame a Tiberius whose early years otherwise provide little to censure.

Tiberius repeatedly dissimulates his inmost emotions, but we are never told how the historian is privy to them. How could Tacitus know that Tiberius's words were "more contrived than he was really thought to feel"?[52] We are also told that the emperor was delighted to see the Senate and his sons at odds; he publicly praised Germanicus, but was secretly unhappy at his adopted son's popularity with the troops; that he dissembled his joy at the funeral of Germanicus but was annoyed at the praise for Agrippina; that he hated or resented or concealed, even though his public actions remained decorous. Tacitus knew the effect he was making, like the lawyer (which he was) who asks leading questions which he knows will be ruled out of order, or who prefaces prejudicial statements with "We will show . . ." He refers near the end of Tiberius's reign to "continual slaughter," but the killings amount to only a handful of judicial executions and seven suicides in a three-year period—unpleasant, but trivial compared to Caligula and Nero, not to speak of the Wars of Religion or modern revolutions and tyrannies. Tacitus records fewer than a hundred treason trials in the twenty-three years of Tiberius's reign: some defendants were acquitted and some were admittedly guilty—this hardly constitutes "continual slaughter." The historian is scrupulous about factual details, but he is willing to select and interpret them to create a false impression.

The gap between fact and impression is greatest in the first six books of the *Annals*—not so much because Tiberius is less monstrous than Nero (though I believe he is), as because Tacitus includes so much positive material on the earlier emperor's reign. Tiberius's generosity to Asia after the earthquake and his grants to impoverished senators; his effective financial administration combined with lack of personal avarice or profligacy; his refusal of excessive titles like "Lord" at home and divine honors in the provinces; his initial scorn for flatterers, informers, and sycophants— all this material recorded by Tacitus led Mommsen to regard Tiberius as the most capable emperor Rome ever had.[53] In his obituary of Tiberius, the historian finally conceded the emperor's merit, but during his actual narrative he treated all attempts at moderation with skepticism and cynicism.[54] That the emperor even used the legend *"MODERATIO"* on his coinage and that he was praised for his moderation by the contemporary court historian Velleius Paterculus would have been scorned by Tacitus as a sham.[55] This negative view of Tiberius was not uniquely Tacitean.

After the terror of Tiberius's last decade, senatorial historians writing under his successors read these aberrations back into the entire reign and thus created his traditional image, which also appears in Dio and Suetonius. Yet Tacitus has gone further; with his literary and dramatic art he has crafted the impression of a desperate, lonely, misanthropic psychopath who has become one of the most vivid characters in Latin literature.

Annals 11–16 contains far fewer transparent rumors, and then only when the target is Nero. "People said" that Nero intended to build a new city and might have been responsible for the burning of Rome; another rumor recounted that Nero sang of the burning of Troy while the capital was in flames. While Tacitus does not vouch for the reliability of this gossip, the repeated stories have the effect of blaming Nero for the fire of 64. But in fairness it should be said that Suetonius reports both these rumors as actual fact, and he also relates numerous additional stories of Nero's sexual depravity. Tacitus may seem cowardly to hide behind rumor and innuendo, but Suetonius shows the immense range of disparaging stories that Tacitus chose not to include.

Besides relaying unverifiable rumors, Tacitus occasionally reported a rumor or report that he knew was false. When reporting Augustus's trip to be reconciled with his exiled grandson Agrippa, he alludes to a rumor that the emperor was killed by his wife Livia to prevent Agrippa's reinstatement.[56] The latter preposterous story is retailed at far greater length by Dio Cassius whence it has found its way into Robert Graves's novel *I, Claudius*. All the components of such a tale foreshadow the murder of Claudius by his wife Agrippina to allow her son Nero to succeed before the emperor reverted to his own son Britannicus. Tacitus is content to use the rumors to besmirch by association Livia and Tiberius who, whatever their failings, never displayed the deranged malice of an Agrippina and a Nero. It is good literature but it can be irresponsible history.

History is constructed of details and the plausibility of any historical work lies first in the accuracy of its details. We have seen that Tacitus does not change his details to fit his conceptual reconstruction of the past. Those details have been confirmed by archaeology in Britain and Germany, by inscriptions, and by other literary sources. But the histories of Tacitus, like all historical writing, also contain the prejudices and personal history of the author. Catholics and Protestants write different accounts of the Reformation; Jewish historians can hardly be wholly dispassionate about the Holocaust. The greatest Roman historians of the last two centuries—Gibbon, Mommsen, Rostovzteff, and Syme—wrote with passion as they saw connections between Rome and their own times. We can hardly demand greater objectivity of a man who had lived through civil war, despotism, and a reign of terror; we can only hope to find professionalism and fairness. It is Tacitus's inclusion of inconvenient facts that even permits us to question the reliability of his judgments. He distinguishes fact from rumor with a scrupulosity rare in any ancient historian. Napoleon thought Tacitus was biased against the emperors whom the Roman people loved. What does "bias" mean? He had studied the actions of Tiberius, Caligula, and Nero; he had seen and heard the suffering which imperial ambitions had inflicted on the Empire during the Civil War; he had observed at close hand the cruelties of Domitian. This was a man who hated emperors passionately, but with good reason. Hatred is no more or less biased than love; either may inspire great history.

We cannot judge Tacitus by the dry, anemic academic history of the later twentieth century that too often collects facts without reaching beyond them to a deeper, moral meaning. Tacitus wrote neither scientific history, nor a bare chronicle of events. There is much about the first century A.D. that we wish Tacitus had told us: how did economics affect political change? what were the effects of social mobility in the bureaucracy? what did the Romans really know about Christianity? But these questions did not interest Tacitus, and it is unfair to impose a modern historical agenda and to regard him merely as a source whose function is to provide us with facts. The most enduring histories are written in passion and are read for their ideas. Truth is sometimes the product of painstaking research, but it may also result from moral resolution or political acumen. Tacitus wrote with passion: a passion to expose official lies and to replace them with a politically and morally true history of the Empire. It is a truth based on factual accuracy but one that transcends it. For only penetrating intelligence, literary genius, and unremitting personal honesty can produce history of such universal power and emotional truth.

*The morality of Tacitus is the
morality of patriotism.*

Letter of
JOHN ADAMS
to Thomas Jefferson *

IV

❖ ──────────────────────────── ❖

The Historian as Moralist

Roman historians always regarded moral teaching as a central function, perhaps the central function, of historical writing. They saw all change in moral terms, and they saw important historical issues like causation as fundamentally moral questions.[1] Thus history must do more than merely tell pleasant stories from the past; it must pass moral judgments. For it was from the study of the past, from the virtues and vices of their ancestors, that the Romans derived their conception of public morality. Crusty Cato the Elder (234–149 B.C.), who was the first to write history in Latin,

---

*Letter of February 2, 1816, in L. J. Capon, *The Adams-Jefferson Letters* (Chapel Hill, 1959) II 462.

had railed against what he saw as the corruption of Roman values by increasing hellenization. A century later Cicero, no historian but willing to pronounce on any subject, affirmed that history must be useful and moral and that it was the *magister vitae*, the guide of life.[2] Sallust saw Rome's decline stemming from the moral flabbiness that followed the destruction of their last serious rival, Carthage, in 146 B.C., and he scathingly attacked the growing personal ambition, corruption, and greed among the ruling elite, despite the fact that he himself had been prosecuted and forced to retire from public life for having amassed a prodigious fortune as governor of Africa. Livy's stirring tales of Lucretia's suicide after her rape, Brutus's expulsion of the Etruscan king, and the Horatii defending their fatherland provided examples of political courage that have inspired poets, painters, and patriots from the Renaissance to the French Revolution.

Roman historians were never the detached and curious observers of the past that Greek historians tried to be. Roman writers became intimately involved with their subject matter in a way that was foreign to the Greek temperament.[3] It would, for example, be difficult to find a character in Homer with whom the author has as strong an emotional connection as Vergil does with Dido or Turnus. Sallust's passionate involvement with Catiline and Livy's with Hannibal is manifest in the moral judgments that abound in their histories.

Tacitus continues this tradition of moral history, but he transforms it into something far more profound. He avoids the shallow moralizing to be found in so many Roman writers and goes beyond the easygoing chauvinism of Livy to show that, in an age of absolute rulers, political virtue consisted in something more complex than fighting to the death to defend the state against a foreign enemy. Of course Tacitus tells tales of *virtus* (manly courage), but a central theme of his history is the link between the decline of *virtus* and the loss of freedom at Rome.[4] Tacitus's bleak, tragic vision of Rome under the emperors leads him to the penetrating and complex moral judgments that so characterize his work.

Sources of Tacitean Morality

Many other societies, from the Greeks and ancient Hebrews up to our own day, derive their codes of moral conduct and their ethical systems from religion or philosophy. But neither religion nor philosophy played an important part in Tacitus's moral system. Despite his occasional expressions of orthodox religious beliefs, it is his skepticism that is pervasive. His hostility toward Christians and Jews is notorious; he is also unsympathetic toward the Druids, Eastern religions, astrology, and the superstitions of the mob. Tacitus was hardly respectful of the imperial cult and avoids the conventional honorific, "the deified Julius," when referring to Julius Caesar. He reports that the German general Arminius sarcastically referred to the "god Augustus," and that, at the funeral of the newly deified Claudius, Nero's inappropriate praise convulsed the crowd with laughter. Even traditional Roman state religion offered him little consolation.[5] The republican state cult had been based upon divine favor which had brought so much success to the Romans. No longer did the benevolent gods smile upon Roman conquests; instead they encouraged the Empire's decline.[6] That anger of the gods first appears in the *Histories* and grows even more relentless in the *Annals* where Tacitus expressly blames the gods for the rise of Sejanus and the continual murders under Nero. These gods are not Jupiter or the other anthropomorphic gods of the Roman pantheon, but such impersonal forces as *Fortuna,* who only punish the guilty; they do not intervene on behalf of the virtuous.

The upper classes in the early Empire were deeply credulous of portents, magic, and astrology.[7] Tacitus's own hostility towards astrologers was certainly shared by some emperors who feared the implications of their forecasts, but his sweeping skepticism about the supernatural was uncommon. Yet Tacitus willingly suspended his disbelief in astrology, magic, and portents if they added to the power of his story. In the *Histories* he presents as credible favorable prophecies of Vespasian's accession: the predictions of the Philistine priest; miracles in Alexandria; and the voices and apparitions at the Temple in Jerusalem which the Jews wrongly interpreted as omens of their victory.[8] But when he comes to write the *Annals*

Tacitus uses supernatural portents only as a dramatic device to foreshadow impending disaster: clouds across the moon, a storm, a comet and bolt of lightning that broke Nero's table, a collapsing bridge, a superhuman female, and the oracular prediction of Germanicus's death. These omens and portents become an integral part of his narrative technique: they serve as metaphors for the punishment of humanity at the hands of superhuman powers.

If the traditional gods who had now abandoned the Roman people did not provide Tacitus with the basis of a moral system, where could he turn? Like all educated Romans of his day, Tacitus was familiar with the major philosophical schools and he discusses the doctrines of both Stoicism and Epicureanism in the *Annals*.[9] But he was deeply distrustful of philosophers, and hardly derived his moral standards from philosophy. He followed Quintilian in preferring oratory to philosophy as the ideal education for a Roman gentleman. He recounts that Agricola

> used to tell us that in his youth he was tempted to drink more deeply of philosophy than a Roman and a future senator should, if his mother's common sense had not reined in his burning enthusiasm.[10]

Tacitus scorns professional philosophers and suggests that most study philosophy "to disguise laziness with a pretentious name."[11] While he defended Seneca and regarded Thrasea Paetus as a brave senator with Stoic views (rather than a Stoic martyr), he was cynical towards the Stoic resistance and said that some even felt the courageous Helvidius Priscus was too eager for fame: "since the desire for glory is the last to be overcome, even by philosophers."[12] Tacitus goes still further in discussing the sanctimonious pretensions of Publius Egnatius:

> Though he professed Stoicism and was trained in manner and demeanor to seem honest, in his heart he was treacherous and crafty, concealing greed and lust. Money later laid bare his vices.[13]

Such charlatans, who remind us of philosophical and religious hypocrites from antiquity through Molière's Tartuffe to the televangelists of today, disgusted Tacitus with their hollow professions of virtue; he was far more interested in noble deeds than empty words.

For Tacitus, as for many other Romans, the bedrock of the Roman moral system was the noble deeds of Romans of the past. Cicero once asked "What is the meaning of a man's life unless it is intertwined with that of our ancestors by history?"[14] The Romans were proud of their ancestral past, and heroic legends were passed on orally for generations before poets and historians gave them literary form. Individual families preserved their own achievements in funeral speeches recounting the real and imagined exploits of centuries of forebears. For the young Roman, duty was defined historically by the important term *aemulatio;* he was to emulate the personal, civic, and martial virtues of his ancestors at the family hearth, in the forum, and on the battlefield. These models of private and public conduct formed the basis of moral and political education at Rome.

The root of our word "morality" is derived from *mos;* its plural *mores* has come over into English with the rather anemic meaning of "customs" or "habits." But for the Romans the meaning was much stronger: *mos maiorum* was "the way of our ancestors" and *mores* are patterns of behavior which set a standard of conduct. The attitude has not entirely disappeared. Contemporary conservatives like Alan Bloom have argued that the teaching of history, particularly a traditional version of Western Civilization, can provide moral guidance for our society,[15] while the liberal historian M. I. Finley suggested that the critical study of the past can give a society cohesion.[16] So too Tacitus saw in the achievements and values of the past the only reliable guide to public or private conduct. He provides exemplars of personal courage in the face of death, devotion to intellectual freedom, dignity in suicide. Likewise, on the dark side of tyranny, we find paranoid leaders, ambitious henchmen, sycophantic flatters, informers, traitors, and executioners. His moral judgments on the virtuous and the vicious are Tacitus's legacy to later generations.[17]

The Romans believed that members of a family (*gens*) were closely linked across generations by a spirit (*genius*) which embodied the values and achievements of the family past. Tacitus projects Roman attitudes onto a barbarian when he has Calgacus conclude his stirring speech to his troops: "As you enter battle, think of your ancestors and your descendants."[18] Romans were often enjoined not to disgrace their ancestors, and Tacitus showed compassion and rare tact towards the impoverished nobles whom Nero paid to appear on the stage: "They are dead; I think their ancestors deserve that I not name them."[19]

At the beginning of the *Annals,* Tacitus makes it clear that he sees the political decline of Rome indissolubly linked with its moral decline:

> How few were left who had seen the Republic? The state had been transformed, and nothing was left of the old, untainted morality (*mos*). Political equality was gone.[20]

Tacitus not only judged politics in moral terms, but he saw political change, especially the loss of senatorial liberty, as deeply affecting moral values. He devotes little time to such details of constitutional change as the evolution of the consulship; he focuses on how the Romans abuse their institutions and how their character has declined from that of their ancestors.[21] One could no longer trust the personal compacts, *fides* and *amicitia,* that formed the basis of political life in the Republic; now flattery and sycophancy towards those in power corrupted all relationships.[22]

Tacitus, like other Roman moralists, idealized the republican past before foreign influences and the wealth of conquest had corrupted traditional values.[23] With his origins in the western provinces, he had a distrust of the East and a sexual puritanism reminiscent of the middle classes in nineteenth-century Europe. He expresses disgust at Nero's theatrical posturing and even condemns his poetry as flaccid and uninspiring. He fully sympathizes with those anonymous critics of the values of the Neronian age:

> "Traditional morality, gradually slipping away, was entirely undermined by imported laxity so that whatever corrupts or can be corrupted would be seen in Rome, and foreign taste would reduce our youth to a bunch of gymnasts, loafers, and perverts. The emperor and senate are at fault; they not only allow these vices, but even force Roman nobles to debase themselves by declaiming or singing onstage. What re-

mained, save to strip naked, put on gloves, and practice box-
ing instead of serving in the army."[24]

Tacitus is also revolted by the trappings of Greek culture: actors,
eunuchs, gymnasia, ballet dancers, singers, astrologers, homosexuality, Claudius's Greek freedmen at court, and the Greek literary
salon at Tiberius's court on Capri.[25]

Tacitus saw the growing sexual license of the imperial court as a
turning away from traditional values. He deplored Tiberius's orgies, Messalina's promiscuity, and Nero's bisexuality; one can well
imagine the outrage in his lost pages on Caligula. The political use
of sexual excess is a particular provocation to Tacitus. His most
notable example is the younger Agrippina who slept her way to
the pinnacle of political power. She seduced her uncle Claudius
into marriage (while also sleeping with his freedman) and then
murdered him so that her son, Nero, could succeed to the throne.
She was later rumored to have had sexual relations with that son
in an unsuccessful attempt to maintain her control over him. Tacitus is certainly repelled by incest, but he is more concerned by
Agrippina's ruthless quest for power. He has Piso link sex with
political power when he says that his rival Otho "dreams of depravity, revelry, and hordes of women; he considers them the prerogatives of the imperial throne."[26]

Tacitus also disapproves of extravagant displays of wealth, as
well as gluttony and indolence that go against Roman aristocratic
traditions. When a senator argued that the growth of private for-
tunes is not new and that the Roman nobility had always lived
more lavishly than the other classes, Tacitus points out that this
hypocritical confession of vice found a sympathetic audience.[27]
Yet there are many more examples of sexual depravity and ostentatious extravagance in Suetonius's *Lives* than in Tacitus.[28] Tacitus
is more interested in political ambition, arrogance, and personal
or public hypocrisy than in sexual behavior or avarice, and he is
more concerned with passing moral judgment than with amassing
sordid details.[29] Sloth, debauchery, and greed are primarily used
by this most political of historians to link the moral failings of the
imperial family and their supporters to the decline of freedom at
Rome.

Moral Character

Tacitus does not engage in abstract discussions of morality; as an historian, he is the judge of men and events, not doctrines, and he studies character in order to show how individuals or groups act in specific situations. Tacitus has long been admired (or deplored) for the vividness of his moral portraits; Francis Bacon ranked him even above Plato and Aristotle as a moralist. He sometimes provides his moral judgment at the first appearance of a character, sometimes in a brief obituary after his or her death. These vignettes capture in a few trenchant lines the moral personality of a character. Thus Tacitus introduces Poppaea Sabina, soon to ensnare Nero as her third husband:

> Poppaea had everything except virtue. She inherited fame and good looks from her mother, the greatest beauty of her day, and her wealth equaled her birth. She was charming in conversation with a sharp wit; while seeming modest she behaved wickedly. At her rare public appearances she wore a veil, either to intrigue the onlooker or because it flattered her. She cared little for her reputation and treated husbands and lovers much the same. No slave to her own or her lover's emotions, she gave her favors where she found the greatest advantage.[30]

In this scathing portrait, he transforms what might elsewhere be virtues (her privacy and modesty) into vices.

Tacitus, like most Roman writers, usually regarded moral character as fixed at birth and the human personality as essentially static.[31] His rhetorical training encouraged him to use the character types found in school exercises (such as the Tyrant or Martyr),[32] much as editorial cartoonists and propagandists in our own century have used instantly recognizable stereotypes (Arab sheik, Russian bear, John Bull, Uncle Sam). Tacitus's portrait of Tiberius's corrupt and bloodthirsty praetorian prefect Sejanus owes much to Sallust's earlier depiction of the unsavory Catiline. Where personality changes are so clearly documented that they cannot be ignored, he attributes them to a gradual revelation of an evil personality previously concealed by hypocrisy. Thus he gradually uncovers the true Tiberius through the first six books of the *Annals;* power corrupts, not because it changes the essential moral character of Tiberius but because it frees him to follow his basest instincts.

Tacitus is not interested in private morality for its own sake, but for the light it sheds on public actions.[33] Where private vices do not affect public life, he passes over them in relative silence. He is slower than most moralists to conclude that private immorality necessarily impairs public competence.[34] He leaves such behavior to the satirist Juvenal or the philosopher Seneca. The depraved private life of Petronius, the "Arbiter of Elegance" at Nero's court and author of the *Satyricon,* does not prevent Tacitus from praising his governorship and consulate. For Petronius—and this is always important for Tacitus—died well. When falsely implicated in a conspiracy against the emperor, he faced death with nobility while avoiding, perhaps even parodying, the sanctimonious suicide of Stoic philosophers. He had the last laugh on Nero. This amuses even our earnest historian whose wry smile is evident:

> He did not rush to take his life, but he had his severed arteries bound up, then opened again, and conversed with friends, but not about serious things nor to win fame for his bravery. He listened to them reciting light songs and amusing verses, not speeches on the immortality of the soul or on the teachings of philosophers . . .
>
> Not even in his will did he praise Nero, Tigellinus, or some other leader, as many did on their deathbed, but he wrote out the emperor's orgies (with his male and female lovers named) with each new act of debauchery, and sent it under seal to Nero . . . Nero was puzzled how the nature of his nocturnal activities had become known.[35]

Virtue under Tyranny

The Romans believed that history, by linking the present with the past, should illuminate the contemporary state of society. Thus moral judgments about the past are intended to provide both moral and practical guidance for the future. Tacitus repeatedly explores this central theme: how good men can live virtuously under evil rulers. His father-in-law Agricola managed to avoid the extremes of the sycophantic informers and the self-admiring ostentation of the Stoic martyrs. For the same reason Tacitus was more sympathetic to Seneca than were some ancient, and most modern, writers. He recognized that, as Nero's tutor, Seneca had successfully controlled the young man (and fended off his power-hungry mother) for more than five years. He reports attacks on Seneca's wealth, and on his complicity in Nero's crimes, but these are voiced by notorious informers.[36] Tacitus understands the necessity of discretion and compromise, and he allows Seneca the redemption of a noble death. Nonetheless, good men cannot simply withdraw; their duty demands that they do all in their power to mitigate the excesses of their rulers. While there is some defensiveness on this issue, there is also insight in his praise for Lepidus as one who could exercise a moderating influence with enough tact to remain in Tiberius's favor.[37] Agricola and Lepidus retained their integrity while working on behalf of their compatriots. That is a noble ideal, but as Tacitus knew well, and as we know again from painful cases in modern history, the line between accommodation and collaboration is rarely distinct.

The Morality of the Masses

Tacitus can see both virtue and vice within the individual characters in his histories, but he invariably passes harsh judgments on people acting in groups. Tacitus followed earlier historians in idealizing the Roman people and the Roman armies of the Republic, but he believed that both had been corrupted by the new regime.[38] When he disapprovingly reports that Augustus had "seduced (*pellexit* in Latin can have a sexual connotation) the army with money, the people with grain, and everyone with the sweetness of peace,"[39] Tacitus knew full well that succeeding emperors continued to woo the armies and the inhabitants of Rome on whose support and acquiescence they depended. Like the aristocratic political theorists of fifth-century Athens who assailed the "rule of the mob," Tacitus was contemptuous of the corrupt Roman mob who were kept in check, in the words of the contemporary satirist Juvenal, with "bread and circuses"[40]—a complaint that recurs in democratic (or pseudo-democratic) states from Periclean Athens to our own day. The crowds who watched Roman armies fighting in the streets in 69 enjoyed the bloodshed as much as if they were celebrating a festival in the Colosseum.[41]

For Tacitus these crowds were no longer the Roman People, but a contemptible mob who had forgotten their ancestors and prostituted their birthright. He attributed army mutinies to recent conscription of troops from the lazy and self-indulgent rabble of the capital who desired luxury and ease rather than the glorious triumphs of their forebears.[42] Roman soldiers had once competed with each other in courage, but now they imitated the selfish and mercurial urban mob in their insolence and insubordination.[43] Discipline was abandoned as centurions plotted against their commanders, generals bribed their way into the favor of potentially rebellious troops. When the troops ran wild in the Civil War, they sacked Cremona like an enemy city and fought in the streets of Rome itself while the temple of Jupiter burned on the Capitol. But Tacitus does not blame the soldiers alone; he also attributes this terrible sacrilege to the "madness of the leaders"—the emperors and generals are themselves acting like an uncontrolled mob.[44]

Tacitus's contempt for slaves, freedmen, and the lower classes displays the traditional Roman connection between morality and social station. When he describes a leader of the mutiny as a professional claqueur in private life, we know Tacitus expects his reader to feel the same disgust as when Vitellius made a knight of his repulsive, ingratiating freedman Asiaticus. Tacitus is at his most condescending in describing the loathsome Sejanus as a "small-town adulterer"; adulterer he certainly was, but his father had been praetorian prefect under Augustus and the family was certainly more distinguished than Tacitus's own.

Yet Tacitus also finds fault with the indolence of the old aristocratic families and applauds the courage of slaves who remain loyal to their masters in distress. After the Pisonian conspiracy, Nero's torturers captured a freedwoman Epicharis who hanged herself rather than incriminate men she barely knew. Her bravery was particularly notable at a time when craven knights and senators betrayed their friends; the aristocratic poet Lucan denounced his own mother in the futile hope of escaping death.[45]

Tacitus's most painful criticism is not for the active criminals, but for all those who, like the centurions of 69, preferred the safe course to the "risks of honor." The betrayal of Galba is "a shocking crime which a few risked, more desired, and all passively acquiesced in."[46] Tacitus knew well that senatorial acquiescence was sometimes far from passive. Despite their oath to the contrary, senators received rewards and honors from their colleagues' downfall. Tacitus regrets having to record the hypocritical senatorial votes of thanks every time Nero ordered execution or exile, but says that "if any senatorial decree reaches new depths of flattery or servility, I will not be silent about it."[47] In his severest self-indictment, Tacitus congratulates Agricola for having been fortunate enough to die before Domitian's terror forced Tacitus himself and the other senators to recognize their own cowardice and complicity in the deaths of Stoic opponents of the regime. As Tacitus said of the soldiers who fought a civil war against their own kin, "They said that it was crime—and they did it anyway."[48] Even more humiliating for the proud Senate, Domitian was finally killed by humble freedmen. Tacitus's is a remarkable confession of collaboration, a confession that has a particular resonance in a century when we have come to realize that the atrocities of popularly supported governments frequently produce just such collective responsibility.

The Danger of Virtue

At the beginning of each of his historical works, Tacitus suggests that traditional Roman virtues have actually become dangerous. He recounts in the prologue to the *Agricola* that he had to seek imperial permission to write such a biography in an era "so hostile to virtue." In the *Annals* a senator who is "rich, energetic, talented and popular, is therefore suspect."[49] It is clear in the introduction to the *Histories* that by 69 things had got worse so that respectability itself brought danger and friends were as treacherous as enemies.[50] Emperors were threatened by examples of republican virtue and they felt more comfortable surrounding themselves with men like the praetorian prefect Tigellinus, whose notorious dissolution Nero found fascinating.[51] Despotic rulers use such loathsome creatures to do their dirty work; then they need not fear invidious comparisons.

If the emperors shunned those who embodied antique virtue, so too did the army, the mob, and even some senators who dreaded the accession of an upright and incorruptible emperor.[52] Piso's dissolute habits made him appealing to conspirators who did not wish to replace Nero with an austere monarch. This is a recurrent theme in the *Histories,* where Galba's integrity caused his downfall. Galba's attempts at discipline and his old-fashioned austerity were hardly welcome to troops used to frequent bonuses and the pandering of their leaders, troops who much preferred the generosity and license of Vitellius. The soldiers now loved the vices of their emperors as they had once feared their virtues. Likewise, the masses resented Tiberius's unwillingness to appear at dance performances (thought not long before to be an example of foreign immorality), and the senators feared that he might impose austerity through stern legislation.[53] It is ironic to see Tacitus reduced to using his *bête noire* Tiberius as an example of republican virtues. But his point is clear: ancient virtue was much praised; few were eager to see its return.

The Decline of Virtue

Tacitus's account of the first century of the Empire makes it clear that "private profit is preferred to the public interest."[54] Examples of greed and selfishness abound, and the "decline of virtue" became a familiar cliché in the literature. In the *Dialogue,* Tacitus has Messala attribute the decline of oratory to the vices of the age: "the laziness of our youth, the neglect of parents, the ignorance of teachers, and the decline of old-fashioned virtue."[55] Like so many moralists, from Athens (where Aristophanes satirized the teaching of Socrates) to our own day, social critics have often blamed parents and educators for a "moral decline" that in fact resulted from wide social and political changes. Even before the fall of the Roman Republic, Cicero and Sallust bemoaned the rise of hedonism and materialism among the young nobles of their time and complained that Catiline, Clodius, and their followers did not heed the example of their ancestors. Rome had been transformed by the vast conquests of the second century B.C., when the evolution of the social, economic, and political institutions of the state produced a quite different moral climate from that of the hardy yeoman-farmer that the Romans idealized. So the changes had hardly all taken place since the triumph of Augustus and the principate, as a naive reading of Tacitus might imply.

For Tacitus the primary cause of moral decline was the concentration of power in the hands of the emperors and their court.

> That old and instinctive desire for power blossomed and burst forth as our Empire became great. In a modest state equality was easily preserved, but world conquest and the destruction of rival cities or kings brought the opportunity to lust after wealth in safety.[56]

Lord Acton was hardly the first to note the corrupting influence of power; Tacitus has a senator say that Tiberius was "transformed and perverted by absolute power despite his experience in public affairs."[57] And the sycophantic flattery of a Sejanus, a Macro, or a Tigellinus encouraged the megalomania of the emperors. The theme of weak rulers and corrupt but strong-willed courtiers has passed from Tacitus through Racine to modern political psychology. Tacitus first showed us how the collapse of laws and the degeneration of civic virtue can be caused by the corrosive influence of absolute power.

If the power of the emperors undermined the laws, their rampaging soldiers brought chaos and anarchy to the Roman state. Tacitus usually appears as an unrepentant imperialist who believed that foreign wars inspired discipline among the Romans, while civil conflict brought out all their worst qualities. But he also saw clearly that even field armies were now corrupt. After a mutiny in the camp, the legions purge their shame by a cowardly attack on the Germans. For Tacitus, there is a symbiotic association between the corruption of power and civil wars, which allow the worst elements to triumph over traditional Roman virtues. "In times of violence and strife, the worst man gains great power; peace and quiet demand virtue."[58] His account of the second battle of Cremona is a powerful reminder of the inhumanity of civil war: one soldier accidentally killed his own father while another claimed a reward for having killed his brother. The soldiers cursed it as the cruelest of wars, but they continued to commit atrocities against their friends and relatives.[59]

Although Tacitus was repelled by the cruelty and cowardice of Roman soldiers in battle, he always applauded examples of military and personal courage. He manifests an almost Vergilian admiration for those who show courage even in defeat. He admires the heroism of the German chieftains and countless individual Roman soldiers or senators are praised for their willingness to risk danger or death. Courage in the face of death is perhaps *the* great virtue for Tacitus. Courageous deaths had made Brutus and Cato martyrs for the Republic while Cicero's death after his vacillating flight had tarnished his memory.[60] While Tacitus despised the way of life of Petronius, he admired the courage of his death, and even the loathsome Agrippina regains a measure of imperial dignity when she heroically resists and finally confronts Nero's assassins. She revealed the nobility of her birth in the manner of her death.

Tacitus highlights the decline of virtue among the Romans by contrasting it to the natural morality of the Britons, Gauls, and Germans. Tacitus creates speeches for barbarian leaders which inspire their troops to acts of heroism, as when Civilis exhorts the Gauls to revolt:

> "Let Syria, Asia, and the Orient accustomed to kings be slaves; in Gaul there are many who were born in the days before tribute . . . Nature has given liberty even to dumb animals while courage is a special gift of men. The gods favor those who are braver."[61]

Nor are these empty words. The Britons fought to the death at Mons Graupius, Civilis swore to let his hair grow until he had defeated the Romans, and Arminius, "the liberator of Germany," destroyed three Roman legions. When Tacitus says that Thracian princes did not wish to outlive freedom, he implicitly compares them to cowardly Romans like Vitellius who tried to negotiate for their lives after defeat.[62] When two German emissaries came to Rome and were taken sightseeing at the Theater of Pompey,

> They noticed a few men in foreign dress seated among the senators. Asking who they were, they were told that it was an honor given to ambassadors of those peoples who had shown exceptional courage and loyalty to Rome. Exclaiming that no one surpassed the Germans in bravery or loyalty, they went down and sat among the senators. The spectators enjoyed their primitive impulsiveness and honest competitiveness. Nero gave them both Roman citizenship.[63]

Tacitus obviously admired such pride and courage.

The ethnographic sections of the *Germania* provide an admiring picture of the German family, and give Tacitus ample opportunity to lament sexual promiscuity at Rome. The Germans were content with a single wife, and in rare cases of adultery, severely punished the offenders. Tacitus extols German women:

> They are uncorrupted by the temptations of the games or by the excitement of banquets. Neither men nor women send secret love-letters . . . No one there laughs at vice, or calls it fashionable to seduce or be seduced . . . Morality is stronger there than laws are elsewhere.[64]

The comparison to the sophisticated debauchery parodied in Ovid's *Art of Love* is evident. The Suebians prefer to deck themselves out for battle rather than for seduction, unlike the foppish young Romans. In Germany families are much prized, and mothers do not fob children off on wet-nurses, but breast-feed their children themselves. They obviously do not share the growing Roman penchant for divorce and childlessness. Tacitus's monograph contrasts the austere moral world of an idealized Germany with the corruption of first-century Rome, and even with the Britons' servile acceptance of Roman civilization. Tacitus was not writing a simple ethnographic treatise to inform the Romans about German life. Rather, he was describing those aspects of German life which shed a bleak light on the mores of contemporary Rome.

Other apparent "digressions" also enable Tacitus to comment on Roman political life. Just as he idealizes elements in German society to cast an unfavorable light on contemporary Rome, his extended discussions in the *Annals* of wars and treacherous dynastic disputes in the East comment on the court intrigues on the Palatine. The rivalry of brothers for the Parthian throne foreshadows the murder of Claudius and the conflict between Nero and Britannicus.[65] Tacitus exploits a powerful irony when he shows Claudius advising the Parthian prince to act, not as an autocrat, but as a leader of free men. Though Tacitus never uses the despised title of "king" for Roman emperors, his digressions make clear the parallels between Roman and Eastern monarchs.

Good and Evil

Although Roman historians had long held *exempla* of both vice and virtue before their readers, their emphasis had been on positive models, just as family funeral eulogies praised the moral standards and political achievements of their ancestors. But such noble achievements are easier to find for historians who write about the remote past. The surviving books of Livy, whose treatment of the decline of the Republic is admittedly lost, are filled with illustrations of personal and public virtue. Livy provides few examples of Roman cowardice and evil; he usually reserves vices for Rome's enemies.

Like Livy, Tacitus finds examples of virtue, even in the terrible year 69:

> Mothers followed their children into flight; wives their husbands into exile. There were bold relatives, courageous sons-in-law, and slaves whose loyalty defied torture. Famous men bravely endured the final torment and rivaled those admired death scenes of antiquity.[66]

But for Tacitus, such acts of courage are minor, almost futile, assertions of human dignity in a world in which all traditional Roman values are being destroyed. In Livy, the courageous actions of Lucretia or the Horatii freed the Roman people or saved the

Republic: individual virtue contributed to the common good. But Tacitus's view of the Roman Empire and the human condition is so bleak that virtue exists only in the private sphere. A woman refuses under torture to disclose her son's hiding place, but that noble act in an ignoble age has no lasting impact. Virtue is admirable, but futile; it is cruelty and evil that determine the fate of the Roman people.

Tacitus was neither the first nor the last Roman historian to express a deeply pessimistic view of the human condition. His great model, in bleakness of moral vision as in style, is Sallust whose picture of Rome's gradual decline casts a pall of fatalism over his books. The pessimistic vision moves from Sallust through Tacitus to the fourth-century historian Ammianus Marcellinus and finally to St. Augustine: an intellectual thread which expresses the moral conscience of the Roman people far better than the works of poets or Stoic philosophers.[67] The corruption of human behavior only depressed the pagan writers, but it inspired the Bishop of Hippo to turn away from the City of Man to the City of God. Tacitus and Augustine, very different men in so many ways, shared the same view of the human condition in this world.

While Tacitus generally believed in the fixity of character, he does make exceptions. Writing of Vespasian, for instance, Tacitus observes that "he alone of all the emperors before him changed for the better."[68] And the historian also sees change when he depicts ordinary citizens and soldiers enboldened to riot, loot, and murder when given the opportunity. Thus Tacitus sometimes seems to regard circumstances as more influential than innate character; he comments on the conflict between Otho and Vitellius that "the only certainty was that the worse man would win."[69] Tacitus clearly believes that the rise of tyranny at Rome has brought about a moral decline. Evil seems to come, not only from the innate character of citizens, soldiers, or freedmen, but from the social and political conditions of autocracy.

Tacitus's early works had shown the conflict between virtue and vice: the struggle of Agricola to live a life of traditional Roman virtue under the regime of a monstrous tyrant; the idealized picture of barbarian Germany with its implied (and sometimes overt) critique of Roman morality; and the linkage between morality, culture, and political life that constitutes the central focus of the *Dialogue*. And yet, despite some individual moral insights, these books remain conventional in tone and purpose. We do not find in them the vivid powers of description, the total command of language, and the bleak moral landscape of the two great histories of his later life. In the earlier works Tacitus was an interesting writer with a particular political perspective; only in the *Histories* and the *Annals* did he become the most profound moral and political philosopher that pagan Rome ever produced.

Other Roman writers described political decline and moral decay; Tacitus's dark meditation raises political and moral failure to an existential level of despair. That despair colors all his texts; what Erich Auerbach saw in the early Empire as "a darkening in the atmosphere of life" is both a metaphor and an exact description of the palette of the historian.[70] The pervasive physical darkness of the *Histories* and *Annals* exactly conveys Tacitus's vision of an age bereft of morality and infused with the blackness of evil.

While individual crimes like Nero's murder of his mother Agrippina may particularly shock Tacitus (and his reader), it is the continual failure of *virtus* and the triumph of evil that gives his work its special character. Not only monsters like Nero and Agrippina are moral failures. Even their victims are guilty of a craven retreat from the high standards of the Roman nobility. Late in the *Annals*, Tacitus interjects what is almost an excuse for this slavish passivity: the fault lay not with individuals but in "the anger of the gods toward Rome."[71] Tacitus's pessimism derives from the conviction that virtue may no longer be possible, that the appearance of virtue may only be fictitious, and that vices were certain to return.

Tacitus believed that a pervasive gloom afflicted the Roman people. Though he occasionally pays lip service to the gods, his diagnosis of the evil of the Empire concludes that Rome had lost her moral compass, one might even say, her soul.[72] Or, if not lost, "it was covered with wounds and lacerations" as Tacitus says of the soul of Tiberius.[73] The corruption encompassed individuals, the state, oratory, literature, and, as he saw with remarkable discernment, language itself. The debasement of language makes it impossible to distinguish freedom from tyranny, cowardice from bravery, good from evil. It is perhaps for this reason that Tacitus has little hope for the future.[74]

Of course this melancholic vision is closely related to Tacitus's own biography in which moral, political, and psychological motives intertwine. He admits that he prospered under Flavian rule and that, even when he withdrew from public life under Domitian, he never confronted the tyrants or their agents. Despite his dismissal of the grandstanding suicides of Stoic philosophers, much guilt and shame lie just below the surface of Tacitus's moral pronouncements and exhortations to courage.[75] He wrote his great histories in an era of "rare happiness" under Trajan, under whom he served as consul and who gave him an important governorship. His good friend Pliny delivered a eulogistic panegyric to the emperor, without reproach from Tacitus. The gloom and anger of the *Annals* are far distant from the comradely spirit of the letters that Tacitus exchanged with Pliny. Could Tacitus have remained so bitter through two decades of Trajan's benevolent rule, or do we see instead a lawyer and orator prosecuting his greatest case with posterity as the jury? Is his pessimism heartfelt, or is it a fire-and-brimstone rhetorical tour de force to prevent the Romans from returning to the autocracy of a Nero or a Domitian? Or has the advent of Trajan's protégé, the philhellene Hadrian, revived Tacitus's fears of another Caligula or Nero and ignited his moral and rhetorical passion?[76]

There are no easy answers to these questions. Both the *Histories* and the *Annals* lack their concluding books, and it is difficult to understand fully a moral message without a clear sense of the ending.[77] We can only speculate about Tacitus's personal feelings when writing the *Annals* near the end of his life. But whatever his motives, his surviving text is an extended meditation on evil in its widest social and political context, and as such it lays claim to great moral authority. Greek philosophers were far more interested in the "Good"; they viewed evil merely as the absence or negation of good. Roman writers like Sallust and Lucan dwell more insistently on the power of evil. But Tacitus goes far beyond the philosophers and his Roman compatriots in his focus on political, social, and psychological evil. And, for him, it was Rome's own moral failure engendered all the evils that led to the decline of freedom. Of all ancient writers, perhaps only St. Augustine goes further than Tacitus in his concentration on evil; in so doing the Christian philosopher has transformed the Western intellectual and spiritual tradition.

*In the delineation of character, Tacitus
is unrivaled among historians, and has
few superiors among dramatists and
novelists.*

THOMAS MACAULAY,
Essay on History*

V

❖ ———————————————————————— ❖

The Historian as Psychologist

The social sciences did not exist as an independent field of inquiry
in the ancient world; they were the province of historians, philosophers, and even poets. For anthropology we look to Homer,
Herodotus, and Tacitus's *Germania;* for social analysis, the sati-
rists and the comic poets; for political theory Plato, Aristotle, and
Cicero; and for political science Thucydides and Tacitus.

Ancient psychology began when Greek poets created the splendid characters—Oedipus, Electra, Medea, Penelope, Achilles—
who have long been analyzed and psychoanalyzed for the light

* *The Complete Works of Thomas Babington Macaulay: Critical and Historical Essays* I (New York, 1910) 262.

they shed on the human condition. Yet, when the p
character, they rarely pondered its source: an indi⸴
to fate or divine intervention. It was the philosᴄ
subjected personality to systematic study: Are ⸴
born with certain moral and psychological traits or are ⸜⸍
result of social formation? In more popular terms, can the leopard
change his spots?[1] Greek thinkers had begun to wrestle with the
issue of genetic determinism versus environment which has continued down to the present day. Likewise, the moral debate over
whether evil springs inevitably from the human personality (nature), or whether it is the product of the pressures of social environment (nurture), has been argued from the ancient Greeks to
the op-ed pages in contemporary newspapers.

It is a scholarly commonplace that ancient philosophers focused
on character types which they believed were determined at birth,
and that belief in the constancy of human nature influenced historians and biographers.[2] Yet there is much evidence that the philosophers *acted* as though education could effect important
change, and the formation (*paideia*) of leaders was an important
theme in Greek literature from Telemachus's voyage of self-
discovery in the *Odyssey*. Socrates hoped that philosophy would
make men better citizens, and was himself accused of corrupting
the young through his ideas. Plato traveled to Sicily to educate a
Syracusan prince, and Aristotle went to Macedon to teach the
young Alexander the Great. All these young aristocrats may have
had innate *arete* ("virtue"), but they had to develop it through
their own self-awareness as Shakespeare's dissolute Prince Hal did
on his road to becoming Henry V.

Psychological development was inextricably linked to moral
formation in antiquity. The Greek word "character" encompasses
both elements. Modern historians, in an attempt at objectivity,
often prefer to describe the personality—from the Etruscan–
Latin "persona" meaning mask—which allows them to portray
psychological traits without passing moral judgment.[3] As a moral
historian, Tacitus would see little difference between the mind and
the soul, yet his focus on individual action and motivation made
his work a handbook for political psychology in later centuries.
Since psychology today is not a moral science, I prefer, at the risk

of some duplication, to devote a separate chapter to the historian's psychological insights and analysis.

The complex tension between nature and nurture helps to explain some of the contradictions in Tacitus's treatment of character. Tacitus cites the prevailing Roman belief that moral character is fixed at birth and the human personality is essentially static: "Most men believe that the future is fixed at each person's birth."[4] Most may well have believed in astrological determinism, but Tacitus is skeptical and leans toward the possibility of change and personal responsibility for one's actions. He elsewhere makes quite explicit his belief that while power corrupted Tiberius, it improved Vespasian.[5] Above all, we must always remain aware that Tacitus used psychology as a tool in his rhetorical and historical arsenal.[6] Consistency was hardly as necessary as it is for a modern analytical social scientist; Tacitus was an advocate and politician by training—men who hardly prefer rigid consistency to persuasiveness or effectiveness.[7] The overall picture of Tiberius is riveting; it seems of little consequence that Tacitus here says he was born bad and there says he became worse. Neither Tacitus, nor any other ancient historian, thought of his work as a series of facts (or judgments) to be quoted out of context. His historical judgments and his ideas derive their value precisely from the narrative, and a hunt for minor discrepancies misses the value of ancient historiography.[8]

Psychological History

While Cato, Sallust, and Livy all rejected Greek detachment and wrote morally and politically committed history, Tacitus carries this subjectivity further still: he is less interested in the external events or even their causes than in the inner emotional dynamic of the Roman people.[9] He describes the bodies and limbs strewn across a battlefield only for the psychological effect it has on the spectator/reader.[10] His is an internal, psychological drama; Tacitus enters into feelings of his characters much as Vergil had done. Rome's greatest historian, poet, and philosopher all partake of the characteristic introspection that is the central original feature of Latin literature.[11]

If Vergil and Tacitus were the most accomplished Roman psychologists, the poet was preeminent in examining human emotions, while the historian linked public action to private thoughts, feelings, and moods. To our modern eyes, Tacitus's psychology might at first seem rather superficial as his characters fall into the stereotypes learned in the rhetorical schools: tyrant, collaborator, noble savage, philosophical martyr, etc.[12] Philosophers and essayists from Theophrastus to Addison and Steele have described such characters, and comic geniuses from Menander, Plautus, and Molière to Charlie Chaplin and Lily Tomlin have amused audiences with portraits of familiar characters from everyday life. Like comedians, cartoonists and even historians sometimes resort to cultural or ethnic stereotypes no less distorted than ancient "characters." Tacitus certainly uses the philosophical and rhetorical tradition, but his imagination allows him to alter these stereotypes: Tiberius and Nero are quite different as tyrants; Messalina and Agrippina have little in common psychologically save that they are both treacherous imperial wives. He uses the character types of his time, but he goes well beyond their narrow boundaries and even uses literary antecedents in his portrait of Tiberius's corrupt and bloodthirsty praetorian prefect Sejanus which owes much to Sallust's earlier depiction of the unsavory Catiline.

In any authoritarian political system, where the policies and institutions of the state depend on the personality of a single ruler and his entourage, political analysis and psychology must go hand in hand.[13] Tacitus saw history in terms of the individual emperor; his personality could hardly be separated from the process of government.[14] Just as modern autocracies keep the highest political activity hidden from their subjects, so the Roman senators understood the paramount importance of the emperor's thoughts and moods and the danger of discussing such "state secrets." One man, accused of being a friend of the discredited Sejanus, defended himself by pointing out that Tiberius himself had showered honors on Sejanus as his own friend and all he had done was to believe what he saw: "Research into the emperor's secret thoughts is hazardous."[15] A bit disingenuous, but still a brilliant defense: he was acquitted and his accusers exiled. But the historian must cover precisely this territory: the connection between private thoughts and public action. There we find the core of Tacitus's psychological perception.

The characterizations in the *Annals* are psychological and moral observations which gradually produce powerful images of Tiberius, Nero, and Agrippina. Characterization becomes political analysis. Tacitus rarely provides a direct portrait of his leading characters, and the few direct characterizations (Sejanus; Poppaea) are quite brief. There are a few crisp descriptive phrases at the introduction of a character, or a brief, acute obituary.[16] Those few lines focus on the moral stature of the character, often forever delineated by a single word or phrase: "fierce-tempered" Agrippa; Tiberius with his "haughty leniency"; Sejanus, the "small-town adulterer."[17] Tacitus allows the most vivid characters in Roman historical writing to reveal themselves in action rather than from extended authorial descriptions.[18] The collective personalities of rebellious soldiers, the fickle masses, and reptilian freedmen are also sharply defined in moral and political terms.

Tacitus's strong narrative and dramatic sense and his penetrating style give his characters far more life than would a large number of physical details.[19] Tacitus is not interested in physical appearances or even lurid anecdotes; moral physiognomy is more important than baldness, acne, or sexual aberrations. He does not care about warts or body odor (as Suetonius often does), he prefers to assess the importance of a character as an historical paradigm.

TIBERIUS AND NERO

Tacitus's rhetorical training in character-types sometimes leads him to try to reconcile, unconvincingly, the internal contradictions in his characters.[20] We can see this in the most brilliant and complex of all Tacitean characters, the emperor Tiberius, who has had such a powerful effect on modern readers. Autocrats do not intend to be fully understood, and Tiberius has succeeded in remaining something of a puzzle. "Complex and devious in the best sense of those words" said Ronald Syme, quoting in 1974 then-President Nixon's description of former President Eisenhower.[21] He has been admired, emulated, deplored, and even disbelieved as too monstrous. Our own century, familiar with far greater political horrors, has resorted to psychoanalyzing both Tiberius and his biographer Tacitus as clinical cases who are not to escape Dr. Freud's ministrations (any more than Oedipus or Moses did) merely by having lived a few millennia too early.[22]

Where personality changes are so clearly documented that they cannot be ignored, he attributes them to a gradual revelation of an evil personality previously concealed by hypocrisy. Thus he gradually uncovers the true Tiberius through the first six books of the *Annals;* power corrupts, not because it changes the innate cruelty of Tiberius, but because it frees him to follow his basest instincts. These were hidden until he came to power or, to be precise, until Sejanus encouraged him to allow despotism full reign. The emperor's obituary is quite explicit:

> His character also had different phases. His life and reputation were excellent while he was a private citizen or an official under Augustus. As long as Drusus and Germanicus lived, Tiberius was secretive and craftily affected decency; he was still a mix of good and evil while his mother was alive. As long as he loved or feared Sejanus, his cruelty was hated but his lust was hidden. Finally, when shame and fear were removed, he followed his own true inclinations and plunged equally into crime and dishonor.[23]

Thus the many good actions by Tiberius must be attributed to hypocrisy, just as self-serving and foolish ones on the part of Germanicus and Agrippina are excused. The *a priori* nature of this judgment is clear. Tacitus elsewhere provides evidence that Tiberius, after an exemplary early military career, became tormented by the fact that his mother Livia and stepfather Augustus had used him for their own political aims. He was forced to divorce a beloved wife to marry the emperor's promiscuous daughter Julia, whose scandalous behavior must have made him a laughing stock in Roman society and finally caused him to seek voluntary exile in Rhodes. Though Tacitus regards his moodiness and lack of sociability as innate flaws, he also makes it clear that Tiberius was cruelly mistreated. The emperor's accession to the throne at the age of fifty-five could hardly erase decades of humiliation. This desperately lonely man placed in Sejanus—a man, let us recall, who saved Tiberius from a cave-in at Sperlonga—an understandable, if unwarranted, confidence. When he was betrayed in turn by Sejanus, his bitterness overwhelmed him. In Tacitus's account, Tiberius even without inborn vices might have developed into a monster. A modern psychologist would regard him as a human tragedy—a creation of his family and his circumstances.

Tiberius was certainly enigmatic and devious, but so are most men (and women) who achieve and maintain absolute power. Tacitus understood that depths existed, but he often tries to resolve the contradictions in the sources and in the man himself. Authors writing under Caligula, Claudius, and Nero, would naturally have blackened Tiberius's reputation and bolstered those of Germanicus and Agrippina. Tacitus was shrewd enough to discount those crude attacks, and he does recount admirable or effective actions by Tiberius; yet when he reports them he still proceeds to undermine them. Tacitus wrestles quite publicly with the contradictions in his portrait: he loathes the emperor while he remains fascinated by his intelligence.[24] If all historians tend to present characters with excessive consistency, Tacitus's honesty subverts the unity of his artistic creation—and yet that very ambiguity makes the character of Tiberius, in the words of Macaulay, "a still higher miracle of art."[25]

Tacitus's Nero is a far simpler character than his Tiberius, and more understandable to the modern reader. Nero's aesthetic pretensions may have baffled contemporary senators, but there is little psychological complexity in this presentation of his personality. Tacitus traces the development of this budding monster from his gilded youth to a cruelty that far exceeded that of Tiberius. His murder of his mother Agrippina seems understandable, even inevitable, in the context of Nero's petulant, willful hedonism. Whatever his flaws, Tiberius was struggling to ensure his own power and that of his successors; Nero merely sought pleasure and acclaim. He was a shallower tyrant, without the dissimulation and secret plans of Tiberius or Domitian. Unworthy of Tacitus's innuendo or complex analysis, he is merely the object of satire and vitriol.

PORTRAITS OF VIRTUE

Tacitus's bleak vision of imperial Rome had little room for the profiles in courage that abound in Livy's history of the Republic. There are, of course, noble figures, but they sometimes seem to have been introduced primarily for contrast. Most victims of tyranny play minor roles, introduced only to be cruelly dispatched. But there are several Stoic philosophers—Seneca, Thrasea, and Helvidius—whom we are allowed to see before their condemnation. Seneca had been Nero's tutor and never publicly opposed his protégé, but Thrasea and Helvidius took a principled stand against tyranny and paid with their lives. Despite his agreement with their views, Tacitus distrusts their stubborn self-righteousness as they glory in their martyrdom.

Even the most positive characters in the *Annals,* Germanicus and his wife Agrippina, certainly are not traditional Roman ideals. Though Tacitus's portrait of Germanicus is often seen as an idealization of an attractive, but mediocre, prince, the historian's purpose here is more complex.[26] The tradition on Germanicus was encomiastic: family memoirs and funeral tributes as well as histories written under Caligula, Claudius, and Nero—his son, his brother, and his grandson. Tacitus created from this material a dramatic foil for his monster Tiberius: a rival, at least in the mind of a paranoid tyrant, for the imperial throne. But Tacitus's picture is more ambiguous, even more derogatory, than in other sources.[27] There is much in Germanicus that he would have found hard to admire. No one can read Tacitus's account of Germanicus's disastrous sea voyage without feeling that the prince was terribly irresponsible to sail "a thousand ships" down the Ems to the North Sea where a gale swept men, animals, and baggage into the water.[28] Though Tacitus ludicrously compares Germanicus to Alexander the Great for his "conquests" in the East,[29] a Roman reader might recognize instead his grandfather Marc Antony:

charm and popularity, willfulness and a weakness for oriental trappings, and an unfortunate involvement with Egypt.[30] His military
exploits were dubious and several times Tacitus describes him as
weeping in a most un-Roman way, first when his family has to flee
a rebellious camp, and shortly afterwards when his soldiers kill
their mutinous comrades in a fit of fratricidal carnage. The image
of Germanicus weeping recalls Tacitus's admiring comment that
among the Germans women weep and men remember.[31] He was
impractical, romantic, emotional, and filled with self-pity: qualities he shared with his son Caligula and his grandson Nero.[32]

Yet Germanicus served as a candid and affable counterweight to
the guarded and suspicious Tiberius, and there is little doubt that
he was genuinely popular with the army and the masses. He and
his imperious wife Agrippina understood what the crowds
wanted, but the implication that they wished to restore freedom
and the republic is absurd. It is wise to remember that Caligula
and Nero also had charisma, but no democratic illusions. Like his
descendants, Germanicus also had the markings of an (initially)
popular tyrant.[33] Tacitus alone records the oriental interests and
demagoguery of Germanicus, and yet he presents him as a dramatic contrast to Tiberius. His portrait is imbued with that Roman love of leaders who died too young—Marcellus, Drusus, and
later Titus—but the favorable impression does not disguise the
many faults in the man. Though he could have done so if he chose,
there is nothing in Tacitus's romantic fantasy to convince us that
he would have made a more effective emperor than Tiberius.[34]
Tacitus provides a more balanced, more nuanced picture of this
failed Roman golden boy than any other ancient source.

Nor was proud and headstrong Agrippina the ideal Roman ma-
tron. She ignores her husband's prudent deathbed orders and repeatedly confronts and embarrasses Tiberius who, we should recall, was her adoptive father-in-law and the head of her family. Her
arrogance brought disaster on herself and her sons Nero and Drusus; Tacitus was hardly unaware that her surviving children included Caligula and the younger Agrippina. Germanicus and
Agrippina were idealized under Caligula and they remain among
the few positive characters in the *Annals*, but Tacitus primarily

employs them to censure Tiberius; they are certainly not figures of traditional Roman virtue.

Agricola is the most intimately wrought portrait in Tacitus. The warm personal qualities of the historian's father-in-law carry conviction, as does a genuine self-effacing modesty that contrasts with the melodramatic false modesty which abounds among senators and courtiers. Agricola carries out his assignment in Britain admirably and never challenges Domitian or the imperial system. He had a Stoic endurance, but he was neither a philosopher nor an opponent of the regime. He is a man of principle, but he will tilt at no windmills in defense of abstract ideals. A patriotic pragmatist, this sensible man embodies the values Tacitus would like others to see in himself.

THE CORRUPTION OF POWER

The use and abuse of politicical power lie at the heart of Tacitus's writings. Before committing suicide, the senator Arruntius responded to the anticipated accession of Caligula with these words:

> "If Tiberius has been transformed and perverted by absolute power despite his experience in public affairs, will Caligula do better? . . . I now foresee an even harsher slavery."[35]

Tacitus believed that virtually all the emperors had been corrupted by power. It was not just power, but the desire for power, that Tacitus found dangerous. He recognized that even in the Republic men had known the desire for domination—a desire that resulted in decades of civil war. He, like many modern voters, distrusted those who obviously hungered for power; the most deserving, like Verginius Rufus, refused the throne. As with Galba, some men seem capable only until they receive power; then their defects become glaringly obvious. Power corrupts, but power also reveals.

DISSIMULATION

Augustus had defeated Marc Antony at Actium and devoted the next forty-four years to securing his power base. Other earlier Roman autocrats (Sulla; Julius Caesar) had died without being able to ensure their succession, and Tiberius could not expect to inherit Augustus's full authority. Thus he took on Augustus's powers tentatively, even offering to forego the imperial throne.[36] But what had begun as a necessity became his political *modus operandi*, perhaps even a pleasure. "Of what he regarded as his virtues, Tiberius valued none more highly than dissimulation."[37] Thus, with a duplicity that rivaled Augustus in the thirties B.C. and many tyrants since, Tiberius pretended to be hesitant in assuming supreme power "in order to discover the feelings of the aristocracy. Twisting words and looks into offenses, he hid them in his memory."[38] The hypocrisy of power, and the psychological consequences of deceit, form one of the central themes of Tacitus's histories, and the one for which he was most remembered through the centuries.

RESENTMENT

Tacitus is the great historian of the psychology of resentment: the resentment of the senators towards the emperors and their creatures, the resentment of Tiberius and Nero toward popular senators and toward their own domineering mothers, and the historian's festering resentment towards emperors, sycophants, and philosophers alike. But if he was unable to overcome his own resentment, Tacitus understood the destructive power of that emotion. His father-in-law Agricola was known for his candor:

> Some described him as a scathing critic: as unpleasant toward bad men as he was agreeable to the good. His anger left no repressed resentment, and you need not fear his silence: he thought it more honorable to hurt than to hate.[39]

Not so Tiberius, within whom every affront was allowed to grow into bitter resentment. And not only affronts, but even favors could be dangerous. Gaius Silius had put down a rebellion in Germany and boasted that he had saved Tiberius's throne. Tacitus shrewdly recognized that his loyalty sealed his doom: "For assistance is welcome as long as a reciprocal reward seems possible, but once it goes beyond that point it produces hatred instead of gratitude."[40] Before Freud taught of the dangers associated with repressed feelings, Tacitus had the native psychological insight to see quite clearly that such repression, whether from political expediency, shame, or fear, led to a dangerous, even murderous, resentment.

FEAR

Even during the collapse of the Republic, the courage of old Roman heroes could still be found: the Gracchi, Sulla, Caesar, Brutus, Antony, and Augustus were all prepared, finally, to risk their lives for power, dignity, or freedom. But that Roman *virtus* has given way in Tacitus to a prevailing terror that allows the tyrannical emperors to consolidate their rule. A tone of fear and secrecy pervades court life as Tacitus weaves carefully selected facts into an impressive tapestry of poisonous dissimilation and paranoia. He recognizes that the survival instinct inhibits political courage.[41] In a remarkable foreshadowing of the electronic devices of the modern police state, Tacitus says:

> Never had there been more anxiety and terror in Rome. People were secretive to their own family, and they avoided meetings, conversations, and the ears of friends and strangers alike; even the inanimate walls and ceiling were looked on with suspicion.[42]

In a society ruled by fear, Tacitus presented men who grovel before the powerful and bully their inferiors, an all-too-familiar pathology in modern political and corporate bureaucracies as well. Tyranny brings its inevitable companions: sycophancy and treachery. Thus Caligula, who fawned on Tiberius and remained in favor while his mother and brothers were eliminated, in turn became even a crueler tyrant.

SHAME

Tacitus acutely recognizes that even the apparently shameless have some shame and the very presence of a victim of a crime might be unwelcome. "It is human nature to hate one whom you have injured."[43] A former partner in crime could be troublesome as well. Thus Anicetus who had assisted in the murder of Agrippina fell from Nero's favor. Nero wished to keep such unpleasantness at arm's length, and so he was shocked when the conspirator Flavus had the courage to say to him:

> "I began to hate you when you murdered your mother and wife and became a charioteer, an actor, and an arsonist."[44]

Tacitus wryly concludes that Nero was quite ready to commit crimes, he was only disturbed when he heard them described. It is the utterance that brings shame, not the act itself.

MOTIVATION

Motivation often remains in the realm of historical reconstruction, or historical speculation. In discussing motives, historians have the opportunity to justify disaster, or to condemn success. Tacitus often provides psychological explanations for the actions of both individuals and groups. When Germanicus moved among his troops by night in disguise, he claims to wish to test their morale, but he knew he would hear—and doubtless enjoy—the soldiers singing his praises.[45] Tacitus recognized the "bitter hatred often felt among relatives"[46] when soldiers turn on their comrades. And he understood the rage that could drive men to a self-destructive course of action. In our own day some are puzzled by those who, embittered by oppression or fired with ideological or religious zeal, are prepared to sacrifice society and even themselves to destroy their opponents. The martyr's single-minded pursuit of immolation seems irrational and thus uncongenial, and so it was to Tacitus who disapproved of the confrontational tactics of Stoic philosophers. But he understood the forces driving the Gauls into revolt in 21 despite the danger from the Germans: "Many so hated the existing regime and desired change that they even rejoiced in their own dangers."[47]

Tacitus often uses a discussion of motivation to invest his history with that characteristic dark and suspicious tone. Even when the historian disavows his own belief in some pernicious motive, his text cynically keeps it before the readers' eyes. In describing Tiberius's son Drusus, his love of gladiatorial combat, and the pleasure he took at the public shedding of blood, Tacitus concludes:

> I am not inclined to believe that the emperor gave his son the opportunity for displaying his brutality and for arousing the outrage of the people, though that was rumored.[48]

GROUP PSYCHOLOGY

Tacitus went beyond the moods and pathologies of individuals to a vivid evocation of the psychology of groups. Soldiers, the urban mob, sycophantic senators, and barbarians are shown with their individual characteristics subordinated to the uncontrolled emotions of the group. They quickly switch from misery to joy: "The crowd is unrestrained in either emotion."[49] With a naive credulity the Roman crowds believe the rumors that Germanicus has recovered from his illness; a mob rarely pauses and never thinks before jumping to conclusions, and often, to action. Tacitus's contempt for the irresponsibility of collective action recurs frequently: "It is customary in a mob, that each blame the others for his own faults";[50] "As happens in a panic, all give orders; no one obeys";[51] "A crowd has less discretion and fewer dangers."[52] Despite his romantic idealization of the Senate and Roman people of the Republic, Tacitus believed that under the Empire these groups usually acted from base and selfish motives; he rarely understood that they might have justifiable grievances.[53]

While Tacitus is a champion of Roman imperialism and the army, his Roman soldiers are as irresponsible as the urban mob. His psychological analysis of mutinies and civil wars engaged Tacitus more than Rome's foreign wars.[54] The bleakness of this portrait of contemporary soldiers is one of the striking features of

Tacitean history. He finally saw the collapse of military discipline as a failure of leadership. Though the recklessness of the troops might sometimes be directed against the enemy as the Flavian general Antonius did at Bedriacum,[55] more often the volatility of the soldiers turned them against civilians, their officers, or even their own comrades, and Tacitus presents extreme swings of mood in the German mutiny. Germanicus was only able to control the troops by shaming them. Mobs and armies will run wild if leadership does not assert itself, but a Germanicus or an Agricola can use his own courage and psychological insight to control his men. The fish, the Italians still say, rots first from the head, and Tacitus saw the corruption emanating from the center of power. His analysis of group dynamics is yet another indictment of the political system and its leaders.

PSYCHOLOGY OF WOMEN

Tacitus has at times been linked with his contemporaries Martial and Juvenal as a misogynist, and the *Annals* certainly paints a bleak picture of Julio-Claudian wives and daughters.[56] And there are aspersions cast on other aristocratic women as well; in 21 Aulus Caecina Severus delivered in the Senate a fierce indictment of senatorial wives when he proposed that wives not accompany their husbands abroad on official business:

> "A retinue of women brings extravagance in peacetime and panic in war, and it turns a Roman marching column into a barbarian procession. That sex is not only weak and easily exhausted, but given the chance they become cruel, scheming, and power-hungry. They walk among the soldiers and dominate the centurions . . . Now they have cast aside their chains and rule the home, the courts, and now the army."[57]

But Tacitus provides no word of approbation and we know that the historian's own wife accompanied him on his provincial command. The scene is not intended to criticize women as to indict the Senate for its inability to conduct business effectively.[58]

Though Tacitus is undeniably hostile to many women, it might be useful to examine more carefully his understanding of the virtues and vices of women. There is certainly a fear of women that runs through Western literature, from Gilgamesh and Homer's Calypso, Circe, and the Sirens, down to our own time. In Greek myth, Zeus created the first woman, Pandora, to entice men and to punish them with all the evils contained in her vase. Men may have physical force; women's power lies in magic, poison, sexuality, and cunning. Tacitus too follows these stereotypes. He shows that women use poison—Plancina arranges poison for Germanicus, and Agrippina gets poison for her husband Claudius—but these are few among the imperial murders. Though Tacitus often links a woman's sexual activity to her political corruption, there is no single pattern. The first century was a time of enormous flux in gender-relations among the Roman upper classes. Aristocratic women were able to exercise unheard-of political, financial, and sexual power while the heroism of the British warrior queen Boudicca affected Roman perceptions of female docility. In an age of such extraordinary changes, it is difficult to distinguish between genuine female power and the paranoid imaginings of the male sources.

Tacitus presents us with a gallery of Julio-Claudian empresses and princesses. Poppaea is straightforward; she sexually teases Nero and uses her attractions to provoke his murder of Octavia. Agrippina too entices Claudius into marriage, and perhaps even tries to seduce her son Nero out of a desire for power. But other imperial wives do not have such control and are destroyed by their sexual desires. Open promiscuity led Augustus to exile his only child Julia, and Livilla was so captivated by Sejanus that she murdered her husband, Tiberius's heir Drusus, and risked certain succession to the throne for an insane passion. Tacitus's explanation—"When a woman has parted with her virtue, she will refuse nothing"[59]—needs some qualification, but Livilla certainly was out of control. Messalina too may have been unwittingly entangled by a lover in a political plot; she could manipulate Claudius, but she herself was sexually or emotionally vulnerable. Livia was completely above sexual reproach and resembles a republican Roman *matrona* in her austere private life and her strict control of her household. There is no clear pattern: some Julio-Claudian women are strong and some are weak; some control through sex and others are destroyed by it. Sex is a convenient shorthand for female corruption, and Tacitus (perhaps like his sources) was less interested in sexual mores than in women becoming involved in political intrigue.

Roman women were far more independent than in Greece, and yet a Roman was thought to be responsible for the conduct of his wife. Her conduct could bring glory or contempt: "a good wife merits as much more praise as a bad wife does blame."[60] Agricola is thus praised by Tacitus while Claudius is held in contempt for being controlled by his wives. As one senator put it: "If a women behaves badly, it is her husband's fault."[61] Even if Julia had begun her infidelities before she was married to Tiberius, he was still shamed by her conduct. It is hardly surprising that Tacitus should share such an attitude; a wife's adultery is a humiliation for her husband, from Homer's Menelaus down to our own day. Tacitus's attitude may be chauvinist, but he has had a great deal of company.

But if the stereotype was that women could not control their emotions and would weep while men remained firm—a stereotype that achieved its greatest expression in Dido and Aeneas—Tacitus recognized that women often showed greater courage and tenacity than men. The elder Agrippina was strong, even if headstrong, while her husband Germanicus openly wept, and their daughter Agrippina was said to have no feminine weakness, merely a thirst for power and unbridled audacity, while her brother Caligula and her son Nero often gave way to their emotions. Young Octavia tried to survive by hiding her feelings from her husband Nero, and other women found the exceptional courage to defend their family or their masters. Agricola's mother inculcated the antique virtues into her son; Vitellius's mother lived by them while her craven son could not. And after many allusions to Livia's insidious intrigues, Tacitus finally admits in her obituary that she had been a moderating influence and that Sejanus had not dared to defy her. Tacitus begins from the traditional Roman stereotypes, but much of his account undermines those assumptions and makes women the more resolute sex. Can he fairly be called a misogynist?[62] Certainly he is biased against women by the standards of our own day, but so are all Roman writers.

The text hardly supports the extreme view that Tacitus truly hated women and blamed their immorality for the decline of Rome.[63] Tacitus is surely uneasy with female sexuality, but he is no Juvenal. Agricola's mother, wife, and daughter—Tacitus's own wife—are all mentioned warmly, and Tacitus can even admire a woman as strong as the elder Agrippina. He is conservative about social change and in general distrusts assertive women, but he often transcends his prejudices. And that struggle with cultural prejudices gives the historian a far greater insight into women than his more sour contemporaries.

The Psyche of the Author

Tacitus was cursed with an acute intellect; when he studied the history of the Empire he understood, and he despaired. His pessimism—or realism, it has been called both—led him to examine the dark side of the psyche: the psychopathology of evil. Most ancient writers with his cast of mind turned to tragedy or epic, and many readers have considered his dark portraits exaggerated beyond belief. But, as Ronald Syme noted, earlier times were more innocent; our own century has seen the dark side of politics and power, and the emotional truth that Tacitus conveys in his portraits of Tiberius and Nero does not strain our credulity.[64]

Any great work of psychological analysis, and the *Annals* is one of the greatest, must also be a work of self-analysis. If it is dangerous to seek an author's personality in his work, few would disagree that elements of cynicism, suffering, pessimism, frustration, and anger were present in Tacitus the man. Tacitus's motives in writing history are complex: his claim is moral and political, but the passionate intensity of his writing stems from deeper psychological sources. Perhaps his own shame and even guilt are reflected in his passionate, but ambivalent, reactions to those who stand up to the tyrants. Some scholars have gone much further and claimed to find evidence of the historian's melancholia, sadism, femininity, homosexuality, paranoia, or even madness.[65] Though such claims are exaggerated, it is easy to see how critics can be led astray. Tacitus's own psychological sensitivity enables him to enter into the emotions of sadists and madmen. His obsession with Tiberius, albeit based on hatred and moral disapproval, is so powerful that we may even sense a psychological link between them: a penetrating mind, a sarcastic tongue, and an abiding bitterness define them both. Tacitus could understand Tiberius, but no more than he could understand himself. His own political accommodation suggests greater ambiguity than a superficial reading of his histories will provide.

Tacitus is a strong-willed moralist, but his works are not simple black-and-white morality plays. He did not have the twentieth-century's vocabulary for psychological analysis, any more than did Catullus a century earlier when he wrote a brief poem:

> I love and hate her; I don't know why,
> but I feel it happen and am torn apart. (Catullus 85)

An ancient writer could only express those polarities, not explain them as a modern might. Likewise Tacitus might express his ambiguities in contradictions: his desire for freedom and his contempt for the people; his admiration and contempt for self-appointed martyrs; innate vs. acquired character traits, etc. With so much inner conflict in the historian, it is little wonder that there are "contradictions" in the text. Despite the illusion of rationality, his historical understanding is often on an emotional level and his literary expression captures the violence of these feelings. In the days before professional psychology, Tacitus was an important source as writers like Bacon and Montaigne began to develop the language of introspection. So Stendhal, who can also be seen as a psychological historian, mentions Tacitus dozens of times and was said to have read him on his deathbed.[66] Tacitus transferred, as great writers do, his own ambiguity and his own anguish to a more universal canvas. It was a poet's instinct rather than a philosopher's analysis that brought him to an understanding of men, their emotions and their actions.[67] The result is a psychological history that has influenced, directly or indirectly, all subsequent historians.

Tacitus . . . of all others the
greatest Enemy to Tyrants.
JOHN MILTON
Defense of the People of England *

VI

❖ ———————————————————————— ❖

The Historian as Political Analyst

Tacitus was a politician before he became an historian; his political passion drove him to history. During the preceding century republican government had collapsed and power increasingly rested with the emperors and their courtiers, while the once-powerful senators were reduced to docile administrators or odious flatterers. An entrenched aristocracy had collapsed. Tacitus links these political changes to the widespread moral decline that affected every circle in Roman society—from the emperor to the army, from the Senate to the mob—and even corrupted the Roman family itself. Tacitus says much about this political transformation,

---

* *The Works of John Milton* (New York, 1931–1938) VII 317.

and the raw power of his political vision transcends imperial Rome to shape for centuries the terms of European political discourse.

The Theory of Politics

Each nation and city is ruled by the people, by the nobility, or by an individual . . . When there was democracy, it was necessary to understand the nature of the masses and how to control them; when aristocrats ruled, those who had the best insight into the minds of senators were thought wise and astute about their times. Now, after a revolution, when Rome is nothing but a monarchy, it might be useful to collect and report this material.[1]

After Augustus dropped the title of triumvir and made himself consul, content with the tribune's authority for the protection of the people, he seduced the soldiers with bonuses, the people with cheap food, and all with the sweetness of peace. Gradually growing stronger, he took over the functions of the Senate, the magistrates, and the laws. No one opposed him, since the bravest men had fallen in battle or by proscription and the remaining nobles received wealth and offices for eagerly accepting servitude. Enriched by the new regime, they preferred the safety of the present to the dangers of the past.[2]

Tacitus, like other Romans, distrusted political theory.[3] The varied constitutions of Greek city-states provided Greek philosophers with ample material for comparative analysis. Theorists produced models of utopian government—Pythagoras and Plato even participated in attempts to realize those theories—but few Romans were concerned with such speculation about oligarchies or democracies. Rome had a traditional, unwritten, and therefore adaptable constitution; theories were less important than specific legislative proposals which effectively changed that constitution. Thus we look in vain for an explicit or even implicit utopian political ideal in Tacitus; he is less concerned with principles than with personalities. In the first passage above, he turns quickly from abstractions to point out that "it might be useful to collect and record these facts." Tacitus does not present a theory in the Greek sense; rather he analyses the use and abuse of power.

The second passage reports Augustus's *coup d'état* with a bitterness which has caused some to regard Tacitus as a "republican" who wished to turn back the clock to the days of senatorial power. Here too the power of Augustus is far more important than his titles or constitutional trappings. Tacitus certainly retains republican sympathies, but he had few illusions about the Republic, which contained so much class conflict, corruption, bribery, and the rule of brute force that "decency sometimes led to a death sentence."[4] That violent and corrupt Republic offered no real alternative to the Principate. Tacitus was a republican in writing history, but he remained a monarchist in practical politics.[5] The historian did not yearn for republican government; he rather sought to revive republican values.[6] The Republic was for him less a political system than a moral golden age of individual courage and senatorial independence. His heroes are moral exemplars like Cato and Brutus, whose political ineptitude helped to bring down the Republic, while Cicero, who valiantly struggled to preserve it, is ignored. When Augustus brought an end to a century of civil war, both Vergil and Livy were able to reconcile their republican principles with loyalty to the new regime.[7] Admiration of republican ideals did not imply republicanism; Seneca found it possible to preserve his veneration of Cato while serving as tutor of the emperor Nero. Tacitus also understood that the restoration of the Republic was an absurd fantasy, something about which the crowds at the funeral of Augustus can only "talk idly."[8] He saw a continuity from the kings of early Rome through the dynasts of the late Republic to the Julio-Claudian emperors: the domination by individuals. One-man rule is inevitable; Tiberius was a hypocrite to pretend otherwise. It is not monarchical power that most offends Tacitus, but the arbitrary use of that power: there was no security of life or property under a Caligula or Nero. He understood that the Stoic idea of freedom under a philosopher—Nero tutored by Seneca—was a dream that became a nightmare: Liberty and the principate were incompatible.[9]

Is Tacitus opposed only to tyrannical emperors or to the principate itself? He gives no easy answer and he has been variously interpreted through the centuries as a "black" Machiavellian who told rulers how to maintain power or a "red" revolutionary who incited resistance to those same rulers.[10] He was popular both with Italian princes and with French and American republicans, and was quoted in support of absolute monarchy and by the English regicides.[11] How can the text of Tacitus be open to such a range of interpretation? His individual insights can be illuminating, but they do not necessarily form a coherent pattern. As he wrote his histories, his evolving attitude toward tyranny produced inevitable change. Since Tacitus sometimes tempers his deep emotional hostility to the emperors with realism and resignation, his pithy aphorisms can easily be quoted out of context to contradictory purposes.[12] His ambivalent view toward political power adds to the confusion: Tacitus is both obsessed and repelled by power; he admires those who use it well and hates its ability to corrupt. Tacitus accepts the principate as necessary to maintain peace, stability, and order over Rome's empire,[13] but he would agree with the Boston pastor Jonathan Mayhew who wrote in 1750, "Rulers have no authority from God to do mischief." That mischief, for Tacitus, consisted in the subtle humiliation or brutal subjugation of the senatorial class, despite the illusion of senatorial authority.

The historian explores the dark, irrational force through which political power determines the fate of the powerful and powerless alike. Absolutism is unavoidable and absolutism corrupts. It is not merely that bad men come to power; Tacitus is the first to suggest that evil is inherent in political power. We can sometimes overlook the fact that Tiberius had been an effective general and a superb administrator, that Claudius was a passable historian, that even young Nero showed the self-discipline to turn a thin, reedy voice into an acceptable musical instrument. They all had genuine talents; spared the imperial purple, these men might have found success and fulfillment.

If the corruption of power is by now a familiar theme, Tacitus particularly illuminates the ways in which absolutism perverts the ruled as well. Freedmen and equestrians curry favor with the emperors while jealous senators outdo each other in groveling servility, for in slavery they hope to find security. Much of the gloom of the *Annals* lies in the progressive degeneration of senatorial values. Tacitus was proud of the Senate and its traditions, and he struggles to keep the senators at the center of political history when freedmen, equestrians, and the armies thrust them to the sideline. It is with anger he reports that to remain members of the nobility, senators must become ignoble: treacherous, venal, and mendacious. When Tiberius might have shared power with them, the senators refused to shoulder the responsibilities of freedom. Where they once competed in political and military achievements, they now compete in abject flattery. The literary critic Longinus quotes a philosopher of the first century who complains that now "there is genius only for flattery."[14] The corruption of his own class affects Tacitus deeply; the issue is very close to home: his friends, his father-in-law, himself.

If Tacitus opposed the emperors' autocratic rule over the Roman people, he also scorned anything resembling democracy. He praised the "Roman people" of the Republic, but we have seen that he repeatedly showed contempt for the masses of his own day: they are fickle and credulous of every omen and rumor, and are equally ignorant of politics.[15] "The degraded plebs who haunt the circus and the theater."[16] They called for an emperor's head as though they were in the circus watching the games; they did not appreciate the accomplishments of the noble but modest Agricola; and they preferred young Nero to the aged Galba because "in the manner of the vulgar, they compared the emperors by their looks and physical attractions."[17] Urban mobs and rebellious soldiers are much the same: they are swayed by appearances and are content to be coddled by their masters. The soldiers now had little use for the Senate or any appeals to republican traditions. When on rare occasions the mob sought freedom, freedom soon became license and inevitably led to violence. Popular government was not an option; the only alternatives were autocracy and anarchy.

Imperial Politics: Secrecy and Sycophancy

Sallustius . . . advised Livia that palace secrets, the advice of friends, and the services performed by soldiers should not be made public. Nor should Tiberius weaken imperial power by referring everything to the Senate. It is a requirement of imperial rule that the books only balance if there is a single accountant.[18]

Even when Tiberius was not intentionally evasive, his words were, either by nature or habit, always hesitant and unclear. And now that he decided to hide completely his real feelings, his language became even more twisted, uncertain, and ambiguous.[19]

If Tacitus provides no coherent theory of an ideal state, his astute analysis of the realities of political life eclipses all others that have come down from antiquity. He recognized, for example, that power in the Roman Empire rested upon secrecy and deception: *arcana imperii*—the secrets of imperial rule.[20] The theme first occurs at the death of Augustus when a courtier warned Livia and it becomes a recurrent theme under Tiberius who hated above all to disclose his real desires. In our age of "disinformation," secrecy hardly seems extraordinary. Tiberius's unforthcoming silence at meetings of the Senate is a form of control popular among Renaissance princes and modern business tycoons. Tyrants from political dictators to football coaches prefer to instill insecurity through control of information and calculated ambiguity. They perceive such widespread uncertainty as increasing their own power to manipulate others. Secrecy and its attendant paranoia were a disease gnawing at the very vitals of the Roman state. It was dangerous to inquire what the emperor really thought; public debates were for display and all genuine disagreements were resolved behind closed doors by imperial advisors. Even the use of astrology was regarded as threatening to the emperor, since the stars might provide knowledge of the emperor's destiny, and thus power over it.[21] As in modern police states and democracies with "official secrets," truth was regarded as treasonous. Knowledge is power; both ancient and modern rulers jealously guard it.

The courtiers also had their secrets. Much was kept from Tiberius by Sejanus—not least his murder of the emperor's son. Claudius's terrified freedman kept his wife's outrageous behavior from the emperor; they were certain she could convince him of her innocence and destroy her accusers. Nero seems to have been as oblivious to the discontent of the legions as Caligula was to that of the praetorians. Truth does not easily penetrate the veil of flattery which surrounds powerful political figures; no one wishes to be, like the messenger in Greek tragedy, the unwelcome bearer of bad tidings. Thus Tacitus tells us how Vitellius abandoned some of his best troops:

> The most experienced centurious disagreed and they would have told him the facts if they had been consulted. But Vitellius's courtiers kept them away. The emperor's ears were so formed that what was practical sounded harsh; he would only welcome what was pleasant, and harmful.[22]

This is hardly surprising. Far more startling are powerful rulers like Augustus and Vespasian, who distrusted flattery and encouraged honest appraisals of a political or military crisis. They were the exceptions; shrewd men who collected sufficiently accurate intelligence to make rational decisions. Perhaps not coincidentally, they were among the few emperors who died of old age in their beds.

Tacitus identified it as a "secret" that emperors could be made away from Rome, but even that disclosure cloaked a deeper political reality.[23] With the Civil War of 68–70, when Galba was acclaimed in Spain, Vitellius in Germany, and Vespasian in Egypt and Judaea, it became obvious that the Senate and people now had little to do with the proclamation of a new emperor; it was the army alone which determined the rulers. The great secret was no secret at all to the perceptive: emperors derived power not from law nor from tradition but through naked military force. The shrewder emperors disguised this fact, not least from the armies themselves and their ambitious generals. Since the reign of Augustus, the army had stood quietly behind the throne; later all could see that it not only protected emperors but created and destroyed them as well.

Tacitus is less concerned with the specific secrets of long-dead emperors and their officials than with the way in which language is used to disguise the truth and deceive the unwary. Calgacus comments that the phrase *Pax Romana* disguises much violence,[24] and Cerialis warns the Gauls that the Germans use the rallying cry of "Freedom" and other "deceptive terms" (*speciosa nomina*)[25] merely in order to become their new masters. Tacitus relishes the exposure of official lies and the misuse of language. Augustus retained the republican titles for his magistrates, even though they had none of their former authority.[26] Galba calls his stinginess "economy," and his cruelty "severity."[27] Elsewhere defeats were celebrated as triumphs; "facts were scorned in favor of appearances."[28] For those who have read George Orwell or witnessed a modern political campaign, all this is hardly surprising. Tacitus regarded the words and feelings of Nero's ghost written (by Seneca) speeches to be equally counterfeit: what the Senate heard was not Nero, it was a lie.[29] The debasement of language in the service of politics is a recurring Tacitean theme, and one that remains relevant today.

Despite the scorn Tacitus shows for Tiberius's secrecy, he certainly did not think public policy should be discussed truly *publicly*.[30] The mob was credulous and untrustworthy, and reading dispatches to the troops was also dangerous.[31] Like senatorial Stoics, his political field of vision encompassed fewer than a thousand senators and high officials. Tacitus sought *libertas* only for the elite; only his own senatorial class should be privy to state secrets. Though a seventeenth-century Jesuit denounced Tacitus for undermining government by revealing its secrets,[32] the historian disclosed few actual secrets that were not already known by his contemporaries. Tacitus did not reveal secrets; he only made clear the power, and necessity, of secrecy itself.

Public secrecy begets private intrigue—that is the image Tacitus conveys of the imperial court. He is the historian par excellence of court politics and this has given him a lasting popularity, for courtiers have a remarkable psychological similarity across space and time. The authoritarian ruler, mistrusting his social equals as possible rivals for power, gathers about himself men and women whose position depends on his good will: eunuchs and mistresses, jesters and childhood cronies, priests and slaves. French kings chose as ministers cardinals, who could not aspire to the throne; recent American presidents populated their White House staffs with old friends who had no national political base and no other possible loyalty. Roman emperors turned to their freedmen or their equestrian henchmen who were socially inferior to senators. Equestrians controlled the praetorian guard and eventually freedmen controlled access to the emperor himself.

Strong courtiers inevitably intrigue to assert their power against one another and sometimes even over their master.[33] Roman senators were outraged at the vast power of such political outsiders—at Rome they were usually Greek slaves who had been freed to make use of their talents in the imperial bureaucracy. A western provincial like Tacitus had little use for Greek freedmen, craven Greek servility (which Romans called *adulatio Graeca*), nor for that Greek literary culture espoused by Tiberius, Caligula, and Nero.[34] Thus a bitter contempt pervades his account of the vacillating Claudius and his exceptionally forceful freedmen Pallas and Narcissus.[35] Pallas had become one of the richest men in the empire while feigning poverty. Tacitus well understood the symbiotic relationship that grew up between weak and indecisive rulers and strong-willed courtiers. He provides the first, and perhaps the deepest, analysis of paranoid government, in which freedmen play upon the fears of the emperor to gain temporary bureaucratic victories (although "bureaucratic victory" may seem a rather tame description for Sejanus's taking control of both the praetorian guard and all access to Tiberius isolated in Capri). There have always been Rasputins, eager and ready to lead their insecure masters to disaster. Though suspicion was a standard character trait of tyrants in formal orations practiced in the rhetorical schools of the first century, Tacitus invested Tiberius with a paranoia that grows not just from his own personality but from the patently insincere flattery of the Senate. And if Tiberius did not believe such adulation, Nero unfortunately did. The *Annals* was regarded as a bible of flattery that in later centuries was repeatedly cited in guides to court life.[36] It is a chilling reminder of the dangers of mendacious courtiers and secret government.

This adulation, inspired first by ambition and later by fear, soon spread to the senatorial class. Tacitus dissected the political basis of the terror that paralyzed all at court. They feared the emperor, but they were also frightened that a new emperor might be worse.[37] "Passivity," he said, "was taken for wisdom."[38] While few would stand up to a Caligula or a Sejanus in his lifetime, Senate and mob alike were eager to condemn their memory and even assault their surviving relatives after their murder.[39] Such universal cowardice disgusted Tacitus: "The mob fell upon Vitellius's corpse with the same baseness with which they flattered him while he lived."[40] Tacitus was the first of his family to sit in the Senate and like Cato and Sallust, earlier Roman "new men" who came to write history, he found many senators unworthy of their aristocratic forebears. Tiberius himself felt contempt for their servility and was said often to leave the Senate exclaiming, "Men fit to be slaves."[41] It was the final degrading irony that, after the assassination of Julius Caesar in 44 B.C., no senators ever participated in the murder of imperial tyrants. All senatorial conspiracies came to naught; only soldiers and freedmen had the courage to strike down an emperor.[42]

Servility and fear soon assumed a more ominous character. No longer merely harmless cowardice, they inspired the aristocrats to mutual recriminations and baseless prosecutions against each other to curry imperial favor. Tacitus dates the beginning of the "treason trials" to the year 16, soon after the accession of Tiberius, when Libo, a foolish young aristocrat who dabbled in astrology and magic, was denounced and committed suicide amid hypocritical senatorial resolutions of thanksgiving.[43] His estate was divided among his accusers, and senators, like freedmen, saw in flattery and denunciation a path to wealth and influence. Informers multiplied, and undistinguished senators discovered opportunities to gain imperial recognition through political prosecutions. Tacitus recognized that there was more danger from unjustified prosecutions for treason then from treason itself. "As the state once suffered from its vices, it now suffered from its laws."[44] Tacitus preached the salutary but often ignored lesson that the fabric of society can be endangered more by the hunt for political dissidents, as in the Terror of the French Revolution, or Joseph McCarthy's smear campaigns, than by actual subversive activity. We need only think of the trial of Socrates to recall that unfair trials hardly began in the Roman Empire; but Tacitus's vivid account of treason trials contrasts justice and ruthless expediency in a dark expression of tyranny that reaches its apex in Dostoyevsky's Grand Inquisitor.

The Art of Survival

I think that Lepidus was for his time a wise and principled man . . . Nor did he lack discretion since he retained his influence and friendship with Tiberius. This makes me uncertain whether the favor shown by emperors to some, or the hatred visited on others depend, like other things, on the destiny of birth; or whether our own decisions allow us to steer a path, safe from intrigue and dangers, between abrasive obstinacy and disgusting groveling.[45]

Tacitus's portrait of tyranny has undoubtedly inspired those fighting for political freedom, but the historian himself counseled cautious compromise rather than rebellion. To survive under a tyrannical regime requires not only luck, but also guile and political dexterity. That is, of course, easier said than done. It is all very well to proclaim *moderatio*—the middle course between fawning collaboration and stubborn self-immolation—but it is difficult to find such a path in the real world of tyrants; Tacitus calls it *rarissima*.[46] Would such advice have been of much use to those who lived under Caligula, Stalin, or Hitler? Dissimulation is likely to be more effective than moderation, and Tacitus regards Tiberius's moderation as feigned.[47] Tacitus himself says that in the reign of Tiberius a certain Piso was "exceptional for one of his reputation in that he died a natural death."[48] In his own day Tacitus adhered to a political program of compromise and criticized both sycophants and martyrs.

The historian is certainly sympathetic to the Stoics who chose death in the last years of Nero. He clearly admires Seneca, often reviled as Nero's tutor and advisor, who finally chose the death by suicide of a Stoic sage.[49] The philosopher had compromised with tyranny in order to improve Nero's rule and, when he could no longer collaborate, he tried to withdraw quietly from public life. But he was too close to the emperor to be allowed to live. Nero condemned Seneca to death; the philosopher merely chose to assert his liberty by dying with dignity by his own hand.[50] Tacitus, who held high office before withdrawing from public life during the Domitianic terror, had far more sympathy for Seneca than for the "ostentatious martyrs" of his own day who refused to compromise their principles.

The *Agricola* indicates that accommodation is possible:

> Even quick-tempered Domitian . . . was mollified by the moderation and discretion of Agricola . . . Let those who are inclined to admire disobedience know that even under bad emperors men can be great. Obedience and self-control, joined to hard work and vitality, leads to the fame that most people attain through a dangerous life and find glory through an ostentatious death, which brings no benefit to the state.[51]

Is this truth or merely special pleading? Tacitus draws a fine line between holding office for the good of the state under a tyrannical regime and becoming an active agent in the repression of freedom. Vespasian was a sensible man and his son Domitian, though unstable, followed many of his policies. They promoted men of merit like Agricola and Tacitus, particularly those from Gaul and Spain whose provincial ancestry made them seem less dangerous as rivals. They relied far less on astrologers, singers and actors, Greek freedmen, and corrupt praetorian prefects than had the Julio-Claudians. Resistance was foolish; compromise seemed possible.

It is possible that Tacitus, who wrote these words before he had begun to do research on the reigns of Tiberius, Caligula, and Nero, was not yet aware of the full horror of those reigns for the noble, the competent, and the virtuous. As he wrote, he plunged into the psychopathology of tyranny and his political perceptions became more acute. In the *Annals* Tacitus is more sympathetic to the kind of rebels and martyrs whom he had characterized as self-dramatizing in his accounts of his own lifetime. The courts of the Julio-Claudians gave little scope for compromise, less for freedom.

Neither time, prayers, nor satiety, which soften others, could deter Tiberius from punishing doubtful, outdated offenses as though they were flagrant new crimes.[52]

Tacitus rarely condemns the dissident or the suicide in Tiberius's reign, but under Domitian he counseled accommodation. Did he fundamentally change his view of the state and the price of survival or has he merely calibrated degrees of tyranny? We cannot tell, but his different books certainly give different pictures of monarchy, collaboration, and resistance. And we must remember that to suggest that principled compromise in his own day was impossible would be an indictment of Tacitus himself.

The notorious informer and collaborator Eprius Marcellus, like others throughout history, justified himself in the same vein:

I admire the past, but I acquiesce in the present; I pray for good emperors, but I endure whatever we get.[53]

Tacitus may despise Marcellus, but his own views are not very different. He too had advanced under Vespasian and Domitian, and he disdained the stubborn opposition of the Stoics. He had resigned himself to the principate; it is only the character of the emperor that really matters. The Stoics might well have seen that as the hypocritical rationalization of a collaborator.

Freedom of Speech

"It was clearly permissible to speak without check about those whom death has placed beyond hatred or favor. Are Cassius and Brutus now in arms at Philippi? Am I at a meeting rousing the people to civil war? Didn't they die seventy years ago? As they are known by their statues (which even the victor spared), so they are remembered in the historians. Posterity accords everyone his due honor. If I am condemned, there are those who will recall not only Brutus and Cassius, but me as well."

Cremutius then left the Senate and starved himself to

death. The senators ordered that the aediles burn his books, but copies were hidden and published later.

It makes us laugh at the stupidity of those who believe that today's tyranny can also obliterate the memory of a future generation. On the contrary, the suppression of genius increases its authority; foreign kings and those who imitate their cruelty achieve nothing but glory for their victims and their own infamy.[54]

The connection between political liberty and freedom of speech became obvious in the early Empire. The unrestricted freedom of republican senators to vilify their opponents could be said to have ended when Antony displayed the head and hands of Cicero on the rostrum in the Forum. Senators and emperors had now to negotiate the "tolerable" limits of freedom of speech. Numerous anecdotes in ancient authors show that Augustus demonstrated considerable restraint in the face of intellectual dissent; he light-heartedly called his friend Livy a "Pompeian," alluding to the historian's republican sympathy for Pompey, and Seneca praised the first emperor's tolerance in allowing his son-in-law Agrippa to be ridiculed. Even Tiberius was initially thick-skinned toward political jibes:

He was calm and tolerant in the face of abuse, slander, or lampoons about himself and his family, and would often say that there should be free speech and free thought in a free country.[55]

But, as an historian, Tacitus had a different perspective. He was not concerned with satiric verses or scurrilous lampoons. He regarded the prosecution of writers as a political attempt to control language and thus suppress free thought. The theme first appears at the beginning of his first book, where Tacitus laments that he had to seek permission to write Agricola's biography. The police believed that censorship and book burning "could destroy the voice of the Roman people, the freedom of the Senate, and the accumulated knowledge of the human race."[56]

In A.D. 25, 68 years after the assassination of Caesar, the historian Cremutius Cordus was prosecuted in the Roman Senate on a new charge: in his history he had praised Brutus and had called Cassius "the last of the Romans." After the stirring speech on censorship which Tacitus wrote for Cremutius, he goes on to point out that book burning and persecution give an author a mythic dimension. Books are less dangerous than martyrs; neither the praetorian guard nor a single rebellious legion was ever inspired by the writings of intellectuals. Cremutius is not remembered for his ideas, but for the reflected glory that Tacitus used him to cast Tiberius into disrepute.

Tacitus thought freedom of speech was a central element in the political struggles of the first century. It was a view that endeared him to Jefferson and made him hated by Napoleon. As heirs to Jefferson's ideals, we read Tacitus with admiration and delight—but we should be cautious: his conception of freedom of speech was that it should be limited to the intellectual elite. Tacitus is far less concerned about Tiberius's abolition of public assemblies than the prosecution of one writer. The struggle between the Senate and the emperors was less over freedom of speech than over political power and ancestral pride. Book burning and censorship did happen, but as a by-product of the attempt to suppress political discontent. Like so many politicians, the emperors found it easier to deal with the symptoms of discontent—books—than the causes.

At least one emperor not only tolerated free speech but glorified in it as reflecting favorably on his own rule. He was hardly typical. The philosopher-emperor Marcus Aurelius was born about the time of Tacitus's death and ruled from 161 to 180; Tacitus had never seen his like and the Empire never would again. But he had surely read Tacitus when he wrote in his autobiography that it was an advantage to have studied

Thrasea, Helvidius, Cato, Dio, Brutus, and to have conceived the idea of a state based on equality, fairness, and freedom of speech, and of kingship respecting above all else the liberty of the subjects.[57]

The Stoic sage loyally restricted his list to Stoic thinkers, all suffered for their devotion to liberty. Our understanding of free speech and politics derives not from this prudent philosopher, however, but from the suspicious historian Tacitus.

Tyranny and the "Good Emperor"

"If our immense empire," said Galba "could stand and remain steady without a helmsman, I would be suitable to launch a Republic. But we have now reached a point that my old age cannot give the Roman people any more than a good successor, nor your youth any more than a good emperor. Under Tiberius, Gaius, and Claudius we Romans were the legacy of a single family so it will be a kind of freedom that emperors will begin to be adopted. And since the Julio-Claudian dynasty has ended, adoption will choose whoever is best. For to be begotten and born of emperors is mere chance, and not of much value. In adoption there is genuine choice . . .

The most practical and quickest way to decide between good and bad policy is to consider what you would or would not approve if another were emperor. For unlike nations ruled by kings, here there is no fixed ruling family and the rest slaves; you will rule over men who can bear neither absolute slavery nor absolute freedom."[58]

The Civil War of 69 and the dangers of 96–97 drove Tacitus to welcome a new regime, but he did so with his eyes wide open. Nerva's adoption of Trajan effected a peaceful transition of power and furnished a model for the selection of a qualified successor from the Senate rather than merely from the ruling family. For Galba's adoption of Piso in 69, Tacitus provided the above speech that spells out the theory of the adoptive principate. For Tacitus, the last phrase is the most poignant. No longer are Romans distinguished from servile Greeks by their rejection of kingship; now they can only hope that their rulers will be, in Tacitus's words, "good emperors." Like the informer Marcellus, Tacitus too can hope only for a "good emperor." The only freedom now possible is the freedom from arbitrary rule, by an emperor who respects the position and prerogatives of the Senate. There is surely some irony in the speech Tacitus wrote for Galba,[59] since his choice of Piso as a successor was to prove calamitous. Galba, a virtuous emperor who lacked political skill, was no less disastrous for the state in Tacitus's eyes than an accomplished villain.[60] Despite the irony in Galba's case, as one who held high office under Trajan, Tacitus could hardly have publicly mocked the concept of adoptive monarchy.[61]

In 97 Tacitus promised to "record our former slavery and the testimony of our present happiness."[62] In the *Histories,* he wrote of Flavian repression, but he never did record the happier times of Nerva and Trajan; he chose to go farther back to the Julio-Claudians. Some attribute this to disillusionment with Trajan and a turning in old age toward a bleaker view of imperial power.[63] Bleakness there was, but Trajan was Tacitus's ideal emperor: respectful of the Senate and a successful imperialist. But even that wise and polite emperor retained autocratic power; he merely chose not to exercise it openly. The extraordinary euphoria that welcomed Trajan's succession as an age of rare happiness would yield to the realization that good emperors are eventually followed by bad ones.[64] As Tacitus's historical research for the *Annals* taught him how bad they really could be, he moved towards a darker, more fatalistic assessment of the principate. While writing the *Histories* the historian discovered his particular métier: his incisive art was suited to unmasking lies and his dark appraisal of human nature made him better at scouring the wicked than praising the virtuous. He was a moralist, and moralists are more interested in iniquity than in merit. He was a tragedian whose subject was the dramatic conflict between freedom and tyranny. He understood that "good emperors" were better than any realizable alternative; but he did not have to like them or write about them. A Tacitean history of the "happiest age" is unimaginable; the horrors of the Julio-Claudians were more to his literary taste.

In that age the powerless Senate first descended to groveling adulation; there the malignant power of tyrants was first unleashed; there *libertas* was truly lost. Tiberius transformed what might have been Augustus's temporary dominance, like that of Sulla or Caesar, into permanent tyranny, and for this Tacitus loathed him. Tiberius's secrecy, his sexual depravity, his reliance on informers, and his humiliation of the Senate established a pattern for his Julio-Claudian successors. And yet this Tiberius retains considerable stature in Tacitus's eyes; he may be bitter, angry, and finally corrupt, but he is no sniveling incompetent. He had no Caligulan madness, Neronian frivolity, or Vitellian sloth. Tacitus reports that he led the armies well, that he balanced the imperial budget, that he chose good administrators, that (except in a handful of treason trials) he enforced the laws, and that he did not raise taxes.[65] Few rulers can boast such a record, much less in an account from an admittedly hostile source. We must recognize that there was much in Tiberius's actual achievement that Tacitus admired, or would have admired if he had not hated the man so much.

Yet only deluded optimists believed that the Republic might be restored by a Drusus, or that a Germanicus might restore freedom. "*Libertas*" was the password of the conspirators against Caligula, and the word appears on coins after the murders of Caligula, Nero, and Domitian.[66] But it means little. The popular assemblies were emasculated by Augustus and abolished by Tiberius, and the Republic could hardly exist without those legislative and electoral bodies. The conspiracies against Nero and Domitian sought only to replace those lunatics with some gentler tyrant. Tacitus implicitly contrasts those brave barbarian princes who choose death over slavery with the craven senators (including, of course, himself) who prefer survival and wealth to freedom, dignity, and other ancestral values. The poet Lucan proclaimed that "liberty has retreated beyond the Tigris and the Rhine."[67] What price were these noble Romans willing to pay for such *libertas*? Neither Tacitus nor his aristocratic colleagues were willing to withdraw to their provincial estates out of sight of the emperors where they could live peacefully and honorably, but obscurely. The blunt conclusion must be that they preferred humiliation and servitude not only to death, but even to boredom. *Libertas* seemed to them a reasonable price to pay for personal security and entertainment. The senators were little different from the Roman proletariat whose loyalty or at least passivity were purchased with "bread and circuses."

Since Tacitus wrote much on tyranny but little on the "good emperors," we must infer his image of such a ruler. The fundamental quality was successful military leadership: "The merits of a good general were imperial qualities."[68] As a provincial, Tacitus was little impressed by family pedigree. The most successful emperors in his lifetime, Vespasian and Trajan, had no distinguished family tree; they were, quite simply, successful generals. He scorned Tiberius for being unwilling to expand the Empire, whereas Vespasian and Trajan had extended Rome's northern and eastern frontiers. There were other generals whose success in the field brought praise from Tacitus and whom he certainly saw as potential emperors: Corbulo with his victories in Armenia and Parthia, Suetonius Paulinus who had success in Mauretania and Britain, Verginius Rufus who twice declined acclamation as emperor and whose funeral address Tacitus himself delivered in 97, and of course Agricola for whom Tacitus certainly nursed great ambitions. But he knew well that military achievements alone did not insure success on the imperial throne: both Tiberius and Galba had splendid military records and blameless personal reputations but power revealed or, more likely, fostered their all too many human failings.

Tacitus rejoiced in the murder of Domitian, and proclaimed that "Nerva has joined things long incompatible: the principate and freedom."[69] But he knew what the idealistic Brutus had not: the removal of a tyrant does not eliminate tyranny. The king is dead; at the propitious time chosen by the astrologers and the politicians, after the necessary deals had been made, a new ruler would be proclaimed. So it was with Tiberius, and so it continued. The system would survive. Tacitus knew political reality. The system would not produce an ideal ruler; he would settle for a "good emperor."

Tacitus and Roman Imperialism

Tacitus is an imperialist. He believes it is Rome's destiny to conquer other peoples; the Roman Peace is an imposed peace. Peace is not the goal; it is merely the by-product of subjugation. The peace of Tiberius was contemptuously dismissed; the historian even suspected Augustus of jealousy for the advice in his will not to exceed Rome's frontiers.[70] The loss of three legions to the Germans in A.D. 9 may have sobered Augustus, but Tacitus wished to push on in all directions. He criticized Augustus and Tiberius for not pursuing Caesar's invasion of Britain[71] and taking up his plans for the conquest of Parthia.[72] In fact, Tacitus has the Parthian prince Tiridates boldly state the case for imperialism:

> "Inaction does not preserve great empires; that requires armed struggle. At the height of power, might makes right! A private family should protect its goods; a king's renown lies in fighting for the property of others."[73]

We can take these lines as a tribute to Trajan who was campaigning in the East against Arabia, Armenia, and Parthia during the years in which Tacitus wrote the *Annals*. Finally a Roman emperor had taken up the challenge of republican conquerors like Pompey and Julius Caesar.

Tiridates argues for a purely selfish imperialism: conquest not only satisfies pride, it is what defines a great power. But Tacitus provides a more reasoned defense of Roman imperialism in the great speech that the general Petilius Cerialis delivers in the rebellious Gallic city of Trier. Rome protects Gaul from the Germans and such protection requires troops and taxes; emperors, even cruel ones, do more harm in Rome than in the provinces. Cerialis warns that the revolt led by Julius Classicus would leave the Gauls in the hands of their traditional German enemies and reminds them of the benefits of Roman rule:

> "There were always kingdoms and wars throughout Gaul until you submitted to our control. Though often provoked, we used the right of conquest to impose on you only the cost of keeping the peace. For there can be no peace among nations without armies, no armies without pay, and no pay without taxes: the rest is shared between us."

He then draws a chilling picture of what life would be like after a Roman defeat:

"For if the Romans are driven out—which the gods forbid!—what will there be except wars among all nations? The providence and discipline of eight hundred years have consolidated this fabric of empire which cannot be destroyed without the annihilation of the destroyers . . . Let the models of good and bad fortune warn you not to choose defiant ruin over obedient safety."[74]

This is a ringing defense of Roman rule, despite the final words which eerily recall Tacitus's sneer at those who prefer the "safe and present" age of Augustus to the "old and dangerous" ways of the Republic.[75]

Yet in the *Agricola* Tacitus also provides cogent critiques of Roman imperialism. He justifies the British rebellions:

The Britons themselves readily comply with conscription, taxes, and other burdens imposed by the Empire as long as there are no abuses. Those they do not endure: they have been reduced to obedience, not yet to slavery.[76]

Here Tacitus speaks in his own voice; elsewhere he makes it clear that the rapacity of the Roman tax collector provoked Boudicca's revolt in 60. His denunciation is more incisive in the speech he writes for an anonymous Briton on the eve of that rebellion:

"Once we had a single king; now two are imposed—a governor ravages our lives and the tax collector, our property . . . Nothing is now safe from their greed and lust. In war the braver man takes the plunder; now weak cowards take our homes, seize our children, and enforce the draft . . ."[77]

Similar criticisms are made by Calgacus in his speech to his forces before he confronts Agricola at Mons Graupius. It is a brilliant performance, more suitable to a Roman rhetorical school than a Scottish battlefield. Tacitus's anger ran deep, and he draws upon it in words that a bitter Roman senator might think appropriate for a barbarian leader. Ironically, his emotions and his art here joined to create in the mouth of an enemy a diatribe against imperialism:

"They are the plunderers of the world; now that the earth lacks booty for their looting, now they look to the sea. A rich enemy arouses their greed, a poor one their desire for power. Neither East nor West has satisfied them . . . To robbery, to slaughter, and to theft they give the false name of 'Empire'; where they create desolation, they call it 'peace.'

It is the law of nature that each man regard his children and relatives as his dearest possessions: they are taken in conscription to serve as slaves far away, and our wives and sisters, even if they escape rape by an enemy, are debauched by our so-called friends and guests. Our goods and money go in taxes; our land and harvest go to their granaries; our hands and bodies are worn out in making roads through forests and swamps, lashed by their whips and their insults. Those born to slavery are sold once, and then fed by their masters: Every day Britain must buy and feed its own slavery."[78]

How much of this did Tacitus believe?[79] We might suspect that Tacitus emphasized the incompetence and corruption of the Roman administrators in Britain to provide a backdrop that highlights the efficiency and virtue of Agricola. As such, it would underline Agricola's wisdom, leadership, and humanity without telling us that Tacitus agreed with Calgacus (or any other barbarian) on the evils of Roman rule. After all, Calgacus was defeated; his analysis was hardly irrefutable.

If Tacitus did not subscribe to the provincials' view of Roman imperialism, he did have some sympathy for some of their criticisms.[80] He was dubious about the claims that romanization brought schools, baths, arcades, banquets, and the toga; "The simple natives called it 'civilization,' when it was part of their enslavement."[81] Gandhi's insistence on homespun cloth and recent anti-Western cultural revolutions in China and Iran reflect a similar view that an alien "civilization" is merely a form of oppression. He often attributes revolts to Roman faults: official venality, inadequate leadership, and civil war. While Roman officials should not pander to the provincials, Tacitus approves of Agricola's policy of trying to understand the provincials' grievances.[82] He remains an imperialist, yet amidst his jingoistic catch-phrases he provides a thoughtful analysis of the reasons for the revolts in Britain, Gaul, and Germany.[83]

Tacitus admires imperialism for he feels that foreign wars and conquests are to the moral advantage of the Roman people, but he also respects resistance rather than docile compliance. While he has no illusions about the Roman Peace and the "benefits" of Roman rule, those without the courage to resist deserve no more than to be Roman slaves. The Germans and the Britons who fought against Roman injustice earn his sympathy, in contrast both to the Romans' own acquiescence in tyranny and to Greek acceptance of Roman rule. The pride and courage of an Arminius and a Calgacus mute even Tacitean cynicism. Thus Civilis appeals to the Gauls to rebel in 69: "Nature has given freedom even to dumb animals, and courage is the special merit of man. The gods help the braver side."[84] Of course racial and cultural bias is also at work here. Tacitus has little sympathy for easterners; he scorns sycophantic Greeks and hates the proud, rebellious Jews. While he sometimes admires the independent Parthians, he preferred to provide fiery speeches to provincial rebels in the murky forests of Germany or on barren Scottish hillsides. His is a romantic image of freedom closer to Schiller or Sir Walter Scott (who doubtless derived much from Tacitus) than to their German or Briton ancestors.

The Teacher of Politics

The ancients believed that historians must have political acumen; politics and history nourished each other. History was the guide to public life, but the political was so intertwined with the moral that it would be impossible to disentangle the loss of political freedom from moral decline. Thus the study of the past helps us to "distinguish good from bad." Tacitus's work is a meditation on freedom (as Machiavelli's is a meditation on power), but the study of freedom and tyranny soon involves questions of corruption and virtue: the decline of Rome's constitution is a moral failure. Greek thinkers had earlier linked moral values and political rights; Plato's ideal Republic where the virtuous rule has long raised the question, "Who will keep the good rulers good?" Or, in the language of a modern totalitarian regime, "Who will police the secret police?" It is clear from the decree which conferred power on Vespasian in 69 that the emperor's actions had the force of law; there were no effective legal constraints on his power. Only the ruler's self-restraint will spare his people; the Romans now must hope for mercy rather than justice. Tacitus seems to accept the inevitability of the corruption of power and is deeply concerned with the immoral ruler. He calls the desire for power "a dominant and uncontrollable force,"[85] which drove tribunes and consuls alike to destroy the Republic and resulted in the despotism of the Empire. It is not only the desire for power but power itself that corrupts; the senator Arruntius chose suicide rather than witness the accession of Caligula; if the mature, experienced Tiberius was unhinged by power, how could the callow youth Caligula do better?[86]

Few ancient writers were more concerned with the sources of power than Tacitus, and he dissects the nature of that ambition that reduced the Roman state to civil war. Tacitus sweeps aside claims of patriotism and high ideals; the motives are merely ambition and self-interest. The emperors therefore distrusted all signs of ambition: popular sons and successful generals found themselves out of favor, or worse. Tacitus himself distrusted the ambitious; those who grasped for the imperial crown were by definition unworthy. He disliked, distrusted, and exposed blind ambition. The only deserving winners refuse to run the race. As he said of Galba, *Capax imperii nisi imperasset*—"He would have been thought capable of ruling if only he had never held power."[86a] The cauldron of power will expose the most promising as lacking moral strength or deficient in political acumen. It is a lesson history has taught us again and again, most recently in the shipwrecked presidencies of Richard Nixon and Jimmy Carter.

The lessons of Tacitus instructed both the rulers and the ruled, Though Tacitus surely intended to teach good men how to live well and to defend their freedom, Guicciardini points out that he teaches men both how to live under tyranny and tyrants how to govern.[87] The ambitious can learn from him that success often follows those who best disguise their ambitions. When he warns against political ambiguity and secrecy, he demonstrates its utility. Nero contrived the coronation of an Armenian king and the attendant celebrations to distract attention from the conviction of a prominent senator: "with public discussion turned to foreign affairs the domestic crime might be hidden."[88] These were not new political techniques first uncovered by Tacitus; but his incisive maxims and powerful characterizations made his lessons easier to learn.

The bleakness of Tacitus's moral vision is matched by his fatalistic political despair. Like the epic poet Lucan, Tacitus provides the counterpoint to Vergil's epic of Rome's foundation: a myth of political decline. Lucan's famous dismissal of the Augustan Peace which followed the long Civil War—"Such a peace comes with a master"[89]—is in the same spirit as Tacitus's scornful comment that Augustus had seduced everyone with the "sweetness of peace." We can trace Tacitus's lineage as a political pessimist to Sallust and Lucan.[90] Despite his obvious gratification in the *Agricola* at the selection of Trajan, his later research on the Julio-Claudians and Flavians taught him how unlikely the survival of a "good emperor" would be. Galba had republican virtues, but the troops cared little for such things. Trajan might truly be the "best of emperors," as his propaganda machine called him on the coinage, but who could tell what would come next? Tacitus found in the accession of the crippled, slow-witted Claudius an indication that malign forces toy with mankind for their own amusement:

> The more I think about the present or the past, the more an element of farce appears in all human affairs. For in public opinion, expectation, and respect, everyone was marked down as more likely for the imperial throne than the future emperor whom fate held in the background.[91]

A political Gresham's Law was likely to bring the basest men forward, men who appealed to the armies. Tacitus lived in Gibbon's "Happiest Age" but his political shrewdness foresaw the horrors of the third century, when dozens of brutish soldiers were quickly crowned emperor and as quickly deposed by rogue armies whose narrow self-interest brought the Empire to the brink of collapse. Since it is unclear "whether human affairs are controlled by Fate and changeless necessity—or by luck,"[92] Tacitus could only face life with resignation and play Cassandra, using his art to teach and warn as best he could. He could prophesy the evils that would follow; try as he might, he could not prevent them. And if he could not save his own people, his passion for freedom and loathing of tyrants and their creatures made a deep mark on the political thought of future ages.

Time that is intolerant
Of the brave and innocent,
And indifferent in a week
To a beautiful physique,
Worships language and forgives
Everyone by whom it lives.
W. H. AUDEN
In memory of W. B. Yeats*

Men and dynasties pass, but style abides.
SIR RONALD SYME
Tacitus**

VII

❖ ─────────────────────── ❖

The Historian as Literary Artist

History and Rhetoric

In the reign of Nero when young Tacitus was beginning his education, the Romans regarded rhetorical training as the basis of all literary and intellectual activity. Neronian poetry, philosophy, drama, and even Petronius's sprawling comic novel, the *Satyricon*, all display the rhetorician's hand. And history too, as Cicero had written a century before, "needs the orator's voice"[1] since it was the orators who understood human nature, ethics, and history it-

The English Auden, ed. E. Mendelson (New York, 1977) 242.
**(1958) 624.

self.[2] Quintilian, who soon became the first official professor of rhetoric at Rome, understandably saw rhetoric, not philosophy, as the basis of all education, while history was the subdivision of oratory "nearest to the poets and may be regarded as a prose poem."[3] It was in the intellectual shadow of Quintilian that Tacitus grew to maturity as a self-described "groupie" who followed orators around the city.[4] He acquired all the arts of an advocate and deployed them in his earliest writings, but Tacitus also recognized that, for all its public power, rhetoric in his own day was often merely a rote training without the broad liberal education that Cicero so well exemplified: barren rhetorical skill had replaced reading.[5]

Every page of Tacitus shows the effects of this rhetorical training, and the speeches he wrote for the *Annals* constitute a history of political oratory from 14 to 68 A.D.[6] Yet Tacitus ultimately turned away from public oratory. The only successful practicing orators of the times were the informers and prosecutors whom he so scathingly depicts. While he might on occasion speak publicly in the Senate or courts, Tacitus regarded oratory as intellectually obsolete and politically irrelevant: sterile tricks used to flatter tyrants and destroy good men. When Longinus has a philosopher assert that orators can only be "grandiloquent flatterers" in such a servile age, this also alludes to conditions in the first century of the Empire.[7] The great political speakers of Athens and republican Rome required freedom under which to flourish; Sparta had no orators.[8] Tacitus in the *Dialogue* clearly admires Maternus's decision to abandon oratory for poetry—a politically charged poetry that cost him his life under Vespasian. He himself chooses history as a suitable vehicle for linking his literary talents to the real political and moral issues of the day.

But if Tacitus chose to forswear an oratorical career, he could hardly expunge the very basis of his intellectual formation. That rhetorical training informs every page of his histories, but it is most obvious in his reliance on speeches to shape the historical narrative. Some speeches are direct, others are indirect; some delineate the psyche and values of his characters, while others provide political or moral analysis.[9] Even Rome's enemies are granted an opportunity to speak, and to speak more effectively than they ever did in Britain or Germany. The speeches and speech itself are the building blocks of Tacitus's histories.

In the *Histories* many speeches have the leisurely amplitude and the ringing patriotism of Livy. Others mark out important political positions in the time of turmoil. Galba spoke in favor of an adoptive monarchy, a policy which failed for Galba but which had produced a peaceful transition to Trajan in Tacitus's own time.[10] In a speech pervaded with Realpolitik, Mucianus urges Vespasian to reach for the imperial throne and not to worry about the constitutional niceties: the army creates the emperor.[11] And at Trier, before his eloquent speech in defense of Roman imperial rule, Cerialis expresses the traditional Roman preference for deeds over words:

> "I have never practiced oratory; Romans prove their merit in war. But since you give such weight to words, and not judge good and evil by the facts but by the talk of troublemakers, I have decided to say a few things, now that the war is over, which it is more useful for you to hear than for me to say."[12]

In the *Annals* the speeches mirror Tacitus's own developing voice: trenchant, analytical, and self-confident. Yet he does not necessarily misrepresent the attitudes of the speakers. Tiberius's canniness and common sense appear in his speeches, and we have seen that the tyrant's ambiguity is perversely congenial to the historian.[13] All ancient historians created speeches; the originals, if they were ever delivered, had long been lost since speeches were rarely preserved in the archives. Even the most scrupulous historian only attempted to satisfy the demands of plausibility. Yet one Tacitean speech does survive: Claudius's oration in favor of the admission of Gallic nobles to the Senate which has been preserved both on a bronze tablet in Lyons as well as in Tacitus's version.[14] The original reminds us of the Claudius of Suetonius (and Robert Graves): digressions laced with historical pedantry.[15] Tacitus downplays the personal idiosyncrasies of Claudius; the speech is briefer and the arguments are more cogently presented.[16] The historian has generously placed his rhetorical skill at the service of an emperor whom he despised to present a powerful statement on behalf of the inclusion of provincials in the Senate. By his own lights Tacitus has been faithful to Claudius's arguments and to the occasion; any modern desire for verbal exactitude would have seemed to him pedantic and unworthy of the literary artistry expected in serious historical writing.

The rhetorical innuendo of the politician and the advocate proved congenial to the imperial historian.[17] Tacitus uses rumors and hearsay to attribute motives and secret feelings to his characters, and anonymous comments function as an important dramatic device. The historian retreats behind the mask of the Romar people to provide a critique of tyranny and to set the tone for the accession of Tiberius. Again and again Tacitus uses anonymous comments to paint a prejudicial picture while he maintains a pose of neutrality and detachment.

Some scholars regard the writer's use of innuendo as at variance with the historian's reliability. But no ancient would see a contradiction; the problem rests in the modern definition of history. So too there is no difference between the literary artist and the historian in Tacitus—such false distinctions stem from our confusing ancient and modern genres. Since one of Tacitus's fundamental themes in the *Annals* is the conflict between appearance and reality, some introspection is necessary to penetrate beneath the surface record of "factual" events. Literary tactics are integral to the task of the analytical historian. All ancient historians were expected to be artists and style was as much a part of the historian's intellectual arsenal as logic.[18] We must judge him by the ancient criteria of historical art rather than by the anachronistic criteria of modern historical science. To do less would be to wrench him from his context. His aim, as with all great historians, is not merely to record the past but to recreate it for the reader.

Literary Structure

Ancient storytellers from Homer onward used digressions to introduce variety into their narrative and to serve a structural purpose. The historian was expected to show the same invention that the orator used in constructing a persuasive speech. The digressions of the *Histories* are exotic and entertaining, but in the *Annals*

Tacitus skillfully uses digressions to comment on his primary story. His account of Claudius's eastern wars and the internal power struggles in the Parthian royal family foreshadow the dynastic struggles at Rome.[19] The digressions often focus on historiographical issues or Roman antiquities which highlight the political conditions of his history, or ethnographic asides which are themselves comments on contemporary Roman society.

Narrative lay at the heart of ancient historiography, and in the *Annals* Tacitus displays his mastery of literary narrative. Despite the appearance of the traditional annalistic method of recounting events year by year, he weaves together certain themes that recur from book to book: treason trials; dynastic intrigues; foreign wars; the personality of the emperor.[20] He can depict mutiny and war with breathless rapidity or he can linger over the emotional scene of Germanicus's death. His transitions are often elegant literary devices: Tigellinus's vast orgy in the Campus Martius leads directly to the great fire of 64.[21] The collapse of the amphitheater at Fidenae (with 50,000 killed or injured) is immediately followed by a fire in Rome that leads the mobs (and so the reader) to connect the disasters with Tiberius's retirement to Capri.[22] The narrative not only relates the events; it suggests much that lies below the surface.

Many ancient historians enrich their narrative through parallels, allusive comparisons of situations and the doubling of characters. Tacitus often uses these literary tactics to evoke the desired response from his reader. Some parallels are quite explicit: dynastic intrigue in Rome and Parthia; Germanicus compared to Alexander the Great; a treacherous death for both Germanicus and Arminius. Other parallels are literary allusions, as when the Vergilian language of the *Histories* links the death of Galba with that of Priam and the burning of Rome in 69 with the conflagration that destroyed Troy in the *Aeneid*.[23] Pairings of characters are used (Germanicus and Tiberius) to highlight their moral contrast.[24] Even the peaceful and beautiful setting of Capri sets off the repellent description of Tiberius in old age, the emperor's disgusting sexual perversions as well as the emotional and moral torment he suffered there.[25]

The most notable parallel is between Tiberius (who is sometimes referred to by his cognomen "Nero") and his vicious successor Nero. Both were dominated by imperious mothers (Livia and the younger Agrippina) and manipulated by their murderous praetorian prefects. Tacitus makes the connection clear in his introduction of their reigns: "The first crime of the new regime was the murder of Agrippa Postumus";[26] "The first death of the new principate was that of Junius Silanus."[27] In Tacitus's day all would have acknowledged the viciousness of Nero and the murderous immorality of Agrippina who had seduced, married, and murdered her uncle Claudius to gain the imperial throne for her son. Tiberius and Livia were another matter, however much Tiberius may have declined in his last years. But Tacitus uses the overt and subtle parallels between the couples to cast a deadly pall over Tiberius from the very day of his succession. It is unfair, most of all to Livia, but it is a brilliantly successful literary device.

Dramatic Effects

Despite Tacitus's evident contempt for Nero's stage performances, readers through the centuries have recognized in the historian himself a master dramatist who moves his extraordinarily vibrant characters across the grand stage of the Roman Empire.[28] Like Dickens, Tacitus creates characters who demand to be transported into the theater, and so they have been from Ben Jonson (Sejanus and Tiberius), Monteverdi (Nero and Poppaea), and Racine (Agrippina, Nero, and Britannicus) in the seventeenth century to the BBC mini-series, *I, Claudius,* in our own day. Though no dramas survive from Tacitus's own maturity, he lived in a theatrical age in which drama permeated much of the art, architecture, and literature. Tacitus followed the taste of his time and his work was, in the words of his sixteenth-century editor Lipsius, "the theater of everyday life."

Though there are dramatic scenes throughout Tacitus's work, it is in the *Annals* that drama is all-pervasive. There the individual books often seem to begin or end like an act of a play. *Annals* 3 begins with the younger Agrippina returning to Italy with her children and the ashes of Germanicus with the crowds surging along the dock (and commenting on the events) as the flotilla sailed into port, and greeting the cortege as it made its way to Rome. On another note, *Annals* 4 begins with the introduction of the arch-courtier and arch-villain Sejanus who was to pursue and destroy the wife and children of Germanicus. Like a classical tragedy, *Annals* 2 closed with a set piece of pathos and political martyrdom, the death of Germanicus; Book 11 with the execution of Messalina; Book 12 with the murder of Claudius; Book 14 with the execution of Nero's wife Octavia (after having opened with the murder of his mother); and Book 15 with the executions and suicides following the Pisonian conspiracy.

Tacitus's account of the deaths of the philosophers Seneca and Thrasea dramatizes with obvious theatricality the eulogistic memoirs of their devoted followers. The historian is not merely a dramatist but seems also to play the role of a critic regarding history itself as theater.[29] It is particularly recognizable in his narrative of the self-conscious dramatics of the Neronian age where theatrical metaphors pervade the text and give it an artistic cohesion.[30] While Nero paraded himself in costume and sang arias from Greek tragedies, the conspirators and philosophers of his court were also playing roles of Brutus the assassin or Socrates the martyr. This blurring of the line between theater and reality was hardly new: Brutus modeled himself on a legendary ancestor who launched the Roman Republic, whereas the younger Cato committed suicide while reading of the death of Socrates. The historian sometimes gives dramatic shape to history, but on other occasions he must expose the ways in which historical actors dramatize their own actions and thus delude themselves as the actor John Wilkes Booth theatrically shouted "sic semper tyrannis" after his murder of Abraham Lincoln. Tacitus understood better than any other ancient writer the theatrical fantasies of political life, and his exposure of the ambiguous relations between politics and drama remains compellingly relevant.

Though the dramatic set pieces avoid the cathartic pain of tragedy through a tone of philosophical acceptance, the *Annals* is constructed as a series of tragedies: Germanicus and Agrippina, Sejanus (whose story is not complete in the surviving text), Messalina, Claudius, Agrippina the younger, and Nero—whose story contains as much incest and matricide as the traditional Greek tragedies about the house of Atreus in which the emperor liked to perform. But the great, overarching tragedy which shapes the first half of the *Annals* is that of Tiberius. He was a complex man of great abilities whose understandable human weaknesses mixed with absolute power to transform him into a monster: flattered and betrayed, suspicious of the innocent but trusting his greatest enemy, finally loathsome even to himself. In this character, so real that he has even been psychoanalyzed, Tacitus embodies the tragedy of the Roman Empire and the tragedy of his own life.[31] It is no small achievement to have transformed an ignoble age into tragedy.

Tacitus is a master of the vignette, using a few pages or even a few lines to capture the essence of all drama: the sudden reversal of fortune. When Piso, sent to the East as the agent of Tiberius, haughtily returned to Rome to face the accusation of murder and incitement to treason, he saw at the first session of the Senate that the emperor would demand his sacrifice as a scapegoat to popular anger for the death of Germanicus. He went home and immediately cut his own throat.[32] When the rumor of a mutiny of the praetorians sent guests scrambling out of the emperor Otho's banquet, his magistrates hastily cast away their badges of office and avoided their waiting attendants so they could lie low until the danger had past.[33] When the senator Haterius falls to his knees to beg Tiberius's pardon for an offensive comment in a senatorial debate, he accidentally trips the emperor and is almost killed by nervous bodyguards.[34] We can see the drama that Tacitus has inserted into such minor episodes when we compare Suetonius's brief account of the praetorian mutiny in which no mention is made of the panic of the guests at the banquet. Nor does Suetonius's account of the death of Tiberius contain the final dramatic twist of Tacitus:

> On March 16th the emperor's breathing stopped and he was thought to have died. Gaius with a crowd of well-wishers was coming out to inaugurate his rule when it was suddenly reported that Tiberius had regained speech and sight, and he asked that someone bring him food to revive his faintness. There was a general panic and the crowd fled: everyone

feigned sorrow or ignorance. With hopes dashed, Gaius was frozen into silence and expected disaster. The fearless praetorian prefect Macro ordered the old man to be smothered with a pile of clothes and all leave the room. So Tiberius died in his seventy-eighth year.[35]

Tacitus not only provides dramatic vignettes; he includes in his history the devices familiar from Greek tragedy.[36] He makes dramatic use of silence: the silence of shame, the silence of terror, or the ominous silence of abandonment.[37] Omens and portents foreshadow future events, while the weather and other natural phenomena reflect human conflicts.[38] The Olympian gods of Homer or Vergil have no place in such an intrinsically skeptical writer; only Fortune appears as Nemesis might in Greek tragedy. More than any ancient historian, Tacitus delights in reporting rumors, and he uses them as a Greek chorus to comment on the events. On a few occasions, as at the death of Augustus, he uses contradictory rumors as a playwright would split the spectators into a chorus to create a dramatic dialogue.[39] The masses in the streets or on the battlefield are depicted as great, irrational forces which bring a certain terror. In some of the longer set pieces, such as the death of Agrippina, many elements of dramatic structure coalesce: prologue (the appeal of Poppaea for Agrippina's death), tension increased by digressions (differing accounts of incest between Nero and Agrippina), dramatic irony (warm greetings for Agrippina at Nero's villa), reversal of fortune (collapse of the booby-trapped boat with Agrippina's remarkable escape and her welcome by the crowds; Nero's panic), and omens (astrologers' predictions; mysterious trumpet blasts from the grave). Even Agrippina's final ironic comment to her murderers, "Strike here!," pointing to the womb which had borne Nero, seems operatically melodramatic.

Tacitus's history certainly arouses the fear and pity that ancient critics sought from tragedy, or the horror and sympathy of its modern counterpart. The role of tragedy was not only personal catharsis, the cleansing that Aristotle posited, but also an exorcism of evil from the entire community. Vergil, Lucan, and especially Seneca had cloaked pain and despair in an aesthetic of horror, and Tacitus takes it still further.[40] His searing account of the cruelty of absolute power in a prevailing atmosphere of terror may have served both as an expiation of his personal collaboration with Domitian and as an attempt to exorcise forever such monsters from the imperial throne. Like other great tragedians, Tacitus shows his characters with intimacy and passion while his grand moral vision drives the story to an inexorable conclusion. Tacitus was a pessimist: his extraordinary mastery of tragic tone, theatrical characterization, and dramatic technique combine to make him the greatest tragedian of ancient Rome.

Visual and Pictorial Effects

Tacitus's gift for drama is matched by his interest in investing his narrative with vivid images, both of detail and of grand tableaux. He does not provide exact physical descriptions of characters or buildings, and there are few details of landscape.[41] At times he uses generic battle scenes, perhaps from a repertoire of images not unlike those used by the sculptors of the column of Trajan.[42] As in his political analysis, Tacitus looks beyond surface appearance to the grand sweep of the dramatic, moral, or political reality. Scenes reminiscent of the historical paintings of the Renaissance led Racine to call Tacitus "the greatest painter of antiquity," and Napoleon continued the metaphor when he complained that Tacitus "painted" everything black.[43] Poets throughout antiquity had employed striking pictorial effects and Vergil had given new weight to visual elements. Tacitus follows Vergil in using tableaux to evoke the entire gamut of emotions in his reader: fear, pity, horror, and revulsion.

Any Roman historian would be expected to provide a graphic account of the Roman army in battle against the enemy, and Tacitus does so in Britain and Germany. Far more memorable are the scenes of civil war when the historian's bitter irony paints the street fighting in Rome between the Flavian and Vitellian forces as a grotesque parody:

> The people stood nearby and watched the fighters and, as though at a mock combat, they encouraged now one side,

now the other, with shouts and applause. Whenever one side gave way, the crowd shouted that those who hid in shops or houses be dragged out and killed, and they took the bulk of the booty while the troops were caught up in the bloody slaughter. Through the entire city there was a cruel and hideous spectacle: here fighting and gore, there baths and bars, blood and corpses next to male and female prostitutes . . . [44]

Tacitus was less interested than Suetonius in the actual physical appearance of his protagonists, but he adds colorful details at crucial moments to provide a more vivid picture.[45] In his account of Vitellius's attempt to abdicate as the Flavian armies marched on Rome, the weeping emperor first lifts his small son to the crowd and then tries to surrender his dagger to the consul who refuses to take it. The crowd blocks his vain attempts to leave the insignia of office in a temple or to flee to his brother's house, and the pathetic emperor, like a child teased by his playmates, is forced to walk home to the Palace.

The historian is always the moralist, and his moral indignation often inspires his most graphic images. When the governor of Britain led his army against the island of Anglesey,

Along the shore stood a mixed battle line, crowded with armed men and women rushing between. Dressed in black like Furies with wild hair, they brandished torches. All around Druids raised their hands to heaven and shouted terrible curses. Our soldiers were struck by this strange sight and exposed motionless bodies to wounds as though they were paralyzed. But encouraged by their general and each other not to fear a band of crazed women, they brought up the standards, cut down the enemy and engulfed them in their own flames. Next they imposed a garrison on the conquered, and they cut down the groves devoted to savage rituals. For there they thought they must drench their altars with captives' blood and consult their gods with human entrails.[46]

Later Tacitus describes with equal disgust the notorious banquet which Tigellinus gave on a lavishly decorated raft floating in a lake, with brothels filled with noble ladies specially constructed along the shore. With such minor details as Nero's hypocritical embrace and kissing of his old tutor Seneca as he prepares to drive him to suicide, Tacitus makes his point with a memorable image.

The most extraordinary of the Tacitean tableaux is his account of the mutinies in Book 1 of the *Annals*. For almost twenty pages Tacitus provides a descriptive tour de force, not a static painting, but a cinematic drama into which individual scenes and characters are brilliantly interwoven in which menacing darkness sets the mood. Amid the grand movements, gestures, and emotions of the crowds of angry soldiers, Tacitus like a director of grand historical films (Griffith; Eisenstein; Lean) shifts his focus from the sweeping panorama of a faceless mob to glimpses of individual faces until the camera's restless eye settles on particularly telling images: an eloquent mutineer rouses the troops with a fiery speech; aged veterans strip to show their scars and shove Germanicus's fingers onto their toothless gums; rapacious centurions are humiliated and even murdered by the rebellious troops; Germanicus melodramatically threatens to commit suicide until a cynical soldier offered his own "sharper sword"; Germanicus is dragged from his bed as other officers flee into hiding.

Natural surroundings set the mood: soldiers confront each other in the dark and panic at the omen of a waning moon, rebels are driven into their tents by rainstorms, and in the ghostly Teutoburg forest Roman bones from Varus's slaughtered legions still lie amidst the swamps.[47] Tacitus changes focus and tone with the speed and skill with which Shakespeare and Verdi shift from monologue or aria to chorus: mass movement mixed with individual suffering; swift changes from light to darkness, with melodrama elevated to the level of tragedy. Near the end of the mutiny the commander's wife Agrippina and their little son, the soldiers' pet Caligula, accompany a group of weeping officers' wives who leave the camp to seek the protection of Rome's Gallic allies. A contrived scene, and a melodramatic one, as is the final image of Germanicus's weeping at the massacres which he had intentionally incited. These vivid scenes form what is perhaps the most graphic drama produced in ancient Rome.

In a later scene from the war with the Germans, Tacitus depicts

Germanicus wandering through his camp the night before the battle disguised in an animal skin and listening to his soldiers praising him. A few sentences convey the drama inherent in the situation. Shakespeare recognized a brilliant theatrical idea, embellished it with dialogue and humor, and raised it to its full potential when Henry V goes in disguise through the English camp to test his men on the eve of Agincourt.[48] Little more needs to be said of Tacitus's sense of drama if the Bard himself praises through imitation.

Darkness is the predominant atmosphere. The crucial events in Tacitus's histories take place in dark torchlit rooms of the imperial palace or the Senate house. Lights blaze only to reveal the scandalous in the surrounding darkness, as in the chiaroscuro style of Mannerist painting. Firebrands flare at Tigellinus's extravagant orgy on the shores of a lake, as do the wedding torches at Nero's "marriage" to a male lover. These scenes immediately precede Tacitus's description of the great fire (said to have started on Tigellinus's estate) which all but destroyed Rome in 64. But this fire never brightens the city. Outdoor scenes of battle rarely occur in the bright sunshine that we find in Livy. Battles are often nocturnal; the moon is frequently covered by clouds. Even in daytime battles, the sun is mentioned less often than clouds or storms which darken the field of combat. The few scenes of daylight festivity are often heavily ironic. For example, here, as in Anglesey, Tacitus uses Bacchic imagery and maenads to lend an air of oriental depravity when the empress Messalina celebrates her bigamous marriage to Silius while Claudius is away in Ostia:

Messalina was never more abandoned. It was autumn and she celebrated a mock wine harvest on her estate. Presses were working and vats overflowed while women in skins danced like crazed Maenads at a sacrifice. With flowing hair she shook a Bacchic staff while beside her Silius, crowned in ivy, wore theatrical boots and tossed his head amidst the wild shouts of a "chorus." They say that Vettius Valens climbed a tall tree as a joke and, asked what he saw, said "A terrible storm coming from Ostia." Either some such thing had begun, or perhaps a casual phrase became a prophecy.[49]

The storm foretells the return to "normality" in the arrival of Claudius and the execution of Messalina. The agricultural abundance of Italy, often used by Augustan poets and artists as a metaphor for the moral and political regeneration of the Roman people, is here inverted by Tacitus.

Style

Ancient literary critics believed that an author's personality is revealed in his style, an idea best formulated by de Buffon in his 1753 lecture to the Académie Française: "Style is the man himself."[50] Many contemporary critics insist that style is merely a mask, another literary stratagem in the arsenal of the writer. And yet pseudonymous authors can be recognized; powerful authorial voices cannot be disguised. To be sure, Tacitus deliberately composed his *Dialogue* in Ciceronian Latin, but the historical works show the clear development of an intense personal style culminating in the *Annals*.[51] While his use of the first person is rare, the reader is always aware of the author's critical, astringent personality conveyed through his style.[52]

To speak of originality is not to deny antecedents. Tacitus's contemporaries doubtless found his style less peculiar than does a modern reader, taught for so long to regard a smooth Ciceronian Latin as the classical norm; he in fact shares many characteristics with other silver-age writers like Seneca. Tacitus was known in the seventeenth century as the "Prince of Darkness" ("prince des ténèbres"), not for his mood but for the obscurity of his style.[53] Even Napoleon complained vehemently of that obscurity to Goethe at Weimar in 1808—a time when political and literary giants took matters of style very seriously indeed.[54] If Tacitus rejected the genial candor, abundant prose, and buoyant patriotism of his greatest historical predecessor Livy, he found in Sallust a political cynicism combined with an intense and acerbic style suitable to his subject and his temperament. Rhetoric can embellish and conceal, but this is a rhetoric of exposure in which acute political diagnosis reveals the hidden truths of the Empire. His aggressive ferocity of syntax was embellished by a Vergilian richness of diction to produce in the most politically charged Latin ever written a remarkable marriage of style and content. He opens the *Annals* with all Rome rushing into servitude, Latin words ("consules, patres, eques") tumble breathlessly forward as the sense shapes the style while verbs and conjunctions are swept aside in a way that poets would rightly envy.[55] In the words of Pascal, "When we see a natural style, we are quite surprised and delighted, for we expected to see an author and we find a man."[56] It is not a literary tactic, it is Tacitus himself.

In the second century, the Greek essayist Lucian wrote in "How to Write History" that the use of poetry in historical writing was as meretricious as painting an athlete like a harlot.[57] That spurious beauty, scorned by Thucydides and Polybius, also revolted Messalla in the *Dialogue* who said "it is undoubtedly better to clothe what you have to say in rough homespun than to parade it in the gay-colored garb of a whore."[58] In theory Tacitus would have been sympathetic; in fact he made much use of a wide poetic vocabulary. Like most rhetoricians, his language becomes more sensational where his facts or conclusions are most shaky. This is often the case in the emotional books of the *Annals* that recount the reign of Tiberius. Though many of Sejanus's allies survived his fall, Tacitus depicts an orgy of slaughter hardly justified by the details of his narrative:

> Excited by these executions, Tiberius ordered the death of all those held in prison for complicity with Sejanus. It was a massacre with every age, each sex, noble, unknown, all lying scattered or in piles. Relatives and friends were not allowed to stand near, nor lament, nor even to look for very long. Guards stood all around the corpses and spied on the mourners until the rotting bodies were dragged to the Tiber where they floated away or were washed to the bank with no one to cremate them or to touch them.[59]

This is exceptional. The final six books of the *Annals*—more controlled or not yet revised, according to one's scholarly taste—are less eccentric and less colorful.

Tacitus has made his own a tone of the utmost gravity with intimations of melancholy and violence lurking just under the surface. It carries a moral and political authority that impresses, even intimidates the reader.[60] The intimacy with his characters and the passion for his story recall the tragedies of Euripides, Shakespeare, and Racine. Yet there is far more to Tacitean style than grandeur. The reader is constantly disoriented by shifts of syntax as Tacitus avoids the hackneyed expression and pursues the surprising turn of phrase that upsets the grammatical balance. That stylistic asymmetry also reflects the changes of mood, now by the breakneck speed of the narrative, now by the extended portrayal of a static nocturnal scene with vivid, if somber, poetic diction. This remarkable combination of nobility and intimacy, of gravity and violence is enormously effective at conveying the underlying sense of fear that pervades the *Histories* and the *Annals*.

In his style Tacitus created an extraordinary intellectual instrument of description and analysis, something which is even apparent at times in translation. Tacitean style is not a literary sugarcoating on the bitter pill of imperial tyranny; it is an integral part of his narrative, his characterization, his political ideology. For style is not merely language; it includes tone and rhetorical structure as well. Style both grows out of the content and in turn transforms the substance of the histories; the relation is symbiotic. But his literary art has its dangers as well: Tacitus uncovers political hypocrisy, but the power of his own rhetoric can distort the truth and his images can take on a reality of their own.

Scholars have fixed on different passages as examples of Tacitus's literary genius: the political clarity of his speeches or his impressionistic treatment of the German mutiny; the restrained grandeur of the beginning of the *Histories* or the transformation of cliché into moving philosophical statement at the conclusion of the *Agricola*. I am most dazzled by the sudden flash of mordant wit, the epigram that undermines the political burlesque of imperial Rome: that ingratiating Otho "played the slave to become the master."[61] There we see the imagination and delight in verbal skill that characterizes great poetry, the remarkable linguistic variation that reaches its apogee in the *Annals*. And, as in poetry, a word or phrase may evoke larger themes.[62] When he describes one leader as *occultior, non melior* ("more devious, not better") he provides the central theme of political life in a paranoid age.[63] Historian or poet, Tacitus's ideas are inexorably intertwined with his style, and it is through his style that his moral vision survives.[64]

Irony and Humor

Voltaire, who did not like Tacitus, admired him as a "fanatic scintillating with wit."[65] Irony, the orator's stock in trade, served Tacitus particularly well in his histories. The historian can hardly be regarded as a jovial fellow; his humor is nearly always black with what Kenneth Quinn calls "the savage economy of the political cartoonist."[66] His bitter jibes are often understated but rarely missed by the attentive reader who learns to await, and savor, the ironic flashes that illuminate the otherwise unrelenting darkness of his story. Sometimes his irony has a wistful sadness as when he laments the premature deaths of Drusus and Germanicus with the thought that "Those loved by the Roman people are short-lived and unlucky."[67] There is an implied nostalgia for better days when he describes the age of Domitian as one in which "courage and freedom were lost at the same time"[68] and when "a great reputation was as dangerous as a bad one."[69] Sometimes his angry contempt is evident, as when Nero was reported to sing of burning Troy while Rome is in flames, or when Roman envoys are assaulted by rebellious troops when even barbarians would not dare such an outrage.

There are innumerable scenes in which Tacitean irony would elicit a smirk or a sad shake of the head from the Roman reader. While many Roman aristocrats included the emperor in their wills to ensure that the will was validated and their families provided for, Petronius's last joke before his suicide is his inclusion of Nero's "secret" vices in his will.[70] The crowd at Augustus's funeral jeered that the emperor, who had held so much power for so long, needed a military guard to ensure his peaceful burial.[71] A grimmer example is the contrast between the courageous freedwoman Epicharis and the cowardly aristocrats who betrayed their friends to save their own lives.[72] In all of these examples, one might argue that irony was inherent in the situation; it was not a verbal quip of the historian. But it is no less Tacitus's irony. The past may be a series of paradoxes and every historical event does contain an ironic element.[73] But the historian, unlike the poet or novelist, cannot write in a purely ironic mode; he must structure his narrative to highlight and give meaning to the ironies which he finds (or thinks he finds) in the historical record. Neither the physical beauty of Capri nor the gross depravity which Tiberius engaged in there is itself ironic, but when they are juxtaposed the historian has created in a few sentences an irony that will pervade his entire account of Tiberius's self-imposed exile. Likewise, the contrast between chaste and heroic barbarians and the corrupt and craven Romans is Tacitus's own ironic creation. The deepest irony, which underlies the wit and the structure of all Tacitus's historical writing, is a moral one: the traditional Roman virtues are no longer desirable for those who wish to survive and succeed. As with Sejanus and Tigellinus, corruption is the road to power in an absolutist state. From that basic irony, the historian imbues his narratives with humor, melancholy, and despair as he examines the moral pathology of the Empire.

While he preferred irony, Tacitus also enlivened his narrative with jokes.[74] These are more prevalent in the *Annals*—but it hardly indicates a mellowing in the writer's old age.[75] That pleasant thought is hardly borne out by the context of the jokes. Plutarch takes pleasure from the many jokes he reports in his biographies as does Suetonius in his often coarse jibes against the emperors; Tacitus seems to take but a grim satisfaction from the jokes he reports or invents. He is, in the words of Peter Gay, "both witty and humorless."[76]

Tacitus includes a number of attributed jokes, as when Gaius Crispus reflected on his brother-in-law Caligula's silence while Tiberius destroyed his family: "There had never been a better slave or a worse master."[77] One of the few coarse jokes in Tacitus is made by the distinguished ex-consul Asiaticus who, when he heard that the list of his crimes included effeminacy (passive homosexuality), mocked his accuser: "Ask your sons, Suillius. They will testify to my masculinity."[78] Another joke is a bit too good to be true, but whoever invented it, Tacitus tells it with relish. A slave of the murdered grandson of Augustus, Agrippa Postumus, pretended to be his master and attracted crowds of supporters. When arrested and brought to the palace, Tiberius asked the slave how he had made himself Agrippa, he cheekily answered "Just as you made yourself Caesar."[79] If a slave made the joke, he was remarkably quick-witted and politically aware; it was more likely the creation of a senatorial wag or even Tacitus himself. *Se non è vero, è ben trovato.*

There are other jokes which are clearly Tacitus's own. When Otho and Vitellius accused each other of debauchery, Tacitus dryly comments, "Neither was lying."[80] Such a sardonic postscript to a speech or a confrontation is typical Tacitean humor. After a hypocritical speech of admiration by Nero, Seneca expressed his gratitude and Tacitus adds: "So end all conversations with tyrants."[81] A few pages later after Nero accused his wife in an edict of seducing the fleet commander and having an abortion, Tacitus jokes "He forgot his recent charge of sterility."[82] And he takes aim at some of his favorite targets: "Astrologers will always be banned and always kept,"[83] and there are always "gloomy philosophers willing to be displayed as royal entertainment."[84] Few of these jokes produce gales of laughter, but Tacitus reports at least one (inadvertent) joke that may have. When Nero spoke at the funeral of Claudius of his predecessor's wisdom and foresight, "nobody could help laughing."[85] Even if the laughter was tinged with bitterness, we can well imagine Tacitus laughing at Seneca's parody of Claudius's deification, in which the dead emperor becomes, not a god, but a pumpkin. A much later source mentions a joke book written by Tacitus, which itself seems to have a touch of unintentional black humor about it.[86] Tacitus was no natural jokester; he only liked jokes with a dark edge.

From Cato onward Roman historians had the gift for aphorism and Tacitus grew to maturity among the orators of the Flavian era who prized the witty epigram above all else.[87] In the first century Rome remained an oral society in which rhetorical skill (which included verbal repartee) was highly prized. From the vantage point of a less witty age, we might think that the early empire, like Parisian and British salons of the eighteenth century, prized superficial cleverness over substance. But wit was as essential a component of intellectual discourse as correct grammar is in a less flamboyant and more prosaic age. Poets like Ovid and Lucan were much attracted to the epigram, and we see in Suetonius's lives how the emperors and their senatorial opponents really did use a witty riposte to drive home a metaphorical dagger. The Senate and the imperial court were little more than a large village in which particularly pungent jibes and skillful aphorisms quickly made the rounds and became commonplaces of the political culture. When Tiberius responds to the grieving crowd at the funeral of his popular nephew Germanicus, "Princes are mortal; the state is eternal," [88] the phrase has the ring of something Tiberius might well have said and probably did. With Tacitus, as with a vaudeville comedian, the question is not the novelty of his jokes, but how he uses his material.

Tacitus's fondness for epigrams is evident in his earliest writing. He says that British chiefs "fight separately and are conquered together." [89] The *Germania* also gave ample scope to Tacitus's skill with those moral judgments that the Romans called *sententiae*. Amber was junk "until Roman luxury gave it value" (45); and, "Weeping is fine for women; men must remember" (27). Such pithy judgments were collected into books of maxims in the sixteenth and seventeenth centuries when Tacitus was held in high regard as a moralist and a political sage. [90]

It is through political analysis and occasional witty quips that Tacitus blackens the reputation of a Tiberius, Nero, or Vitellius; he does not resort to traditional invective which held a hallowed place in Roman political life. Cicero's own scathing personal attacks on Catiline, Clodius, and Marc Antony show the relative gentility of most modern political polemic. Tacitus disapproved of such gross invective in historical writing—it would display the *ira et studium* (anger and partisanship) which he promised to avoid. If he relinquishes the cannon of Ciceronian invective, Tacitus assails his targets with dozens of witty and precisely aimed darts while seeming to maintain his emotional distance. For the modern reader, the latter literary tactic may well be both more agreeable and more convincing.

A common type of Tacitean epigram is the rhetorical antithesis: "Gratitude is irksome; vengeance is valued." [91] "All claim victory; only one is blamed in defeat." [92] "In foreign wars we learned to spend others' money; in civil wars our own."[93] These verbal antitheses are, of course, merely condensed versions of rhetorical structures which abound in Tacitus as when first sympathizers and then critics speak at Augustus's funeral. Antithesis was commonplace in Roman rhetoric, and similar antithetical epigrams appear in Plutarch and Suetonius—sometimes even derived from a common source. This device is hardly unique with Tacitus, but he found it especially appealing.

One of the most common sources of humor in ancient (and modern) comedy is the reversal of expectations.[94] From Aristophanes onward, Greek and Latin comic poets liked to conclude a line with an unexpected, even outrageous, phrase. Tacitean epigrams often link the unexpected—sometimes to provoke a grim smile, but often to emphasize a novel political or moral point with exceptional verbal vitality. "The reward for virtue was certain doom,"[95] or the poet "was banished because he showed talent."[96] In one case, Tacitus creates an oxymoron—a literary self-contradiction—so striking that it has entered our everyday speech. He closes the third book of the *Annals* with an account of the funeral of Junia, sister of Brutus and once wife of Cassius, the principal assassins of Julius Caesar. As was customary, effigies of famous ancestors were carried in the funeral procession, "but Brutus and Cassius were most conspicuous, precisely because their portraits were not seen."[97] When Lord John Russell in a speech to the electors of London in 1859 used the phrase "conspicuous by its absence," he went on to say "It is not an original expression of mine, but is taken from one of the greatest historians of antiquity."[98] Tacitus's political quip created an image so striking, so universally comprehensible, that it continues to enrich our language two millennia later.

Though most Tacitean aphorisms have a political or moral edge, some are merely *bons mots*. "Rumor is not always wrong; it is sometimes correct."[99] Tacitus sometimes uses a maxim to close a book or chapter, in a manner similar to Jane Austen:

The business of her life was to get her daughters married; its solace was visiting and news. (*Pride and Prejudice* I,i)

Comparable concluding tags occur frequently in the *Histories:*

The remarkable happiness of a time when we may think what we wish and may say what we think. (1,1)

Those who had no enemy were destroyed by friends. (1, 2)

The gods do not care for our safety, only for our punishment. (1, 3)

In the *Annals,* Tacitus increasingly integrates the epigrams into the narrative, but they are no less striking.

Aphorisms in Roman poetry most often treated moral themes—morality in the widest ancient sense which includes not only ethics but also cultural expectations. As such, they are often clichés. Horace's noble line, "It is sweet and proper to die for one's country,"[100]—much quoted in Fascist Italy—was translated from a jingoist poem Tyrtaeus wrote for the Spartans more than five centuries earlier. Tacitus also adapts aphorisms from the past, but his perspective is resolutely skewed and ironic. So we find numerous Tacitean variations on the theme that in a debased age Virtue equals Vice: "Inertia is taken for wisdom";[101] high principles are a character flaw;[102] virtue is punished and crimes are rewarded. As the prestige of Seneca and Thrasea increases, so does their danger.[103] We may admire the verbal skill of these repetitive jibes, but the individual epigrams add little to our understanding. We have all seen cowards who have "savage tongues"[104] even if we cannot formulate a Tacitean riposte. But the occasional epigram brings the reader up short by the wealth of psychological awareness packed into a phrase. Tacitus describes Agricola's candor in dealing with his men: he might be sharp-tongued today, but there was no hidden resentment tomorrow; "He thought it more honorable to give offense than to hate."[105] Against the background of Domitian and Tiberius, Tacitus goes beyond a defensive justification of his father-in-law to deeper truths about emotion and repression.

Some of Tacitus's epigrams are now so familiar to our ears that they seem to be platitudes: "Violence and turmoil gives power to the worst men, peace demands honorable talent."[106] While we cannot tell whether there are specifically Tacitean or rhetorical commonplaces of the time, other aphorisms show Tacitus's own hand. Vitellius was so cowardly that, "if others had not remembered that he was emperor, he would have forgotten it himself."[107] But the most complex epigram is the most peculiarly Tacitean in its terseness and its political and psychological profundity. He said of the elderly senator Galba who ruled briefly in 68–69, *Capax imperii nisi imperasset* ("He would have been thought capable of ruling, if only he had never come to power"). No translation can capture the irony of Tacitus's Latin which Paul Plass compares to Freud's famous quip: "He has a great future behind him."[108] So too had Galba.

Some critics have suggested that Tacitus created a new genre which combined the political aim of history with the ethical goal of ancient biography, and thereby foreshadowed later drama and even the novel. Indeed, the modern novel seems to owe less to the romances called ancient "novels" than to Tacitus, whose treatment of social intrigue would not be out of place in the nineteenth century. Since orthodox modern historical practice pretends that the historian and reader remain objective observers, Tacitus more closely resembles in narrative strategy such "realistic" authors as Tolstoy, Stendhal, and George Eliot where the astute narrator also serves as a moral commentator. Radical historians and biographers who now insert themselves into their stories would have probably shocked Tacitus less than they would have shocked a nineteenth-century, positivist historian like Ranke.

But if the overall form of Tacitus's work resembles the modern novel, the language is that of a poet and a century ago the great German Latinist Frederich Leo pronounced Tacitus "one of the few great poets of the Roman people."[109] The echoes of Vergil and Lucan are evident, and Tacitus has finely honed diction and syntax to capture brilliantly both matter and mood: The *Annals* is the greatest literary achievement of post-Augustan Rome.[110] Some see this literary artistry as poetry; others merely condemn it as failed history.[111]

The central question here is the nature and purpose of history. We can agree that the historian must recreate the past, but is this a didactic or an emotive recreation? For what purpose did an audience assemble to hear a reading by Herodotus or Livy: enlightenment or exultation? Surely both; there is ample ancient evidence that history was intended to delight.[112] The greatest historians, from Herodotus to Gibbon, have been great artists, but is art therefore an essential component of historical writing? It certainly was in antiquity and, though nineteenth-century positivists might demur, even Mommsen classified historians among artists rather than among scholars. Tony Woodman has recently argued forcefully that ancient historians were above all literary artists.[113] Today we acknowledge the sterility of academic monographic history as an unpalatable, but practical, necessity in a world of increasing publication and narrow specialization. But the ideal of history remains the revivification of the past through scholarship and imagination. The historian reaches the mind of his reader by appealing to, and even manipulating, his feelings. Tacitus uses literary power and personal experience to create the most vivid historical tableau that has come down to us from antiquity. It is great poetry and great history, for his imagination has recreated historical truth.

VIII

❖ ─────────────────────────────── ❖

The Impact of Tacitus

Though Tacitus was the greatest Roman historian, it was not among Romans, nor even among historians, that he had his greatest impact. In early modern Europe Tacitus's political vision, dramatic images, and incisive moral aphorisms left their mark on poets and philosophers, princes and popes, painters and political theorists. He was regarded not as a mere chronicler of events but as a moralist worthy to be ranked with Plato and Aristotle, as a political thinker whose influence vied with Machiavelli. His vivid portrayal of the tyranny, brutality, and political paranoia of the Roman Empire seemed disturbingly familiar in the absolutist monarchies and the papal states. His histories lent themselves to varied, and sometimes conflicting, interpretations. Republicans and courtiers alike learned from him; German Reformation humanists and English Puritans used him to forward their own agendas; French and American revolutionaries drew inspiration from him. Since the Renaissance Tacitus has occupied a central place in the evolution of political thought; this chapter will examine some important aspects of that influence.

From Antiquity to Renaissance Florence

While contemporaries like Pliny, Juvenal, and Suetonius knew Tacitus's work, there are relatively few references to him in the centuries following his death, though a third-century emperor named Tacitus claimed the historian as his ancestor and ordered his works to be made available in all libraries.[1] He found few followers in his craft; succeeding Latin historical writers preferred to write the biographies and historical abridgments which made fewer intellectual demands on their readers. Only a fourth-century Greek from Syria, Ammianus Marcellinus, who continued Tacitus's history in Latin from 96 down to his own time, captured something of his master's perceptiveness. Tacitus was scorned by Christians for his supposed bias against them and the Jews, and in late antiquity only occasional references to him or his work occur. In the fifth century the Christian Orosius heaped insults upon Tacitus ("fool," "flatterer," "liar") but he also included many quotations from the *Histories* in his own *History against the Pagans;* this polemical book remained a source for Tacitean quotations in later centuries when the texts themselves were unknown.[2] A century later the historian had become so little known that in the last ancient reference to him the chronicler and administrator Cassiodorus referred to him only as "a certain Cornelius."[3]

Though manuscripts of Tacitus were read, copied, and perhaps even imitated in monasteries during the Middle Ages, few outside saw them. A manuscript containing the *Annals* 11–16 and the *Histories* was copied at Monte Cassino in the eleventh century, but it became widely known only after 1360 when it was brought to Florence (perhaps by Boccaccio) where humanists were able to study it.[4] Those literary scholars were primarily interested in the peculiarities of the historian's style, but Tacitus was soon used to support political arguments.[5] Leonardo Bruni, in his 1404 panegyric to Florence, rejected the medieval exaltation of monarchical rule (as seen in Dante's glorification of Caesar) in favor of republican values, and he cited Tacitus to prove that the emperors had suppressed the virtue, the nobility, and the genius of the Roman people.[6] But Bruni was an exception; fifteenth-century humanists much preferred the ringing orations of Cicero and the stirring tales of Livy—for the amplitude of their style as well as for their moral and patriotic examples of republican virtue.[7] It was only in the sixteenth century that long-ignored Tacitus would burst upon European intellectual and political life.

The first edition of Tacitus, lacking only *Annals* 1–6, was printed in Venice in 1470. The Florentine statesman Niccolò Machiavelli made some use of that edition as he worked on his *Discourses on the First Ten Books of Livy* and *The Prince* after his exile in 1513.[8] In *The Prince*, written to regain ducal favor, Machiavelli provides advice to promote stable rule, but its cynicism caused it to be criticized later as amoral and even atheistic. The book overturned much of humanist political morality (derived from Cicero) in advising the ruler that it is better to be feared than loved.[9] Secrecy and hypocrisy are indispensible to the ruler who may have to violate truth, humanity, or even religion to maintain his government.[10] Though Machiavelli's ruler resembles Tacitus's Tiberius, *Annals* 1–6 was only published in 1515 after the completion of *The Prince* and scholars are divided whether Machiavelli might have seen the manuscript.[11] Despite their close links in the minds of later Renaissance thinkers, Machiavelli was less influenced by Tacitus's ideas than he was attracted by the anti-monarchical aphorisms which could buttress his own arguments in his later, and overtly republican, *Discourses*.[12] Machiavelli's essential pragmatism was his basic link with Tacitus; both men were realists who examined actual (rather than ideal) men and institutions.[13] Both men, writing under the rule of princes, cultivated a certain ambiguity that fostered diverse interpretations. When Machiavelli's works were placed on the Index of Forbidden Books by the Church, it was to Tacitus that Italian political theorists eventually looked for inspiration and authority. His maxims were used to illustrate Machiavelli's theories; what Benedetto Croce saw as an attempt "to hide Machiavelli under the mask of Tacitus, and his prince under the figure of Tiberius."[14]

The impact of Tacitus increased after the foreign invasions of Italy and the brutal sack of Rome in 1527.[15] The republican values of Livy and Cicero were shattered and Italy of the sixteenth century turned to the acerbic style and cynical political ideas of the imperial historian. This movement is known as "Tacitism."[16] Thinkers turned from rhetoric and philosophy to history and politics, and the rediscovery of Tacitus gave impetus to the development of Renaissance Political Science.[17] His histories acutely described the duplicity of princes and their courts, and he could provide guidance for those who lived under them. The Florentine Francesco Guicciardini, like Machiavelli and Tacitus himself, was forced to turn from politics to history and his masterly *History of Italy* (published posthumously in 1561) is Tacitean in its probing analysis of politics, personalities, and events. He learned discretion from Tacitus, but he also warned that history can be a two-edged sword:

> Tacitus teaches those who live under tyrants the mode of life and how to govern oneself prudently, and he teaches tyrants how to establish tyranny.[18]

Tacitus found particular favor with the bourgeois elite who identified themselves with the Roman Senate. The medieval concern with equal justice dispensed by a paternal monarch gave way to countless "Discourses" on the text of Tacitus which explored the more immediate, and more Tacitean, subjects of the nature of arbitrary rule and the character of rulers.[19]

Renaissance and Reformation Germany

If the Italians were slow to make political use of Tacitus, the Germans were not.[20] The humanist Enea Silvio Piccolomini, later Pope Pius II, was among the first to see the manuscript of the *Germania*, and he quoted from it extensively in a long letter to the Chancellor of Mainz in 1458.[21] Ironically, he cited Tacitus to de-

fend the papacy against charges of corruption and to show how
far above their early barbarism Rome and Christianity had raised
the German people. Pius's essay had enormous impact on both his
followers and his adversaries. The *Germania* fanned the fires of
German nationalism and Tacitus became the father of ancient Germanic studies. Tacitus, together with early Germanic law codes
(Salic law) and the medieval chronicler Jordanes's history of the
Goths, provided the basic elements of the myth of "Germanism":
the high standard of German morality and the simplicity of their
customs; their racial purity; and the native freedom of the Germanic tribes.[22] There then arose the heated debate between Ro-
manists and Germanists which has continued down into our own
century.[23] When the anti-clerical and anti-Italian Conrad Celtis
(1492) used Tacitus to show the indigenous virtues of the ancient
Germans, he linked the vices of the ancient Romans to the corruption of the papal court.[24] What had begun as a cultural conflict
between Germans and Italians would soon take on religious importance; the Reformation was only decades away.

While some patriotic German humanists used "our Tacitus" to
praise their barbarian ancestors, others also produced imperial pa-
negyrics praising the Holy Roman Emperors as the legitimate
heirs of Augustus, since the Roman emperors had yielded their
throne to German kings in 476. But, after the 1515 publication
of *Annals* 1–6, it was the ancient German general Arminius who
became the focus of German nationalism and German hostility to
Rome.[25] He appeared (quite inappropriately) on the frontispiece
of the 1519 Basel edition of Erasmus's *New Testament:* there he
confronts the Roman Varus who is depicted as a serpent.[26] A few
years later the extreme nationalist Ulrich von Hutten wrote his
Latin dialogue *Arminius* in which the god Mercury summons Tacitus to the pagan underworld to appear before the judge Minos in
order to bear witness that Arminius surpassed Scipio, Hannibal,
and Alexander the Great![27] This extraordinary canonization of Arminius was praised even by Luther, who argued that the name
"Arminius" was a Roman corruption of the Germanic "Her-
mann."[28]

Tacitus had much that was negative to say about the Germans
and even about Arminius, but this was ignored in newly resurgent

Protestant Germany. His judgment that the ancient Germans were indigenous and racially uncorrupted was much cited; his censure of their drunkenness was generally forgotten.[29] His reports on Germanic practices now became hallowed customs; his creative etymologies became the basic truths of German historiography. Tacitus endorsed a German freedom from law that greatly pleased Luther (who loathed the "plague of lawyers" which he associated with the Roman Church), and Tacitus's report of heroic "ancient songs" were identified with the famous Minnesingers.[30] Tacitus was not regarded as a political thinker; he was the scribe of ancient German history and ancient German virtue, and thus inspired historical and geographical research.[31] More than twenty editions of the *Germania* appeared in Germany alone between 1500 and 1650.[32] Pastors and princes all took pride in what they saw as their heroic ancestors, morally and racially uncorrupted. From the *Germania* German humanists created a potent political myth that has endured into our own century.

Tacitism in the Counter-Reformation

Outside of Germany Tacitus was less used by historians than by the "new science" of politics which was born in the bloody atmosphere of the Reformation and Counter-Reformation as opposing camps of Christians contested their beliefs on the battlefield, in the pulpit, and in the printed word. The terrible civil wars of the *Histories* had an eerie appeal to an age of bitter religious wars and the increasing encroachment of reactionary Spain upon the civic and political life of Italy.[33] The immense anxiety of the age made Tacitean pessimism fashionable to some in the later sixteenth century when true liberty seemed as far from Italy or Paris as it had from imperial Rome.[34] Yet the establishment view remained that Tacitus wrote biased and anti-Christian history in execrable Latin. In a much quoted comment, the great French scholar Guillaume Budé called the historian "the most depraved of all writers."[35] Tacitus still achieved widespread popularity among opponents of absolutism who admired his penetrating critique of despotism and even preferred his sharp prose to that of Cicero which had long been co-opted by political and religious orthodoxy.[36] For them he was describing a depressingly familiar world.

Courtiers used Tacitus's histories as a guide to the art and science of politics, and the proliferating essays on flattery and court life frequently cited his works.[37] Clerical and secular princes alike regarded him as a "master of prudence" in an age when dissimulation was ranked with the highest princely accomplishments, as in the aphorism "*Qui nescit dissimulare, nescit regnare*" ("He who cannot pretend cannot rule").[38] The great classical scholar Marc-Antoine Muret wrote in 1580,

> Although, by the grace of God, our age does not have Tiberiuses, Caligulas, or Neros, it is good to know how good and prudent men lived under them, and how and to what extent men could endure the tyrants' vices and disguise their own feelings. (Lecture 14)[39]

Philip II of Spain, known as the Prudent, revealed more than a few Tiberian characteristics in his bloody suppression of the revolt in the Netherlands, which perhaps partly explains the growing Dutch interest in Tacitus.[40] The king had a Jesuit apologist who denounced Tacitus as "a pagan, idolator, and enemy of Christ our Redeemer."[41] But he also had a learned, but duplicitous, courtier in Antonio Perez. When Perez finally fled to England, he described himself with some pride as "the Sejanus who got away."[42] In an age of intrigue, the *Annals* provided a convenient point of reference.

The greatest Tacitean of the time was neither a politician nor an historian, but the immensely learned Dutch philologist Justus Lipsius (1547–1606) who produced a series of excellent editions of Tacitus whose epigrammatic prose style he loved and imitated. Though he lectured and wrote on the political and moral ideas of the historian, Lipsius admired Tacitus's canny pragmatism more than any political ideology: "a sharp and shrewd writer—the most useful for men of our time."[43] Lipsius, born a Catholic, became in turn a Lutheran in Germany, a Catholic again in Louvain, a Calvinist in Leyden, and died once more a Catholic. He was scarcely a man of hard and fast beliefs, and he sought no fixed principles in Tacitus.[44] When he calls the historian the Prince of Politicians or the Father of Prudence, Lipsius reminds us that what he wished most of all was peace and quiet to pursue his scholarly research. This apolitical man managed to survive by giving his heart and faith only to books and to learning; Tacitus was for him "a Garden of Precepts" who provided the wise counsel necessary for those who wished to survive in a dangerous age of radical change and intolerant rulers.

At the end of the sixteenth century, many Italian thinkers relied upon Tacitus to support theories of statecraft in an Italy dominated by the papacy and its Spanish supporters. The conservative, Jesuit-trained theorist Giovanni Botero published *The Reason of State* (1589) which attempted to provide a moral and theological underpinning for "Raison d'état."[45] Botero linked Tacitus, whom he cites more than any other author, to the Machiavellian proposition that the ruler would do best to pursue his own self-interest, then goes on to condemn him as one who provides evil counsel to rulers. It was Botero who permanently tarred Tacitus with the charge of "Machiavellianism" in the absolutist courts of Catholic Europe.[46] His political opposite, Traiano Boccalini, in his satiric dialogue *News from Parnassus* (1612–1613), used hundreds of Tacitean citations to comment on the princes and courtiers of his own time.[47] (His far more politically explicit *Commentary on Tacitus* was published only long after his death, and then only incompletely.) Boccalini admired the moral commitment of an antimonarchical Tacitus who had gone beyond Machiavelli and brought the art and science of politics to the people as well as to the princes: he has Apollo praise Tacitus for warning people about tyranny.[48] In an age when Spanish assassins and papal poisoners hunted down their opponents across Italy, Boccalini sought the protection of James I of England whom he saw as an enlightened ruler and a fellow-Tacitean. But he died in Venice in 1613, a rumored victim of papal agents.[49] The spread of absolutist rule in the sixteenth and seventeenth centuries brought with it the destruction of humanist values. The papacy established the Inquisition as Italy, Spain, and France increasingly resembled Julio-Claudian Rome; Tacitus replaced Livy as the most popular and relevant Roman historian. In fact the first half of the seventeenth century saw more editions of Tacitus than of any other Greek or

Roman historian, and commentaries on Tacitus became an important genre of political discourse.[50] In his 1662 commentary on the *Annals*, the exiled German diplomat Christophe Forstner wrote "What Tacitus calls the vices of power our politicians call 'raison d'état.'"[51] He too saw links between Tacitus and Machiavelli, but he preferred the withering scorn of the *Annals* to the scientific exploration of *The Prince*. Scholars and politicians of all ideological stripes regarded the *Annals* as a central literary, moral, and political text for their own times.

As knowledge of Tacitus grew, criticism of his ideas also increased. Early in the seventeenth century the Jesuits, who regarded themselves as the shock troops of the papacy, assailed Tacitus as a disloyal subject who undermined government by revealing its secrets.[52] Their view of history—a common establishment view through the ages—was that the historian should merely narrate, not try to analyze or criticize. The Tacitean spirit of inquiry was a threat to the status quo; it might endanger papal orthodoxy and Spanish rule. For them the historian should be the panegyrist of established virtue. Livy was the ideal; Tacitus was nothing more than a bad historian and an evil man. Here we find the "Red" or revolutionary Tacitus, a menace to established authority, but a source of inspiration to the Puritans and to republicans of Paris and colonial Boston.[53]

But there was also a "Black" Tacitus who provided advice to tyrants, and models for sycophantic courtiers. The learned legal and political theorist, Jean Bodin, saw in Tacitus the justification for monarchy and recommended him for judges and magistrates.[54] After Botero's linkage of Tacitus and Machiavelli, later writers increasingly identified the two and Tacitus was castigated for the cynicism of the Florentine. With Machiavelli on the Index and thus theoretically inaccessible even to his opponents, Tacitus was attacked as a substitute.[55] In absolutist Italy and France, dissidents gradually grew increasingly suspicious of Tacitus who, like Machiavelli, seemed to help cynical princes maintain themselves in power. Only in seventeenth-century England did progressive politicians uniformly view Tacitus with enthusiasm.[56]

Montaigne and Racine

Though Tacitus never entered into the everyday political arena of *Ancien Régime* France as he would in Stuart England, French moralists used him to examine character and personality traits.[57] The greatest of these, Michel de Montaigne (1533–1592), turned to the historian again and again in his essays.[58] In his early Stoic phase Montaigne imitated Tacitus's anticiceronian style[59] and he mined the historian for historical examples to illustrate Stoic principles found in Seneca or elsewhere, and he defended Tacitus against attacks by Christian polemicists. In his essay on freedom of conscience, he attacks bookburning in the name of religion and points out that Tacitus's few offensive sentences caused his books to be so savagely treated by earlier Christians that they almost perished completely.[60] In his final decade he turned his interest rather to the moral and political judgments of Tacitus and to the man himself.

Montaigne felt a particular intimacy with Tacitus—an intimacy that causes distress when the historian disappoints his expectations. In his essay "Of the Art of Discussion" he confessed that the first book he has read straight through in twenty years was Tacitus.[61] While he recognized that there was sometimes a gap between the reported facts and the conclusions Tacitus drew from them, it was the judgments that fascinated the moralist. Montaigne was particularly attracted to the introspective approach to historical motivations: emperors may act for reasons of state, but they also act from hatred, resentment, lust, and foolish pride. Montaigne also responded to Tacitus's deep psychological insight into political malignity:

> I know of no author who introduces into a register of public events so much consideration of private behavior and inclinations . . . This form of history is by far the most useful. Public movements depend more upon the guidance of fortune, private ones on our own. This is rather a judgment of history than a recital of it; there are more precepts than stories. It is not a book to read; it is a book to study and learn . . . (His work) is more suited to a disturbed and sick state, as

ours is at present; you would often say that it is us he is describing and decrying.[62]

When Montaigne states elsewhere that "the very laws of justice cannot subsist without some mixture of injustice,"[63] he goes on to cite Plato and Tacitus: "Every exemplary punishment has in it some injustice against individuals, which is compensated by public utility."[64] Montaigne does not seek a cynical precedent for the idea that the ends justify the means, but rather a realism free of political cant and religious hypocrisy.

A century later the greatest French playwrights brought dramas from the pages of Tacitus to the Parisian stage. Pierre Corneille (1606–1684) looked to Tacitus in the darker mood of his old age for material for a drama of despair. In the preface to *Otho*, he says that as much as possible he has translated the characters of "that incomparable author," Tacitus.[65] His theatrical rival, Jean Racine (1639–1699), raised and educated by the Jansenists, shared much with Tacitus: his seriousness and high moral tone, his dark view of life, his sense of pervasive evil.[66] His library contained both texts and translations of Tacitus, and Racine claimed he prepared more for writing *Britannicus* (1669) than for any of his other plays. It is not merely a Tacitean story; it contains Tacitean characters and Tacitean concerns. Racine was nothing if not a supporter of absolute monarchy, and the contemporary controversy over "raison d'état" lies at the heart of the play.

Britannicus closely follows the *Annals*. Both authors show the political conflict that underlay the personal passions of the Neronian court. Atypically for Racine, love plays a relatively peripheral role in *Britannicus;* it is the political ambition of Nero and his jealous mother Agrippina that is the driving force of the drama.[67] In his second preface to the play, Racine wrote:

> I have copied my characters from the greatest painter of antiquity, I mean from Tacitus. And I was then so imbued with the reading of that excellent historian that there is almost no brilliant stroke in my tragedy for which he did not provide the idea.[68]

Racine, like Tacitus, has a grudging admiration for the political skill and courage of Agrippina—"my tragedy is no less the disgrace of Agrippina than the death of Britannicus"—while lavishing nothing but scorn upon the corrupt and corrupting relations between weak rulers and their parasitic, though forceful, courtiers. Here the young Nero begins to develop into the monster he would later become. Racine may have found his characters in Tacitus but his drama came from seventeenth-century Tacitism's focus on the political justification for immoral action.

Tacitus in Tudor-Stuart England

English scholars did not show so early an interest in Tacitus as did the humanists of the Quattrocento or the political theorists of Cinquencento Italy.[69] The Ciceronian or Livian style remained the dominant historical model, though Thomas More had read the *Annals* and used it for the atmosphere of dissimulation in his *History of Richard III*.[70] The Tiberius-like Richard passed from More (via Holinshead's chronicle) to Shakespeare's play which remains distinctly Tacitean.[71] Early English historians adapted sections of the *Agricola*, and even the *Germania*, as sources for their own national history. The royal tutor Henry Savile, presenting his translation of Tacitus (in which he added his own version of the missing death of Nero and accession of Galba) to his pupil Elizabeth I, complained feelingly of the style of his author: "he is harde." The anonymous preface to the second edition (1598), probably written by the Earl of Essex, said "there is no historie . . . so well worth reading as Tacitus."[72] After Savile was knighted for his scholarly labors, his friend Ben Jonson paid him tribute in an epigram:

> If, my religion safe, I durst embrace
>   That stranger doctrine of Pythagoras,
> I should believe the soul of Tacitus
>   In thee, most weighty Savile, lived to us:
> So hast thou rendered him in all his bounds
>   And all his numbers, both of sense and sounds.
> But when I read that special piece restored,

Where Nero falls and Galba is adored,
To thine own proper I ascribe then more,
And gratulate the breach I grieved before.[73]

It was only with the accession of the learned James VI of Scotland as James I of England that Tacitus was much read and cited in English intellectual circles. James, or one of his secretaries, included many Tacitean allusions in his new edition of his *Precepts on the Art of Governing* in his year of accession (1603).[74] When Boccalini sought the king's patronage, he sent the monarch a letter replete with Tacitean quotations that finally compared James to Trajan whose subjects enjoy "happy times as few others have been, for we can think as we please and speak as we think."[75] Even the royal princes read Tacitus, who was not only a font of historical, moral, and political ideas, but he was even regarded as a guide to life at court.

The change in attitude toward Tacitus soon made its impact on the English court and beyond. The seventeenth century was an age of witty repartee and pithy moral judgments; courtiers and philosophers alike found much in Tacitus to their taste. Sir Philip Sidney had earlier praised the historian's wit, and the political epigrams and moral maxims were now collected into popular anthologies.[76] Francis Bacon, who rated Tacitus above Plato and Aristotle as a moral thinker, was one of the first to turn from the amplitude of Cicero to the "pointed, concise style . . . used with more restraint by Tacitus"—a style which he brought to English prose and which found wide favor as the "plain style."[77] Bacon popularized the mordant Tacitean epigram which became characteristic of English prose during the seventeenth century. He regularly quoted appropriate passages of Tacitus in his servile letters to the king, letters which often unsuccessfully sought preferment to higher office. When in 1610 he delivered a speech to James on behalf of the Commons, Bacon compared the king to Nerva and Trajan in that he, as Tacitus says at the opening of the *Agricola,* had reconciled freedom and monarchy—"a compliment paid by one of the wisest writers to two of the best emperors."[78] Bacon uses Tacitus to flatter the king and, not coincidentally, himself. His own *History of Henry VII* owed much to the Roman, and he frequently used Tacitean examples in his essays, as when he discussed intentional political obscurity in "Of Simulation and Dissimulation."[79] The notorious difficulty of Tacitus, known as the Prince of Obscurity, appealed to the erudite Jacobeans.[80] Bacon did much to bring Tacitus to the attention of politicians and the historian became, in the words of the contemporary poet John Donne, the "Oracle of Statesmen."

Ben Jonson, who greatly admired the plain Attic style, regarded Tacitus as the one who "speke best Latine."[81] He wrote his *Sejanus* (1603) for the King's Men at the Globe Theater; Shakespeare, who acted in it, well may have played Tiberius.[82] Jonson knew his classics well—there is even a line of Greek in the play.[83] Jonson's recurring theme is excessive desire—whether for money, sensual pleasure, or power—in the "realistic" and ambitious society of Jacobean London, and in this play he focuses on a world where the lust for power has become the norm and family ties are sacrificed to political advancement. As Sejanus says, "Ambition makes more trusty slaves than need" (1, 366). Tiberius's corrupt courtiers here argue Reason of State to forward their own ambitions, as when the treacherous and syncophantic Macro justifies his actions:[84]

A prince's power makes all his action virtue. (3, 717)

He that will thrive in state, he must neglect the trodden paths that truth and right respect. (3, 736–737)

The play failed and failed badly; in Jonson's words, the play "suffered no less violence from our people here than the subject of it did from the rage of the people of Rome."[85] Perhaps the complex, and cold, intellectual duplicity of the characters and the unremitting bleakness of tone made the play unappealing to the audience, or perhaps it was too much a closet philosophical drama: all talk and few spectacular dramatic effects. Yet the themes were topical enough: the twilight world of spies and informers was well known to the Roman Catholic Jonson who had already served time in prison, and the ambitious courtier Sejanus might well represent the recently fallen Essex.[86] For whatever reason, Jonson was charged before the Privy Council with treason, though (as with so many other such charges) the issue does not seem to have come to trial. The poet saw Tacitus as a guide to the political dissimulation and corruption of his day and annotated the quarto edition of *Sejanus* with hundreds of allusions to the *Annals*, so that Hazlitt called it "an admirable piece of ancient mosaic."[87] Jonson even urged in an epigram that "ripe statesmen" carry a pocket text of Tacitus with them as a guide to the secrets of political power.[88]

Tacitus remained a favored preserve of English republicans and revolutionaries; eventually he was used to attack the very Stuarts who had done so much to foster interest in him. In 1626 the Puritan Sir John Eliot moved to impeach the royal favorite the Duke of Buckingham, quoting Tacitus (in Latin) on Sejanus; King Charles responded "he must intend me for Tiberius."[89] Eliot was arrested the next day and sent to the Tower. In prison he wrote the *Monarchy of Man* which relies heavily on Tacitus to make the case for a constitutional monarchy constrained by the laws. Eliot was not the last Puritan to be punished by Charles for comparing the Stuarts to the Julio-Claudians. William Prynne wrote in *The Player's Scourge* (1632) that the soldier Flavus was justified in plotting Nero's murder since that emperor had debased himself by appearing as an actor and had disgraced Roman noblewomen by bringing them on the stage. Since the Stuart court was fond of participating in masques, Prynne was charged with treason in the Star Chamber, lost his ears, and went to prison.[90]

When in 1627 the poet and courtier Fulke Greville founded the first chair in history at Cambridge, he selected a Dutchman Isaac Dorislaus as incumbent.[91] A friend of Bacon, Greville set Tacitus as the topic for the first lecture and Dorislaus delivered the second on the revolt in the Netherlands.[92] Complaints were made that he spoke "too much for the defense of the Liberties of the People," and the lecturer was soon silenced.[93] The obsequious letter by Dr. Matthew Wren, Master of Peterhouse, to Bishop Laud of London denouncing Dorislaus survives as a model of academic and political slander; he concludes with the request that his name not be used lest he be called a "Delator."[94] His use of the Tacitean term for an informer is both apt and ironic. The same Dorislaus later helped to draw up the charges against King Charles; he was in turn assassinated by English royalists in the Hague in 1649, not long after the king's execution.

Though some Stuart partisans thought that Tacitus should be suppressed as seditious, other royalists, like some continental supporters of absolutism, could support their case with aphorisms from Tacitus.[95] They particularly savored the Tacitean comment on the ancient Britons, "They fight separately, and are conquered together," which was quoted repeatedly to urge unquestioning loyalty to the crown and to suppress dissenting religious publications. Royalists, including such orthodox figures as the condemned Archbishop Laud writing before his execution, typically quoted Tacitean phrases out of their historical context. When the poet and political radical John Milton, Latin Secretary to the Commonwealth, called Tacitus "the greatest enemy of tyrants," he was rebutting the French royalist Salmasius who had quoted Tacitus out of context in support of absolute monarchy.[96] (Milton gave his Satan in *Paradise Lost* clear characteristics of the Caesars, especially Tacitus's Tiberius.)[97] At least one royalist, the Earl of Clarendon, made good use of Tacitus in his *History of the Rebellion* written in exile.[98] In his loathing for Civil War he found in Tacitus a soulmate in gloom and despair.

Tacitus had been used in political polemic under the Stuarts and the Commonwealth, but with the restoration of Charles II in 1660 he came to play a different role in English political life. He was seen as neither a republican nor a supporter of absolute monarchy and, with the Glorious Revolution of 1688, Tacitus was taken as an admirer of the more limited Germanic kingship where great issues were decided by the entire tribe.[99] (This was seen in opposition to continental absolutism brought to England by the Normans.)[100] After the accession of William of Orange, Algernon Sidney and other pamphleteers saw Tacitus's "Gothic polity" as the ideal government for an England where kings could now be made or broken by Parliament.[101]

Tacitus in the Eighteenth Century

In the eighteenth century Tacitus remained far from the center of the political stage; the decline of absolute monarchy had lessened the impact of his penetrating analyses.[102] "Raison d'état" had become an anachronism; Tacitus was now read by historians and thinkers rather than used in the rough-and-tumble of political polemic. In England Tory writers continued to carp, as when Thomas Hunter wrote in 1752 "Tacitus is not a just Writer, though we allow him a great Wit. He is void of Candour, wants Judgment, exceeds Nature, and violates Truth."[103] But the Whigs saw in Tacitus an enemy of tyranny whom they might justly study and admire; "a penetrating genius" in the words of the Scots historian and philosopher David Hume.[104] Thomas Gordon appended essays on liberty to his Whiggish translation of Tacitus, a translation that long remained popular in the American colonies for its sharp criticism of monarchy.[105] Whig writers had found in the *Germania* indications that the Saxon "witan" was a prototype of Parliament and thus gave additional ancient authority for a restricted monarchy.[106] as Montesquieu said, citing Tacitus, the English constitution emerged from the forests of ancient Germany,[107] and the British liked to oppose this northern political freedom to the tyranny of Bourbon France, papal Italy or ancient Rome. The Whigs, like Tacitus (*Histories* 1, 1), believed that the arts could only flourish in a free state.[108] The heroic barbarian chieftain Calgacus was repeatedly brought to the London stage to deliver his splendid indictment of imperialism from the *Agricola*.[109] Such speeches cast no aspersions, of course, on Britain's own Empire; Tacitus had been domesticated as an Englishman, and a Whig at that.

The greatest historian of the eighteenth century was a Whig and a devoted Tacitean, and he was perhaps the first to rewrite the history of antiquity. Edward Gibbon wrote a more luxuriant prose than Tacitus, but his pithy maxims and his recurrent irony give his history a Tacitean tone.[110]

> It would require the pen of a Tacitus . . . to describe the various emotions of the senate; those that were suppressed, and those that were affected. It was dangerous to trust the sincerity of Augustus; to seem to distrust it was still more dangerous. (*Decline and Fall* chapter 3)[111]

His admiration for his great predecessor went far beyond matters of style, for they shared a determination to explain the reality beneath the superficial appearance:[112]

> ... the Germans were surveyed by the discerning eye, and delineated by the masterly pencil, of Tacitus, the first of historians who applied the science of philosophy to the study of facts. The expressive conciseness of his descriptions has deserved to exercise the diligence of innumerable antiquarians, and to excite the genius and penetration of the philosophic historians of our own times. (*Decline and Fall* chapter 9)[113]

Montesquieu possessed the genius that Tacitus had excited, and these two remained Gibbon's great heroes.[114] These philosophical historians had been able to discover moral causes and so too did Gibbon seek to describe the secret poison that was to destroy the Roman Empire.

Writing in an age prone to Germanic sympathy, Gibbon began his history with the "Good Emperors" of the second century in order to identify his reader with the greatness of Rome and develop a sympathy for its corruption and decline.[115] Though Gibbon thus did not overlap Tacitus's account of the Julio-Claudian and Flavian dynasty, he did paraphrase and adapt Tacitus's thumbnail sketch of the fall of the Republic (*Annals* 1, 2) in the third chapter of *The Decline and Fall of the Roman Empire*.[116] Later in life he regretted having begun his history in the "happiest age"; the evils of the Empire would have been clearer if he had begun where Tacitus had, with the tyranny of Tiberius or the Civil Wars.[117] Despite Gibbon's Olympian detachment, which is far from the burning anger of Tacitus, he shared with his Roman master the ability to draw scathing portraits of his characters— actors would perhaps be a better word for the theatrical court personalities created by both these historians.[118]

Far from London in the intellectual backwater of Naples, the philosopher Giambattista Vico studied natural law in his quest for a New Science of politics.[119] Through his study of Francis Bacon, Vico rediscovered Tacitus who had by now long been ignored in Italy. He found in Tacitus (whom he cited over sixty times) the empirical basis for his *New Science* (1725) and his work attempts a synthesis of Plato and Tacitus: "With an incomparable metaphysical mind, Tacitus contemplates man as he is, Plato as he should be."[120] Vico saw in Tacitus's account of the last days of Augustus and the transfer of power to Tiberius a warning: how free republics can become kingdoms. He likewise saw that Tacitus could lead the reader from the "Culture" of civilized Rome to the "Nature" of the Germanic tribes.[121] Vico remained, and remains, an obscure and difficult genius, but he (along with Montesquieu) restored Tacitus to political importance.

The eighteenth century brought to France a new rationalism and some suspected Tacitus of having more poetic emotion than dispassionate analysis. Voltaire, who intensely disliked Tacitus's praise of the Germans, distrusted almost everything he read in the historian.[122] While he admired his stylistic panache, he complains in a 1768 letter to Mme. du Deffand:

> I neither like the translation nor Tacitus himself as a historian. I regard him as a satirist sparkling with wit, who knows men and courts, says memorable things with striking brevity, and in a few words flays an emperor for all time. Still I remain curious; I would like to learn about the rights of the senate, the imperial armies, and number of citizens, the form of government, morals and customs. I find none of that in Tacitus; he amuses me, but Livy teaches me.[123]

Yet Tacitus still inspired those who were looking beyond questions of historical accuracy, wars, and political dynasties to more general issues of cultural history, natural law, and political morality. Baron Charles de Montesquieu in his *Considerations on the Causes of the Greatness of the Romans and Their Decline* (1734) sketched a philosophical history of the Roman people. He followed Tacitus (and inspired Gibbon) in seeking moral causes for social and political change. Later, in his search for the principles of natural law, Montesquieu explored political theory itself in that vast tapestry that is his *The Spirit of the Laws* (1748), which cited Tacitus more than any other author. As he said, "Tacitus summarized everything because he saw everything" (30.2).[124] He is always concerned to distinguish monarchy from despotism, and he cites the *Annals* for the judgment that "monarchy is corrupted when important men are stripped of respect and made into vile instruments of arbitrary power" (8.7). Rather, it is best (as with Nerva) that the government seem benevolent, even gentle. "The prince must encourage and the laws must menace" (12.25). Even in Tacitus Montesquieu was able to find evidence for the separation of powers, an idea which had so much influence on his readers in colonial America.

If the goal of Tacitus was to make history the conscience of mankind, the French Revolution perhaps brought to an apogee his influence in France. French boys read Tacitus's histories at school[125] and the great spirits of the Enlightenment—Rousseau, Diderot, and D'Alembert—all translated him into French.[126] Rousseau admired the historian as a stylist, and he and his contemporaries saw both Tacitus and Machiavelli as republicans.[127] The *Encyclopédie* makes considerable use of Tacitus, either directly or indirectly as in the article "Lèse majesté" which virtually copies Montesquieu's Tacitean pages.[128] Diderot, whose translation emphasizes Tacitean drama, loved him as a political thinker and a hater of tyrants: "of all Latin writers it is he whom intellectuals esteem most highly." But Diderot was also aware of the danger inherent in these texts; they could be used by one's enemies as well: "Distrust a ruler who knows by heart Aristotle, Tacitus, Machiavelli, and Montesquieu."[129]

The Revolution was a Tacitean moment: a passion for freedom acted out in great dramatic tableaux. The revolutionaries conveniently forgot Tacitus's equal contempt for emperors and rampaging mobs; he became one of the authors most cited in debates and the revolutionary press.[130] The mood is expressed by the poet Marie-Joseph Chénier (who later wrote a play *Tibère*) in a letter to Voltaire where he says that Tacitus's "name pronounced makes tyrants pale."[131] When Madame Roland read the *Annals* in prison as she awaited the guillotine, she wrote that the reign of Tiberius with its informers had returned.[132] Camille Desmoulins, a radical antimonarchist journalist who had led the storming of the Bastille, used Tacitus again and again to protest the Terror.[133] His journal printed translations of Tacitus as a critique of his own time and he found Tiberius and Nero more merciful than the Jacobins.

Desmoulins's journal was burned and he was executed, presumably to teach men not to go searching in ancient historians for lessons of mercy.[134] The men and women of the Revolution, like Tacitus and his heroes, trusted to history to vindicate them and indict their adversaries, be they Bourbons, Jacobins, or Bonapartists.[135] They believed, like the Swiss revolutionary La Harpe, that Tacitus "punished tyrants when he painted them,"[136] and hoped the same vengeance would fall on their own enemies. The historian had become, as Marie-Joseph Chénier wrote much later, "the conscience of the human race."[137]

Tacitus and Napoleon

A similar warning was hurled at Napoleon by François de Chateaubriand, the greatest French writer of the romantic era. Chateaubriand had supported Napoleon and even held office until he broke with him over the assassination of the Duke d'Enghien. A few years later in 1807 he wrote in the *Mercure de France:*

> When everyone trembles before the tyrant and it is as dangerous to risk his favor as to earn his disgrace, the historian appears charged with the vengeance of the people. It is in vain that Nero prospers, Tacitus was already born in the Empire.[138]

Napoleon took the point and was angry—Tacitus had already been a *bête noire* of the French emperor who had complained about his style to the secretary of the Académie Française[139]—but, since he admired Chateaubriand, he merely suppressed his journal and banned Chateaubriand from Paris. The next year, in a colorful sequence preserved in the *Mémoires* of Talleyrand, Napoleon again denounced Tacitus to Goethe and Wieland. The emperor sought out the German poets at a conference at Weimar attended by Tsar Alexander and other monarchs and Napoleon turned the discussion to Tacitus:

> I assure you that the historian whom you are always citing, Tacitus, has never taught me a thing. Do you know a greater

and less just detractor of mankind? He finds criminal intention in the simplest acts; he makes complete scoundrels out of all the emperors to make us admire his genius in exposing them. It is right to say that the *Annals* are not a history of the Empire, but a summary of the Roman law courts. There are always prosecutions, defendants, and people opening their veins in the bath. He speaks interminably of denunciations when he is the greatest denouncer himself . . . But I am bothering you; we are not here to talk about Tacitus. Look how well Tsar Alexander dances![140]

Napoleon further complained, as he did on other occasions, about the obscure and difficult style of the historian which wishes to paint everything in black.

> "I myself am not a Latinist," he would say later to Goethe, "but the obscurity of Tacitus is clear in the ten or twelve Italian or French translations that I have read."[141]

But style was only a minor annoyance; the emperor felt himself defamed by this "discontented senator" whose savage portraits of his Roman predecessors belied the fact that "the Roman people was not of the same party as Tacitus; they loved those emperors whom Tacitus meant to have them fear."[142] He expressed his anger most clearly in an outburst to a French diplomat: "Tacitus! Don't speak to me about that pamphleteer! He has slandered the emperors!"[143] Perhaps he had. The vigorous political and intellectual debate over "Caesarism" in nineteenth-century France grew out of Napoleon's own reading of Tacitus.

Tacitus in Revolutionary America

Revolutionaries across the Atlantic also looked to Tacitus for inspiration. Young Ben Franklin had little Latin before he began, at age sixteen, his discussion of free speech in his *Dogwood Papers*, for which he had probably read Tacitus in English translation (though he quoted the Latin).[144] He did master Latin later, not least (like Cato the Elder learning Greek) so that he could help his son learn it. Much later, on July 4, 1776 at the signing of the

Declaration of Independence, Franklin drew on Tacitus in his famous *bon mot* made to John Hancock: "We must indeed all hang together, or, most assuredly, we shall all hang separately." (Tacitus *Agricola* 12: "As long as they fought separately, they were conquered together.") Tacitus's hostility to tyranny, his irreverent wit, and his moral outrage appealed to the colonists in their struggle against the British crown.[145]

The second and third American presidents, John Adams and Thomas Jefferson, once bitter political antagonists but reconciled in the learned correspondence of their old age, loved Tacitus above all the other ancients.[146] They found much in his histories to sustain their long argument about the role of an aristocratic Senate, but both agreed that autocratic rule must be avoided. Jefferson, who argued for the place of Tacitus and ancient history in the curriculum of the University of Virginia, wrote to his granddaughter: "Tacitus I consider the first writer in the world without a single exception. His book is a compound of history and morality of which we have no other example."[147] As an agrarian democrat, he admired Tacitus's Germans who lived on the boundary of an Empire in native freedom while resisting Roman domination.[148] In his first letter to Adams in 1812 after a twelve-year silence, Jefferson wrote Adams that he had given up newspapers for the classics, while Adams wrote back in 1816, "The Morality of Tacitus is the Morality of Patriotism."[149] They had absorbed their classics fully; their letters are unself-consciously sprinkled with allusions to their wide reading and the tone is often as classical as the quotations. Neither had much use for Plato and his ideal states; these were practical political philosophers who had seen the French struggle for freedom turn into a Bonapartist tyranny.[150] Jefferson in a late letter told Adams that to achieve universal republicanism, "rivers of blood must yet flow, and years of desolation pass over; yet the object is worth rivers of blood, and years of desolation." The realism, the courage, and even the weariness, echo the tone of Tacitus's histories.

The Decline of Tacitean Influence

In the early nineteenth-century many still read and revered Tacitus, some for his politics, and others for his literary power. Stendhal, also a devotee of psychological analysis, refers over fifty times to Tacitus and even read the historian on his deathbed, just as Julien Sorel prized his edition of the histories.[151] Macaulay regarded Tacitus as an unparalleled portraitist of character,[152] and John Quincy Adams claimed he read the historian every day and used him in his political speeches: "Think of your forefathers! Think of your posterity!"[153] But through the century the writing of history gradually became professionalized and the universities, especially in Germany, used the scientific model for historical seminars and research. Though the *Germania* remained a central text for early anthropologists and ethnologists, Tacitus's passionate approach to history was scorned by a new breed of academic historians. Only a gentleman historian like Henry Adams would refer enthusiastically to Tacitus in his 1907 autobiography.[154] Tacitus's obvious bias was unpalatable to positivist historians who, not having read Hayden White, did not know how culturally bound their own histories were.[155] Even Mommsen, who admitted that hatred as much as love was a great motivator of historians, found Tacitus wanting: he failed as a military historian and his account of Tiberius was literally unbelievable. But there was an even more powerful reason for the decline of Tacitus's influence on nineteenth-century Europe. With a growing belief in progress and the betterment of mankind, the gloomy vision of Tacitus became much less congenial and a more optimistic age refused to accept such an unvarnished view of human evil. Tacitus was swept to the remote margins of intellectual life and eliminated from practical politics. The romanticism of disillusionment, in Lukács's words, only survived in the great nineteenth-century novels of England, France, and Russia where men and women struggled futilely to transcend their allotted destiny.[156] George Eliot, Hardy, Balzac, Dostoyevsky, Tolstoy—like Tacitus—were students of society and the psyche, and they became his greatest heirs in an Age of Progress.

Tacitus, like most Greek and Latin writers, has remained on the

fringes of intellectual life in the twentieth century. He has surely
had an effect, but it has usually been indirect. The *Germania* was a
revered text under the Nazis but its ideas had already been incor-
porated into the German national consciousness by the German
humanists and Reformation polemicists. The German habit of
obedience, in the words of Meinecke, may be traced back to Tacitus,[157] but no one needed to read the *Germania* to recognize its
existence. In our own time he has been banned in Eastern Europe,
and a 1969 collection of essays on Tacitus was movingly dedicated
"To the People of Czechoslovakia" in the year after the Prague
Spring.[158] The demons of collaboration, corruption, treachery,
and tyranny that inspired Tacitus have not yet been laid to rest.
The atrocities of our century have swept away the smug liberalism
of the Victorian era: rulers can be monsters and something close
to pure evil must be credited. The Tacitean Tiberius and Nero
seem positively benign after Stalin, Hitler, and Pol Pot who murdered not dozens or hundreds but millions. Those horrors have
opened the eyes of historians to other cruelties which have long
waited for our attention. Massacres in the prairie, in the outback,
on the veldt, in slave galleys, or prison camps, from hunger or
neglect, from swords or the highest technology—all now lie naked before us. Tacitus's obsession with evil is once more on the
agenda of historians of the twentieth century.

Conclusion

As a moral historian, Tacitus hoped that his work would be used
by later generations and so it has been, though not always as he
intended. It is the fate of all texts, like all works of art, to take on
their own lives independent of their creators. Still, it is disturbing
that Tacitus has been subjected to differing, even contradictory,
interpretations on such fundamental issues as his view of monarchy. Tacitus describes court sycophancy and imperial paranoia
with irony and contempt and yet, as Guicciardini first noted, he
provided a model for tyranny. The authority of antiquity carried
great weight in the Renaissance: Italian princes imitated Tiberius
and handbooks of court flattery used Tacitean anecdotes as
though the historian had produced a manual for getting ahead,

like *The Prince* or *The Courtier* (both of which cite Tacitus). His description of corruption became a prescription for success. The biting aphorisms on emperors and senators lend themselves to quotation, in and out of context. Politicians once read collections of Tacitean maxims—as public figures and their speechwriters today rely on Bartlett's—so the historian's pithy judgments were cited to buttress every imaginable position. The royalist Archbishop Ussher and the revolutionary Benjamin Franklin use the same phrase from the *Agricola* to justify their positions. That the ironic historian was used by the object of his sarcasm is, of course, the ultimate irony.

However, by the eighteenth century attitudes towards Tacitus were fixed and "red" Tacitus had triumphed: the advocate of free speech and the caustic opponent of tyranny. Thus he appealed to British Whigs, to American revolutionaries, and to French adversaries of the Bourbons, of the Terror, or of Napoleon. Despite the occasional exception, English Tories and Napoleon himself regarded Tacitus as the enemy. This is the image of Tacitus who survives near the end of the twentieth century.

We should not end this brief survey of the impact of Tacitus without an important caveat. Tacitus wrote as an historian, and historians provide, above all, a context for events, personalities, and ideas. When we discuss Tacitus or any other historian, we extract political attitudes and moral principles from the web of their history. This may be necessary to describe his work, but we must recognize that "ideas-in-history," like "ideas-in-poetry" or "ideas-in-art," are very far from the ideas found in a philosopher or social theorist. This does no less violence to the integrity of the historian's vision than do prose descriptions of *King Lear* or the Sistine Chapel—all such abstractions necessarily trivialize the works themselves. History is about particular events and particular men and women, and any generalization the historian provides or the reader imposes functions within a specific context. Tacitus never expected to have his "ideas" summarized, his maxims extracted, his "characters" discussed.[159] All abstract discussion of his work, including this book, distorts his vision; that can only be found in reading his books themselves. That is how he hoped to affect later generations.

We need a man can speak of the intents,
  The counsels, actions, orders and events,
Of state, and censure them; we need his pen
  Can write the things, the causes, and the men.
But most we need his faith (and all have you)
  That dares nor write things false, nor
    hide things true.

BEN JONSON
"Epigram to Sir Henry Savile"*

IX

Epilogue

Tacitus may have been the greatest of the Roman historians and the last great mind of Roman paganism, but his impact today rarely reaches beyond learned journals and graduate seminars. Tacitus, like nearly all historians before the nineteenth century, was a gentleman rather than a professor. But serious history has now become an academic discipline and the professors regard with condescension gentleman-historians: Winston Churchill or Will Durant. Armies of professional historians and their graduate students produce careful, if narrowly focused, research. Such academic monographs appropriately demand scrupulous documen-

**Ben Jonson,* ed. Ian Donaldson (Oxford, 1975).

tation and disinterested impartiality; all in the interest of the grand, but always receding, synthesis. When we judge earlier historians by contemporary scholarly standards, we attach far greater weight to objectivity, to scientific precision, and to original research than they would have done. So Tacitus has become a historical curiosity, an undeniably powerful writer but one who was methodologically naive and inaccurate, if not deceitful.

We should not forget that Gibbon, Montesquieu, Macaulay, Henry Adams, or even Mommsen's *History of Rome* are most commonly read today for their ideas or their style; there are more convenient and more accurate ways to learn the "facts." Every great writer is diminished—and misunderstood—when assessed according to anachronistic norms: Tacitus by those who deplore that he omitted social history, neglected the provinces, and showed unseemly political passion. These standards are not merely anachronistic; they show a misunderstanding of what makes great history. The greatest historians of ancient Rome during the last two centuries are likewise subject to charges of bias and selectivity. Edward Gibbon, a child of the French Enlightenment which affected his views of religion, was issued in "Bowdlerized" editions in Victorian England; Theodor Mommsen, the only professional historian to win the Nobel Prize for Literature, wrote a passionate, multi-volume *History of Rome* in which Caesar became the inevitable solution to republican Rome's dilemma as Mommsen himself yearned for a strongman to resolve the chaos of nineteenth-century Germany; Michael Rostovtzeff brought his flight from revolutionary St. Petersburg to bear on his *Social and Economic History of the Roman Empire* (1926)—a glorification of the Roman municipal bourgeoisie; and Sir Ronald Syme's *The Roman Revolution* (1939) looked at the rise of Augustus through the spectacles of a liberal who saw on his visits to Italy the names and trappings of Augustan Rome used by a new *dux,* Benito Mussolini, and wished to expose in a very Tacitean way the thuggish similarities between the two regimes. These historians were selective; they had prejudices; they wrote their own experiences into the history of Rome; and a student will find the "facts" more briefly set out in a pedestrian textbook. But these were great historians whose insight, learning, and passion have illuminated for all the experience of the Roman people.

We must approach Tacitus as a writer whose art and intellect have translated his personal experience into the most powerful ancient evocation of tyranny—tyranny as both a political condition and a psychological state. If other ancient writers examined the human psyche as affected by war (Homer), by love (Ovid), by suffering (Sophocles), and by religion (Euripides's *Bacchae*), Tacitus above all others probes the individual personality transformed by political absolutism. He writes with that intensity so typical among Roman writers forging the complex link between the past and his own present, his present and our present. He has been criticized because he did not provide a more balanced picture of emperors who (by and large) brought peace and prosperity to the Roman world after decades of civil war. Tacitus certainly lacks the "long" view of history: that *in the long run* the emperors brought better government to the Roman world than the senatorial nobility had ever done, that *in the long run* peace and prosperity are certainly worth a few dozen executions. He does not believe that "to understand all is to forgive all." Rather he gives powerful expression to the "short" view, the howl of the victim for recognition and for vengeance, the view that the freedom of individuals cannot be ignored by their rulers. He saw the need to remember, the historian's duty to commemorate suffering. We should take care lest our own desire to reach a balanced judgment too easily shuts us off from his emotional power and his political insight.

Gibbon and Montesquieu are the great modern practitioners of moral history and they admired Tacitus as their forebear. The moral historian not only wishes to teach moral lessons, but he argues that good and evil are the motors of historical change. Tacitus does not ignore the role of fortune or political realism in Roman history, but the ultimate causes are moral. Moral history is hardly fashionable today, not least because there is little agreement on a common basis of morality. But where moral norms are clear, moral history still plays a powerful role. Historians of the Holocaust may report specific bureaucratic procedures and administrative decisions, but beneath the surface text the historian and his reader understand that a dark, almost inexplicable, evil drove the Third Reich to destroy European Jewry and finally itself. The historian, like the victim, chooses to become a witness. Perhaps in the twenty-first century there will be an increasing place for the moral historian.

Tacitus speaks to us today about the corruption of power, and the ways in which both rulers and ruled are complicit in that mutual corruption. Lies and dissimulation are intertwined with self-deception until the truth of evil is hidden, even from a Nero himself. Power resides in language, and the corruption of language leads directly to the corruption of political life. Tacitus the politician was not a hero; he admits that his courage failed him. But his language is unsparing in its exposure of evil and its devotion to truth. That, rather than a political program, is his lasting legacy.

The *Annals* has been criticized as a "novel," as though truth cannot be found in Balzac or Tolstoy or Dickens. Their truth may not be the whole truth, but no one tells the "whole truth" nor the only truth. The communication of truth is the vital issue, not the genre of the book. Tacitus has recreated the truth of the early Roman Empire, the truth of lost freedom, the truth of intellectual and moral decline, the truth of the sycophancy and dissimulation of court politics, the truth of cowardice and collaboration, the truth of evil. He survived, even prospered, under that regime and his burden of guilt made his perceptions all the more acute. All historical writing is a re-creation of the past through the consciousness of the historian who often reads his own life into his subject. He knew the worst. Like so many great artists, Tacitus was trying in a healing work of self-revelation to exorcise his own demons; his books are to some degree a study of his own troubled soul.

The Annals and *The Histories* are much more than mere self-justification; they are a brilliant and angry analysis of his class, of his age, of the moral condition of imperial Rome, of the ageless corruption of politics, and, finally, of the psychopathology of tyranny—all written from the inside. Tacitus has lifted his story to universal heights: his Roman emperors stand with the Grand Inquisitor as a universal paradigm of oppression. He has attained, as he urged in the *Dialogue,* a connection between literature and life.

Or as that great word-forger James Joyce put it in *Finnegans Wake*,[1] it is "simply because as Taciturn pretells, our wrongstory-shortener, he dumptied the wholebarrow of rubbages on to soil here."

They continue to blossom.

Notes

I. *Introduction*

1. *Annals* 3, 65; on this passage, cf. Luce (1991).
1. *Annals* 4, 33. On the historian as judge, cf. Pippidi (1944) 19; Michel (1966) 12; 249.
3. For another view, cf. Walker (1960) 257: ". . . if Tacitus's outlook had not been cramped by his personal frustration, he might have been qualified to write history of a breadth and impartiality rare among ancient writers."
4. For an example of an excellent modern text which deals almost entirely with the issues absent from Tacitus, cf. P. Garnsey and R. Saller *The Roman Empire* (Berkeley, 1987).
5. Cook (1988) 4.
6. Cf. Chapter VIII below.
7. For Napoleon's views on Tacitus, cf. Chapter VIII below.
8. Von Fritz (1957) 94.
9. *Aeneid* 1, 462.
10. Luce (1991) addresses the historian's duty to preserve memory. Cf. 2921 n. 45 for the Orwell reference.
11. H. White "The Value of Narrative in the Representation of Reality" in *On Narrative* ed. W. J. T. Mitchell (Chicago, 1981) 1–23 concludes with the question: "Could we even narrativize *without* moralizing?"

II. *The Historian and His Histories*

1. Pliny the Elder *Natural History* 3, 31. On the Gallic origins of Tacitus, cf. Syme (1958) 611–624.
2. On the life of Tacitus, cf. Martin (1981) 26f.
3. Syme (1958) 595; 598ff.
4. Syme (1958) 29: "a vindication of the new men from the provinces, setting them up against effete aristocrats and the parochial Italians."

5. Laistner (1947) 131.
6. *Dialogue* 2.
7. *Histories* 1, 1.
8. Bowersock (1992).
9. *Agricola* 3.
10. *Panegyricus* 56, 3; cf. chapter VI below for a discussion of "moderatio."
11. *Agricola* 45.
12. Lucas (1974) 227; also cf. Syme (1958) 428f.
13. *Histories* 1, 16.
14. *Agricola* 3.
15. Pliny *Letters* 2, 1 (Verginius's eulogy); 2, 2 (prosecution).
16. On the dangers of 97, cf. Syme "How Tacitus Came to History" in Syme (1970) 18; also cf. Syme (1958) 130.
17. Syme (1958) 72; now cf. Bowersock (1992) on Tacitus and Asia.
18. For a recent discussion on the date of Tacitus's death, cf. Sage (1990) 960–962.
19. *Agricola* 2.
20. On the *Agricola* as a funeral address, cf. Ogilvie (1991) 1715–1718.
21. Martin (1981) 39.
22. Leeman (1973) 206.
23. Thomas (1982) 124.
24. *Agricola* 10–12.
25. *Agricola* 12.
26. *Agricola* 30–32; cf. Ogilvie and Richmond (1967) 253–264.
27. Sallust *Epistle of Mithridates* (= *Histories* 4, 69). (Loeb edition pp. 433–439.)
28. *Agricola* 30.
29. Livy 21, 40–44.
30. On Agricola's modesty, cf. *Agricola* 8; 40.
31. Dorey (1969) 2.
32. *Agricola* 28.
33. *Agricola* 42: "posse etiam sub malis principibus magnos viros esse."
34. Classen (1988) 98; 116.
35. *Agricola* 44–45.
36. *Agricola* 46.
37. Thomas (1982) 125.
38. E. Gabba "True History and False History in Classical Antiquity" *Journal of Roman Studies* 71 (1981) 50–62.
39. Syme (1958) 126.
40. *Germania* 2.

41. Goodyear (1970a) 9.
42. E. A. Thompson *The Early Germans* (Oxford, 1965) 2.
43. Boissier (1906) 28 argued for moral contrasts. Though Anderson (1983) ix–xix and Laistner (1947) 111 have questioned Tacitus's moral purpose in the *Germania*, most recent scholars recognize that moral comparisons lie at the heart of the book; cf. A. N. Sherwin-White *Racial Prejudice in Imperial Rome* (Cambridge, 1967) 40; Thomas (1982) 126; Dauge (1981) 247–254.
44. *Germania* 19.
45. *Germania* 7.
46. *Germania* 33.
47. Schellhase (1976) 11 ff.; cf. Chapter VIII below.
48. Momigliano (1966) 112. (This is a reprint of a lecture, "Some Observations on the Causes of War in Ancient Historiography," first given in 1954.)
49. *Dialogue* 1.
50. Luce (1992).
51. *Dialogue* 10.
52. *Dialogue* 20.
53. *Dialogue* 11–12.
54. *Dialogue* 28–30.
55. *Dialogue* 26.
56. Williams (1978) chapter 1.
57. *Dialogue* 40.
58. Costa (1969) 31; Murphy (1991) 2295.
59. Winterbottom (1970) 220. Güngerich (1980) collects many Ciceronian parallels in his commentary on the *Dialogue*.
60. D. A. Russell *Criticism in Antiquity* (London, 1981) 61; Luce (1992) 44ff. spells out differences in argumentation between Cicero and the *Dialogue*.
61. Leo (1896) 172ff. first demonstrated this point. I am unconvinced by G. Kennedy's argument that Tacitus's Ciceronianism is ironic; cf. *The Art of Rhetoric in the Roman World* (Princeton, 1972) 516.
62. Woodman (1975) 274 places its composition in 102. Syme (1958) 112–113; 670–673 suggests that the work was composed about 102 and published in 107. Barnes (1986) 244 prefers 97.
63. Mendell (1957) 346.
64. Pliny *Letters* 6, 16.
65. On the sources of the *Histories*, cf. Syme (1958) 176–190; Martin (1981) 189–198.

66. I rely here on Ginsburg (1981), the best recent account of Tacitus's use of annalistic forms.
67. Benario (1975) 108f.
68. *Histories* 1, 18.
69. *Histories* 1, 50.
70. *Histories* 2, 82.
71. *Histories* 3, 36.
72. *Histories* 3, 34.
73. Baxter (1971) 93ff.
74. *Histories* 5, 2–10.
75. Wardy (1979) 613–634.
76. Martin (1981) 68; 101.
77. *Histories* 2, 3 (Venus); 4, 83 (Serapis).
78. On his admiration for Antonius Primus, cf. *Histories* 3, 17; also cf. 2, 38 on lust for power.
79. *Histories* 1, 50 (scoundrels in power); 4, 54 (Druids).
80. *Histories* 3, 11.
81. *Histories* 4, 57.
82. *Histories* 4, 44.
83. *Histories* 1, 16. I do not accept Syme's (1958) 206–207 interpretation that Tacitus uses this speech to demolish the principle of the adoptive monarchy. For a further discussion of this speech, cf. pp. 152f. below.
84. Syme (1958) 265–266.
85. While the hexadic composition of the *Annals* is now widely accepted, Goodyear (1970a) 18 disputes it.
86. Syme (1958) 253.
87. Leeman (1973) 187.
88. Commentary on Zakariah 14, 1, 2. *S. Hieronymi Presbyteri Opera* Corpus Christianorum 76A (Turnholt, 1970).
89. *Annals* 1, 9–10; cf. Miller (1969) 103.
90. *Annals* 4, 6–7.
91. *Annals* 6, 51.
92. Syme (1958) 259f.
93. *Annals* 12, 1.
94. *Annals* 12, 7.
95. *Annals* 3, 34: "it is a husband's fault if his wife gets out of line"; on Claudius, cf. *Annals* 3, 18.
96. *Annals* 14, 15.
97. *Annals* 15, 60–64.

98. *Annals* 6, 6.
99. *Annals* 1, 3.
100. Cf. Chapter VI below.
101. In my opinion, the best discussion of the *Annals* and its historian remains Walker (1960).
102. *Annals* 3, 65.
103. *Annals* 4, 33.
104. Syme (1958) 465–503; against this viewpoint Goodyear (1972) 127; (1981) 387–393.

III. *The Historian's Method*

1. *Histories* 1, 4; *Annals* 13, 31.
2. Sempronius Asellio, cited in Aulus Gellius 5, 18, 8–9.
3. On Nepos, cf. N. Horsfall "Nepos" in *Cambridge History of Classical Literature* II Latin Literature (Cambridge, 1982) 291; Horsfall is more sympathetic in *Cornelius Nepos* (Oxford, 1989) xv–xxi; on Florus, cf. F.R.D. Goodyear "History and Biography" *ibid.* 664.
4. *Annals* 4, 32–33: "quia pauci prudentia honesta ab deterioribus, utilia ab noxiis discernunt, plures aliorum eventis docentur."
5. Momigliano (1990) 113.
6. *Histories* 1, 4.
7. Goodyear (1970b) 101–106.
8. *Annals* 3, 55.
9. Woodman (1979) 148f.
10. Martin (1981) 242. For another view, cf Momigliano (1966) 131 calls the *Annals* the "most conspicuous example of a great work of history written with a minimum amount of independent research."
11. P. G. Walsh *Livy* (Cambridge, 1961) 110ff.; T. J. Luce *Livy: The Composition of His History* (Princeton, 1977) chapter 5 presents a more positive picture of Livy. He correctly argues (154) that he could better display his historical talents in the last seventy-five books, which are lost, than in the surviving books which survey remote antiquity.
12. Pliny *Letters* 6, 16.
13. Wardy (1979) 613–634.
14. For judicious treatments, cf. Martin (1981) 189–213; Syme (1958) 176–190; 271–303. A recent summary can be found in Sage (1990) 893–900 (*Histories*); 997–1017 (*Annals*).
15. *Annals* 13, 20.

16. Martin (1981) 117–118; 204.
17. R. Talbert *The Senate of Imperial Rome* (Princeton, 1984) 333.
18. Syme (1958) 319. I do not agree with Momigliano (1990) 110–112 that Tacitus used the *acta senatus* only for the reign of Domitian.
19. *Annals* 11, 24; H. Dessau *Inscriptiones Latinae Selectae* 212. Cf. Miller (1956) 304ff.; Syme (1958) 317–318; 703–710.
20. Corbulo: *Annals* 15, 16 and Syme (1958) 297; Agrippina: *Annals* 4, 53.
21. Wellesley (1972) 7f.; also cf. A. Breissmann (1955).
22. *Histories* 2, 101.
23. 2, 62: "ne quid falsi dicere audeat? deinde ne quid veri non audeat?"
24. *Agricola* 2.
25. *Histories* 1, 1: ". . . sed incorruptam fidem professis neque amore quisquam et sine odio dicendus est."
26. *Annals* 1, 1: "sine ira et studio, quorum causas procul habeo."
27. 4, 2: "mihi a spe metu partibus rei publicae animus liber." For an illuminating discussion of the Roman equation of impartiality with historical truth, cf. Woodman (1988) 70ff.
28. *Apocolocyntosis* 1, 1: "nihil nec offensae nec gratiae dabitur."
29. I am here greatly indebted to Luce (1989) 16ff. who provides an excellent discussion of ancient views of bias in historical writing.
30. Cook (1988) 63.
31. *Annals* 4, 11.
32. *Annals* 11, 27: "civitate omnium gnara et nihil reticente."
33. *Histories* 5, 5: "nam et necare quemquam ex agnatis nefas."
34. Wellesley (1969) 72.
35. Ginsburg (1981) 96 argues that Tacitus is not in any real sense an annalistic historian, and that he is not restricted by the formal year-by-year organization of his history.
36. T. Mommsen *The Provinces of the Roman Empire* (London, 1886; Eng. trans.) I 181.
37. *Annals* 2, 23f.
38. Cremona: Syme (1958) 168; Wellesley (1969) 92; Civilis: Martin (1981) 95. For a recent survey of the evidence and a positive assessment of Tacitus as a military historian, cf. Sage (1990) 926–935.
39. Perhaps the only serious factual error is his statement on the legionary fortress at Vetera which was destroyed in the revolt of Civilis: "neither the site nor the defenses had labor spent upon them" (*Hist.* 4, 23). Excavations have now proven that the defenses and build-

ings had been vastly improved in the preceding decades. The historian certainly is in error, but he probably reports what was a popularly accepted excuse for the destruction of the most important Roman camp on the Rhine rather than inventing it himself. Cf. E. Birley *Journal of Roman Studies* 20 (1930) 112f.

40. *Agricola* 22; cf. Ogilvie and Richmond (1967) 4–5.
41. On innuendo, cf. Ryberg (1942) 383ff.; Sinclair (1991) 2802ff.
42. Morford (1990) 1624 goes further and pronounces "Tacitus' presentation of the facts, where it can be checked, is generally as reliable as that of any ancient historian."
43. *Apologeticus* 16: "ille mendaciorum loquacissimus."
44. Walker (1960) 82–137 provides the most extensive account of the divergences between fact and impression.
45. *Annals* 1, 3 mentions Agrippa's brutality, but in 1, 5 it is ignored.
46. *Annals* 1, 2.
47. *Annals* 6, 7.
48. Marsh (1931) 11.
49. *Agricola* 30f.
50. *Agricola* 43.
51. *Annals* 1, 10.
52. *Annals* 1, 52: "magis in speciem verbis adornata quam ut penitus sentire crederetur."
53. T. Mommsen *Ges. Schriften* IV (1906) 299.
54. Pippidi (1944) 40.
55. Wallace-Hadrill (1982) 41–42.
56. Syme (1958) 482f. calls the episode "inartistic."

IV. *The Historian as Moralist*

1. Cf. Mellor (1987) 1541ff. For change in moral terms, cf. D. C. Earl "Sallust" in T. J. Luce (1982) 621–641.
2. *De oratore* 2, 9, 36.
3. Otis (1967) 193ff.
4. For an important discussion of *virtus* in Tacitus, cf. F. Klingner (1961) 493ff.
5. But Scott (1968) 4 argues that Tacitus is representative of traditional Roman attitudes to religion.
6. *Histories* 1, 3.
7. J. H. W. G. Liebeschuetz *Continuity and Change in Roman Religion* (Oxford, 1979) 119–125.

8. *Histories* 2, 78–79 (Philistine); 4, 81 (Alexandria); 5, 13 (Jerusalem).
9. *Annals* 6, 22.
10. *Agricola* 4.
11. *Histories* 4, 5.
12. *Histories* 4, 6: "quando etiam sapientibus cupido gloriae novissima exuitur."
13. *Annals* 16, 32.
14. *Orator* 120.
15. *The Closing of the American Mind* (New York, 1987).
16. *The Use and Abuse of History* (London, 1975), 23.
17. In the postwar era, there were several attempts to bring Tacitus to the attention of a wider readership; cf. I. Kristol *Encounter* 5 (1956) 84–87; L. Trilling's essay "Tacitus Now" republished in *The Liberal Imagination* (New York, 1949) 187–192.
18. *Agricola* 32: "proinde ituri in aciem et maiores vestros et posteros cogitate."
19. *Annals* 14, 14: "quos fato perfunctos ne nominatim tradam, maioribus eorum tribuendum puto."
20. *Annals* 1, 3–4.
21. Wirszubski (1950) 163–164.
22. *Histories* 1, 15; cf. Keitel (1991) 2775.
23. Cf. Seneca the Elder *Controversiae* 2, 1.
24. *Annals* 14, 20.
25. On Tacitus and the Greeks, cf. Syme (1958) 504ff.
26. *Histories* 1, 30: "haec principatus praemia putat."
27. *Annals* 2, 33.
28. Löfstedt (1948) 4.
29. Leeman (1963) 351.
30. *Annals* 13, 45.
31. Walker (1960) 47; Woodman (1989) 202 says Tacitus projects different aspects at different points in the narrative. Woodman contains recent bibliography on this topic.
32. Walker (1960) 204ff.
33. Storoni-Mazzolani (1976) 143.
34. Syme (1958) 41–42 cites cases where vicious or frivolous men were effective governors or commanders.
35. *Annals* 16, 19–20.
36. Martin (1981) 168.
37. *Annals* 4, 20.
38. Michel (1966) 191.

39. *Annals* 1, 2: "militem donis, populum annona, cunctos dulcedine otii pellexit."
40. *Satires* 10, 80.
41. *Histories* 3, 83.
42. *Annals* 1, 31.
43. *Histories* 3, 11.
44. *Histories* 3, 32–33.
45. *Annals* 15, 57.
46. *Histories* 1, 28: "ut pessimum facinus auderent pauci, plures vellent, omnes paterentur."
47. *Annals* 14, 64.
48. *Histories* 3, 25: "Factum esse scelus loquuntur faciuntque."
49. *Annals* 1, 13.
50. *Histories* 1, 2.
51. *Annals* 14, 51.
52. *Histories* 2, 37.
53. *Annals* 1, 54.
54. *Annals* 6, 16: "privato usui bonum publicum postponitur."
55. *Dialogue* 28: "desidia iuventutis et neglentia parentum et inscientia praecipientium et oblivione moris antiqui."
56. *Histories* 2, 38.
57. *Annals* 6, 48: "cum Tiberius post tantam rerum experientiam vi dominationis convulsus et mutatus sit."
58. *Histories* 4, 1: "inter turbas et discordias pessimo cuique plurima vis, pax et quies bonis artibus indigent."
59. *Histories* 3, 25.
60. Wirszubski (1950) 128.
61. *Histories* 4, 17.
62. *Annals* 4, 50.
63. *Annals* 13, 54.
64. *Germania* 19.
65. Keitel (1978) 462ff.
66. *Histories* 1, 3.
67. Ferrero (1962) 58.
68. *Histories* 1, 50: "solusque omnium ante se principum in melius mutatus est."
69. *Histories* 1, 50: "solum id scires deteriorem fore qui vicisset."
70. *Mimesis: The Representation of Reality in Western Culture* (Princeton, 1953) 53. Auerbach wrote *Mimesis* in Istanbul during the Second World War, and the first German edition was published in Switzerland in 1946.

71. *Annals* 16, 16.
72. Michel (1966) 112.
73. *Annals* 6, 6.
74. Though many scholars see Tacitus's passionate anger as a sign that he is too involved to be a cynic; cf. Otis (1967) 200.
75. R. MacMullen *Enemies of the Roman Order* (Cambridge, 1966) 46ff. discusses the philosophical opposition under the Flavians.
76. Syme (1958) 465ff. argues that Tacitus's hostility to Hadrian is evident in the *Annals*. Few scholars now see Hadrian as relevant to the *Annals*, though Sage (1990) 960–962 suggests that Tacitus lived beyond 117.
77. F. Kermode *The Sense of an Ending: Studies in the Theory of Fiction* (New York, 1966) 5.

v. *The Historian as Psychologist*

1. Jeremiah 13, 23: "Can the Ethiopian change his skin or the leopard change his spots?"
2. Walker (1960) 47.
3. Gill (1983) 471.
4. *Annals* 6, 22: "ceterum plurimis mortalium non eximitur, quin primo cuiusque ortu ventura destinentur."
5. Woodman (1989) 187.
6. Woodman (1989) 202 says Tacitus projects different aspects at different points in the narrative. Woodman contains recent bibliography on this topic.
7. Goodyear (1972) 38.
8. Luce (1986) 149–150.
9. R. G. Collingwood *The Idea of History* (Oxford, 1946) expresses vehement opposition to the psychological history of both Thucydides (30) and Tacitus (40). He says that psychological history "is not history at all, but natural science of a special kind" (29). Though he never gives persuasive reasons for regarding Tacitus's psychological approach an "impoverishment" or "a declining standard of historical honesty," it is clear that Collingwood believes that psychology demands an *a priori* acceptance of a method that limits the historian's intellectual freedom.
10. *Agricola* 35–37.
11. Otis (1967) 193f.; cf. Segal (1973) 107ff. on the "inner dramatic" of Tacitean narrative.

12. Walker (1960) 204ff.
13. Pippidi (1944) 25.
14. Tacitus *Annals* 4, 33. Cf. A. J. Woodman (1977) 45; Syme (1974) 481.
15. *Annals* 6, 8: "Abditos principis sensus, et si quid occultius parat, exquirere inlicitum, anceps."
16. Syme (1958) 314.
17. Pippidi (1944) 29.
18. *Annals* 1, 3: "rudem sane bonarum artium et robore corporis stolide ferocem"; 1, 8: "remisit Caesar arroganti moderatione"; 4, 2: "municipali adultero."
19. Mendell (1957) 138.
20. Walker (1960) 235.
21. Syme (1974) 495.
22. Marañon (1956) is a controversial book by an Argentine psychoanalyst. Lucas (1974) is a fascinating, but extreme, picture of the paranoid historian. Interestingly, Lucas (1974) 192 compares Tacitus to Proust's Baron de Charlus at the same time that Sir Ronald Syme (1974) 496 links Charlus with the emperor Tiberius in their insane pride, aesthetic tastes, and ferocious sarcasm.
23. *Annals* 6, 51.
24. Syme (1958) 428.
25. Quoted in Martin (1981) 268 n. 36.
26. Daitz (1960) 34ff.; Walker (1960) 118ff. For a re-evaluation, cf. Rutland (1987) 153ff.
27. Ross (1973) 209ff.
28. *Annals* 2, 23f.
29. *Annals* 2, 73.
30. Storoni-Mazzolani (1976) 184.
31. *Germania* 27.
32. Ross (1973) 222 makes the important point that ancient historians attached great weight to lineage in the depiction of character. Germanicus's despotic descendants would be ever present for the Roman reader.
33. Borzsak (1970) 282.
34. Pelling (1992) ms. 123.
35. *Annals* 6, 48.
36. *Annals* 1, 12.
37. *Annals* 4, 71: "nullam aeque Tiberius, ut rebatur, ex virtutibus suis quam dissimulationem diligebat."

38. *Annals* 1, 7.
39. *Agricola* 22.
40. *Annals* 4, 18: "nam beneficia eo usque laeta sunt, dum videntur exsolvi posse: ubi multum antevenere, pro gratia odium redditur."
41. *Annals* 15, 50.
42. *Annals* 4, 69.
43. *Agricola* 42: "proprium humani ingenii est odisse quem laeseris."
44. *Annals* 15, 67.
45. *Annals* 2, 13.
46. *Histories* 4, 70.
47. *Annals* 3, 44.
48. *Annals* 1, 76.
49. *Histories* 2, 29.
50. *Histories* 2, 44; *Agricola* 40 condemns the masses for judging men by outward display.
51. *Histories* 3, 73.
52. *Annals* 14, 60.
53. Auerbach (1953) 52.
54. Grant (1970) 302.
55. *Histories* 3, 15.
56. Baldwin (1972) 83–101.
57. *Annals* 3, 33.
58. Ginsburg (1992).
59. *Annals* 4, 3: "neque femina amissa pudicitia alia abnuerit." Martin and Woodman (1989) 93 finds the editors in disagreement over this passage: Martin considers it a generalization while Woodman prefers to link it specifically to Livilla. There is an ironic verbal allusion here to Livy's virtuous Lucretia ("amissa pudicitia").
60. *Agricola* 6: "in bona uxore tanto maior laus, quanto in mala plus culpae est."
61. *Annals* 3, 34: "nam viri in eo culpam si femina modum excedat."
62. Syme (1958) 534 believes "The documents fall a long way short of proof."
63. As proposed by Lucas (1974) 192.
64. Syme (1974) 496.
65. Especially cf. Lucas (1974).
66. Janssens (1946) 318.
67. Walker (1960) 195.

VI. *The Historian as Political Analyst*

1. *Annals* 4, 33.
2. *Annals* 1, 2.
3. Syme "The Political Opinions of Tacitus" in Syme (1970) 119–140.
4. *Annals* 3, 28: "multa honesta exitio fuere."
5. R. Syme *The Roman Revolution* (Oxford, 1939) 512 ff.
6. Walker (1960) 196.
7. Wirszubski (1950) 127.
8. Classen (1988) 100.
9. *Agricola* 3: "Nerva Caesar res olim dissociabiles miscuerit: Principatum ac Libertatem." Cf. Hammond (1963) 93–113.
10. This terminology was first used by G. Toffanin *Machiavelli e il tacitismo* (Padua, 1921; reprint Naples, 1972); it has been adopted (with criticism) by Momigliano (1947) 91–100; also by Burke (1969) 162.
11. Cf. Chapter VIII below.
12. Luce (1986) 150.
13. Storoni-Mazzolani (1976) 175; Martin (1990) 1576.
14. *On the Sublime*, 44, 3.
15. *Histories* 2, 1; 1, 89. On the crowd in Tacitus, cf. Newbold (1976) 85–92.
16. *Histories* 1, 4: "plebs sordida et circo ac theatris sueta."
17. *Histories* 1, 7.
18. *Annals* 1, 6.
19. *Annals* 1, 11.
20. *Annals* 2, 36.
21. For Tiberius's belief in astrology, cf. *Annals* 6, 20–21. The emperor himself was expert enough to cast the horoscope of Galba and predict he would reach the imperial throne. On the political implications of astrology, cf. J. H. W. G. Liebeschuetz *Continuity and Change in Roman Religion* (Oxford, 1979) 119–125.
22. *Histories* 3, 56.
23. *Histories* 1, 4.
24. *Agricola* 30; cf. Cook (1988) 94.
25. *Histories* 4, 73.
26. *Annals* 1, 3.
27. *Histories* 1, 37.
28. *Annals* 15, 18: "dum aspectui consulitur spreta conscientia."
29. *Annals* 13, 3.

30. *Histories* 2, 1.
31. *Histories* 4, 25.
32. Ramorino (1898) 50; cf. Chapter VIII below.
33. E.g. *Agricola* 41.
34. Syme (1958) 504ff.
35. *Annals* 11, 34.
36. Burke (1966) 149.
37. *Annals* 11, 28.
38. *Agricola* 6.
39. Cf. *Annals* 5, 9 for an account of the murder of Sejanus's young children.
40. *Histories* 3, 85.
41. *Annals* 3, 65: "O homines ad servitutem paratos!"
42. B. Baldwin *Suetonius* (Amsterdam, 1983) 334.
43. *Annals* 2, 27f. *Annals* 1, 73 records even earlier charges brought under the *lex majestatis* (treason law), but those were dismissed by Tiberius.
44. *Annals* 3, 25.
45. *Annals* 4, 20.
46. *Agricola* 7, 3. Cf. Classen (1988) 95ff. H. North *Sophrosyne* (Ithaca, 1966) 291 points to the contrast between the *moderatio* of Agircola with the *ira* of Domitian and the useless defiance (*contumacia*) of the Stoic martyrs.
47. Wallace-Hadrill (1982) 42.
48. *Annals* 6, 10.
49. R. Syme "The Political Opinions of Tacitus" in Syme (1970) 138.
50. Michel (1966) 40.
51. *Agricola* 42.
52. *Annals* 6, 38.
53. *Histories* 4, 8.
54. *Annals* 4, 35.
55. Suetonius *Tiberius* 28.
56. *Agricola* 2.
57. *Meditations* 1, 14, 2.
58. *Histories* 1, 16.
59. E.g. R. Syme "The Political Opinions of Tacitus" in Syme (1970) 132; Luce (1986) 147.
60. Laugier (1969) 104.
61. Keitel (1992) warns against discrediting the arguments in the speech merely because the speaker is unsuccessful at implementing his own goals.

62. *Agricola* 3.
63. Syme (1958) 219.
64. *Histories* 1, 1: "rara temporum felicitate." On Tacitus's growing gloominess under Trajan, cf. Von Fritz (1957) 92.
65. *Annals* 4, 6.
66. Hammond (1963) 93ff.
67. *Pharsalia* 7, 433f.
68. *Agricola* 39: "ducis boni imperatoriam virtutem esse." These words are attributed to Domitian, who had military ambitions.
69. *Agricola* 3.
70. *Annals* 1, 11.
71. *Agricola* 13.
72. Syme (1958) 236f.
73. *Annals* 15, 1.
74. *Histories* 4, 74.
75. *Annals* 1, 2.
76. *Agricola* 13.
77. *Agricola* 15.
78. *Agricola* 30–31.
79. At the 1990 Princeton Tacitus Conference in memory of Sir Ronald Syme, G. W. Bowersock offered the interesting suggestion that the speech of Cerialis was perhaps intended as a response to Calgacus.
80. Roberts (1988) 132.
81. *Agricola* 21: "idque apud imperitos humanitas vocabatur, cum pars servitutis esset."
82. *Agricola* 19.
83. Cf. Martin (1981) 197 on the revolt of Civilis.
84. *Histories* 4, 17.
85. *Histories* 2, 38.
86. *Annals* 6, 48.
86a. *Histories* 1, 16.
87. *Ricordi* ed. R. Spongano (Florence, 1951) Chaper 18; cf. Chapter VIII below.
88. *Annals* 16, 23: "ut versis ad externa rumoribus intestinum scelus obscuraretur."
89. *Pharsalia* 1, 670.
90. Ferrero (1962) 58.
91. *Annals* 3, 18.
92. *Annals* 6, 22: "fatone res mortalium et necessitate immutabili an forte volvantur."

VII. *The Historian as Literary Artist*

1. *De oratore* 2, 36.
2. *De oratore* 1, 165.
3. *Institutio Oratoria* 10, 1, 31: "proxima poetis et quodam modo carmen solutum."
4. *Dialogue* 2.
5. *Dialogue* 29–30.
6. Syme (1958) 322ff.
7. *On the Sublime*, 44, 3.
8. *Dialogue* 40.
9. Miller (1975) 56.
10. *Histories* 1, 16.
11. *Histories* 2, 76–77.
12. *Histories* 4, 73.
13. Syme (1958) 319–320.
14. H. Dessau *Inscriptiones Latinae Selectae* 212 (Lyons tablet); *Annals* 11, 24.
15. Martin (1981) 149.
16. Syme "Tacitus on Gaul" in Syme (1970) 26; Goodyear (1970a) 39; Miller (1956) 304ff.; Wellesley (1954) 13–33 (esp. 32) praises Claudius's idealistic conception of Empire and criticizes Tacitus.
17. Ryberg (1942) 383–404; Sinclair (1991) 2795–2831.
18. Lucian *How to Write History* 34: "the best writer of history comes ready equipped with these two supreme qualities: political understanding and power of expression."
19. Keitel (1978) 463ff.
20. On the strands of narrative, cf. Walker (1960) 17f.; Ginsburg (1981) 78 alludes to the "thematic coherence."
21. *Annals* 15, 38.
22. *Annals* 4, 62.
23. Baxter (1971) 93ff.
24. Keitel (1981) 206ff.
25. Michel (1966) 121.
26. *Annals* 1, 6: "primum facinus novi principatus fuit Postumi Agrippae caedes."
27. *Annals* 13, 1: "prima novo principatu mors Junii Silani."
28. Macaulay *Essay on History* (1828) in *The Complete Works of Thomas Babington Macaulay. Critical and Historical Essays* I (New York, 1910) 262.

29. Fornara (1983) 89 likens Tacitus to a critic studying actors on the stage.
30. I owe much to the stimulating paper by Woodman (1992) on the theatrical language and themes in Tacitus's treatment of Nero.
31. Maranon (1956) has written a psychoanalytical account of Tiberius.
32. *Annals* 3, 16.
33. *Histories* 1, 81.
34. *Annals* 1, 13.
35. *Annals* 6, 50.
36. Walker (1960) 44.
37. *Histories* 4, 62; 1, 40; 3, 84.
38. Miller (1978) 14.
39. *Annals* 1, 9–10.
40. Laugier (1969) 179.
41. Malissard (1991) 2833 ff.
42. Tanner (1991) 2709 ff.
43. "Il n'est pas juste de peindre tout en noir comme l'a fait Tacite. C'est là un peintre habile, je vous l'accorde, un coloriste vigoureux et séduisant, mais qui songe qu'à l'effet qui'il va produire." Quoted by Walker (1960) 145.
44. *Histories* 3, 83.
45. Quinn (1963) 120.
46. *Annals* 14, 30.
47. Woodman (1988) 169ff.
48. G. Bullough *Narrative and Dramatic Sources of Shakespeare* (New York, 1975) vol. IV 362ff. makes *Annals* 2, 13 the source for *Henry V* IV, 1, and provides (410) the Grenewey translation of 1598. In his recent edition G. Taylor *Henry V* (Oxford, 1982) 41ff. is more dubious about the parallel.
49. *Annals* 11, 31.
50. *Discours sur le style* in *Chefs-D'oeuvre Littérare de Buffon* (Paris, 1864) 9.
51. Williams (1978) 241.
52. Storoni-Mazzolani (1976) 144.
53. Croll "Attic Prose in the XVIIth Century" in Croll (1966) 86.
54. Cf. Chapter VIII p. 227.
55. *Annals* 1, 1.
56. *Pensées* (New York, 1941) 1, 29.
57. *How to Write History* 8; on the adornment of history, cf. Wiseman (1979) 3ff.
58. *Dialogue* 26: "fucatis et meretriciis vestibus insignire."

59. *Annals* 6, 19.
60. Walker (1960) 5.
61. *Histories* 1, 36: "omnia serviliter pro dominatione."
62. Segal (1973) 122.
63. *Histories* 2, 38.
64. Miller (1987) 8.
65. *Dictionnaire philosophique* cited in Boissier (1906) 87.
66. Quinn (1979) 237.
67. *Annals* 2, 41: "brevis et infaustos populi Romani amores."
68. *Agricola* 11: "amissa virtute pariter ac libertate."
69. *Agricola* 5: "nec minus periculum ex magna fama quam ex mala."
70. *Annals* 16, 19.
71. *Annals* 1, 8.
72. *Annals* 15, 57.
73. *Annals* 3, 18 is the most explicit statement on the irony of history.
74. On Tacitean humor, now cf. Plass (1988).
75. As suggested by Syme "The Political Opinions of Tacitus" in Syme (1970) 137.
76. P. Gay *The Enlightenment: An Interpretation* I (New York, 1966) 16.
77. *Annals* 6, 20.
78. *Annals* 11, 2.
79. *Annals* 2, 40: "quo modo tu Caesar."
80. *Histories* 1, 74.
81. *Annals* 14, 56.
82. *Annals* 14, 63.
83. *Histories* 1, 22.
84. *Annals* 14, 16.
85. *Annals* 13, 3.
86. The source is Fulgentius *Explanation of Archaic Words* 54, cited in Plass (1988) v.
87. On Cato, cf. Quinn (1979) 202; also cf. Martin (1981) 219.
88. *Annals* 3, 6: "principes mortales, rem publicam aeternam."
89. *Agricola* 12.
90. Burke (1966) 149; Morford (1992).
91. *Histories* 4, 3: "gratia oneri, ultio in quaestu habetur."
92. *Agricola* 27.
93. *Annals* 3, 54.
94. Plass (1988) 32.
95. *Histories* 1, 2: "ob virtutes certissimum exitium."
96. *Annals* 16, 29.

97. *Annals* 3, 76.

98. *Speech at London Tavern* 15 April, 1859. Within a few years the phrase was widely used; s.v. "conspicuous" 2.b in the *Oxford English Dictionary*.

99. *Agricola* 9.

100. *Odes* 3, 2, 13.

101. *Agricola* 6: "quibus inertia pro sapientia fuit."

102. *Histories* 1, 45.

103. *Annals* 15, 23.

104. *Histories* 1, 35.

105. *Agricola* 22.

106. *Histories* 4, 1.

107. *Histories* 3, 63.

108. *Histories* 1, 16; Plass (1988) 62.

109. Leo (1896) 11.

110. Segal (1973) 107 links the *Annals* and the *Aeneid* as the "two great poetic histories" of Rome.

111. Syme (1958) 362.

112. Wiseman (1979) 30; Tacitus's warning (*Annals* 4, 33) that his history will be more useful than enjoyable hardly precludes the strategies of a literary artist.

113. Woodman (1988).

VIII. *The Impact of Tacitus*

1. M. F. Tenney "Tacitus Through the Centuries to the Age of Printing" *University of Colorado Studies* 22 (1935) 341–363. Mendell (1957) 225–238 collects the testimonia. On the emperor Tacitus, cf. *Historia Augusta* "Life of Tacitus" 10.

2. For collected Latin texts, cf. Mendell (1957) 230–232.

3. *Variae* 5, 2.

4. Mendell (1957) 239ff.

5. Schellhase (1976) 17.

6. H. Baron *The Crisis of the Early Italian Renaissance* (Princeton, 1966) 47ff.

7. Syme (1960) 4; Schellhase (1976) 25.

8. Von Stackelberg (1960) 64ff.

9. *The Prince* chapter xvii; cf. Q. Skinner *Machiavelli* (Oxford, 1981) 40; 46.

10. *The Prince* chapter xviii ("How Rulers Should Keep Their Promises").

11. J. H. Whitfield "Livy > Tacitus" in Bolgar (1976) argues that *Annals* 1–6 could not have affected *The Prince*. The only quotation from Tacitus in *The Prince* is from *Annals* 13. Others point out that the manuscript was already known in Italy by 1509.

12. Schellhase (1976) 69f. and 197 n. 12 shows the importance of Tacitus in the *Discourses;* also cf. Syme (1960) 4–6. The parallels are collected in Von Stackelberg (1960) 70f. Toffanin (1921) presented Tacitus as a forerunner of Machiavelli who took a great deal from him. For criticism, cf. Schellhase (1976) 83.

13. Burke (1969) 166.

14. *Stòria della età barocca in Italia* (Bari, 1946) 82. Also cf. Butler (1959) 172; 176; and Etter (1966). Momigliano (1962) 282 cautions that Tacitus "was not just an *Ersatz* for the forbidden Machiavelli."

15. Whitfield in Bolgar (1976) 291.

16. Momigliano (1937) 172–173. Most recent scholars follow Momigliano in his criticism of Toffanin.

17. J. G. A. Pocock *The Machiavellian Moment* (Princeton, 1975) 351; Salmon (1980) 307.

18. *Ricordi* ed. R. Spongano (Florence, 1951) chapter 18. Cf. A. La Penna "Vivere sotto i Titanni: un Tema Tacitano da Guicciardini a Diderot" in Bolgar (1976) 295ff.

19. Medieval monarch: H. Baron *The Crisis of the Early Italian Renaissance* (Princeton, 1966) 49; on "Discourses," cf. H. Baron 143 and Ramorino (1898) 44.

20. On the reception of Tacitus in Germany, cf. Schellhase (1976) 31ff.; Borchardt (1971) 56ff.; Ridé (1977) I 165ff.

21. The letter is translated in G. Strauss *Manifestations of Discontent in Germany on the Eve of the Reformation* (Bloomington, 1971). On this polemic, cf. Ridé (1977) 169–182.

22. D. Kelley *Foundations of Modern Historical Scholarship* (New York, 1970) 201–202.

23. Kelley (1992).

24. Ridé (1977) 229ff.

25. Ridé (1977) I 471ff.

26. Schellhase (1976) 45.

27. Latin text in U. Von Hutten *Opera* (Leipzig, 1859–1861; repr. 1963) vol. IV 409–418; on Von Hutten, cf. H. Holborn *Ulrich Von Hutten and the German Reformation* (New Haven, 1937) 76ff.

28. Schellhase (1976) 47.
29. Borchardt (1971) 180; 208.
30. Kelley (1992) cites Luther's use of the old adage "Good lawyer, bad Christian" and Tacitus *Annals* 3, 27: "The corrupt state has the most laws." Also, cf. D. Kelley *The Human Measure: Social Thought in the Western Legal Tradition* (Cambridge, Mass., 1990) 20.
31. Borchardt (1971) 177; cf. G. Strauss *Historian in an Age of Crisis: Life and Work of Johannes Aventinus 1477–1534* (Cambridge, Mass., 1963) 229 on Johannes Aventinus's emulation of Tacitus as the conscience of his people.
32. Burke (1966) 141; Schellhase (1976) 47.
33. Tenney (1941) 152.
34. Syme (1960) 12.
35. *De Asse* in G. Budaei *Opera* (Basel, 1557—Photoreprint, Farnborough, 1966) 192. Cf. Allott (1980) 33.
36. M. Croll "Juste Lipse et le Mouvement anticicéronien à la Fin du XVIᶜ et au Début du XVIIᶜ Siècle" in Cross (1966) 1–44; Miller (1969) 114.
37. Amelot de la Houssaie's handbook was translated into English as *The Modern Courtier, or The Morals of Tacitus upon Flattery* (London, 1687).
38. Syme (1960) 7.
39. Schellhase (1976) 121f.; on Muret, also cf. Salmon (1980) 322. On the influence of Muret (who converted Lipsius from Cicero to Tacitus) on style, cf. M. Croll "Muret and the History of Attic Prose" in Croll (1966) 103–165.
40. Ramorino (1898) 62.
41. Pedro Ribadeneyra is quoted in Schellhase (1976) 152 and 228 n. 12.
42. On Perez, cf. G. Ungerer *A Spaniard in Elizabethan England: The Correspondence of Antonio Perez' Exile* (London, 1974–1976).
43. "Dedication to Emperor Maximilian II." The passage is quoted in Butler (1959) 173n.
44. For the life of Lipsius, cf. Schellhase (1976) 117–140; M. Morford *Stoics and neostoics: Rubens and the Circle of Lipsius* (Princeton, 1991).
45. G. Botero *The Reason of State* trans. by D. P. Waley and P. J. Waley (London, 1956). For the classic study of Reason of State, cf. F. Meinecke *Machiavellism: The Doctrine of Raison d'Etat and its Place in Modern History* (New Haven, 1957) 66ff.
46. Schellhase (1976) 126f.

47. *I Raguagli di Parnasso or Advertisements from Parnassus* tr. by Henry, earl of Monmouth (London, 1674).

48. Von Stackelberg (1960) 131–146; Tenney (1941) 153.

49. Schellhase (1976) 146.

50. Burke (1969) 162.

51. Quoted in Butler (1959) 174.

52. Ramorino (1898) 50; G. Spini "Historiography: the Art of History in the Italian Counter-Reformation" in E. Cochrane *The Late Italian Renaissance 1525–1630* (London, 1970) 105.

53. The terms "Tacito Rosso" and "Tacito Nero" come from Toffanin (1921).

54. *Methodus* p. 134b: "Nullus profecto historicus magistratui ac judici utilior videtur." Quoted by Von Stackelberg (1960) 182. Also cf. Schellhase (1976) 109ff.

55. Syme (1974) 496; Burke (1969) 166.

56. Schellhase (1976) 157.

57. Momigliano (1990) 123.

58. On Montaigne, cf. Von Stackelberg (1960) 159–186; Schellhase (1976) 128–134. I use D. M. Frame's translation of the essays (New York, 1960).

59. M. Croll "Attic Prose: Lipsius, Montaigne, Bacon" in Croll (1966) 163–202.

60. *Essays* 2, 19.

61. *Essays* 3, 8.

62. *Essays* 3, 8.

63. *Essays* 2, 20.

64. *Annals* 14, 44.

65. Allott (1980) 32–47.

66. For a sketch of Racine's life and education, cf. P. Butler (ed.) *Racine Britannicus* (Cambridge, 1967) 11–17.

67. Butler (1959) 177–178.

68. *Britannicus* Preface of 1676. *Théâtre Complet* ed. J.-P. Collinet (Paris, 1982) 305–308.

69. I rely heavily on the excellent essay by M. F. Tenney (1941); also cf. Schellhase (1976) 157ff.

70. *The History of King Richard III*, volume 2 of *The Complete Works of St. Thomas More* (New Haven, 1963) contains More's English and Latin versions. The editor Richard Sylvester (lxxxviii f.) details the use of Tacitus for Richard's deceitful character. There are also verbal parallels; e.g., "structis in principem insidiis" (p. 23 lines 3–4) recalls "structas principi insidias" (*Annals* 4, 28).

71. F. J. Levy *Tudor Historical Thought* (San Marino, Ca., 1967) 72.

72. Tenney (1941) 154; Levy *Tudor Historical Thought* 251 believes that the Taciteans (including Savile) went into decline with the execution of Essex. Now cf. D. Womersley "Sir Henry Savile's Translation of Tacitus and the Political Interpretation of Elizabethan Texts" *Review of English Studies* 42 (1991) 313–342.

73. Epigram 95 "To Sir Henry Savile"; *Ben Jonson* (Oxford, 1975), ed. Ian Donaldson.

74. Tenney (1941) 156.

75. Schellhase (1976) 147 where Boccalini cites *Hist.* 1, 1.

76. Sidney: Benjamin (1965) 109; Maxims: Burke (1966) 149; Burke (1969) 167f.

77. "Attic Prose: Lipsius, Montaigne, Bacon" in Croll (1966) 163–202; also cf. Miller (1969) 114–115.

78. *The Works of Sir Francis Bacon* ed. J. Spedding; R. Ellis; D. Heath (London, 1868) XI 177ff.

79. Ibid. VI 387ff.; Benjamin (1965)104.

80. "Attic Prose in the XVIIth Century" in Croll (1966) 86; Burke (1969) 152.

81. "Conversations with Drummond" in *Ben Jonson* (ed. C. H. Hereford and P. Simpson) (Oxford, 1925) vol. I 136. Cf. W. Trimpi *Ben Jonson's Poems: A Study of the Plain Style* (Stanford, 1962) 31.

82. J. Barish (ed.) *Ben Jonson: Sejanus* (New Haven, 1965) 1; D. Riggs *Ben Jonson: A Life* (Cambridge, Mass., 1988) 105 notes that it is Shakespeare's last appearance in a cast list.

83. *Sejanus* 2, 330. Line references are to the Barish edition.

84. Syme (1960) 3 comments that the text of Jonson brings together Tacitus and Machiavelli.

85. Jonson's letter to Lord Aubigny; cf. Barish *Ben Jonson: Sejanus* 25.

86. D. Riggs *Ben Jonson: A Life* 100; J. Barish *Ben Jonson: Sejanus* 16f.

87. J. Barish *Ben Jonson: Sejanus* 181 cites Hazlitt and points out that he quotes substantial extracts of Tacitus in his notes.

88. Epigram 92.

89. Eliot's speech is reprinted in John Foster *Sir John Eliot* (London, 1864) 541–552.

90. Tenney (1941) 161.

91. J. Mullinger *The University of Cambridge* III (Cambridge, 1911) 81–89 provides a full account of the Dorislaus affair. For more recent accounts, cf. R. Rebholz *The Life of Fulke Greville, First Lord Brooke* (Oxford, 1971) 292–302; K. Sharpe "The Foundation of the Chairs of History at Oxford and Cambridge: an Episode in Jacobean Politics" *History of Universities* 2(1982) 127–152 = K.

Sharpe *Politics and Ideas in Early Stuart England* (London, 1989) 207–229.

92. From the Dutch revolt Tacitus had been popular in Holland. Burke (1969) 155 reports that the great seventeenth-century historian P. C. Hooft, called "The Dutch Tacitus," had read his Roman predecessor fifty-two times!

93. Dr. Samuel Ward writing to Archbishop Usher, May 16, 1628; cf. J. Usher *Works* (London, 1847–1864) XV 402–405.

94. Mullinger *University of Cambridge* III 87–88 prints the Wren letter. Though Dorislaus' lecture does not seem to have survived, Wren sent excerpts of it to Archbishop Laud and both his rough notes and fair copy survive in the Public Record Office. I hope to publish these at a later time.

95. Tenney (1941) 158ff.; Schellhase (1976) 164f.

96. *Defence of the People of England* quoted in Kliger (1952) 147–148.

97. S. Davis "Triumph and Anti-Triumph: Milton's Satan and the Roman Emperors in *Paradise Lost*" *Etudes Anglaises* 34 (1981) 385–398.

98. Tenney (1941) 162.

99. *Germania* 7; 11.

100. Kliger (1952) 126.

101. Kliger (1952) 190ff.

102. La Penna in Bolgar (1976) 303.

103. Quoted by Miller (1969) 99.

104. Gay (1974) 25.

105. H. Benario "Gordon's Tacitus" *Classical Journal* 72 (1976–1977) 107–114.

106. H. T. Colbourn *The Lamp of Experience* (Chapel Hill, 1965) 7.

107. *The Spirit of the Laws* 11, 6. Borchardt (1971) 316 points out that Tacitus's Germans were the ancestors of the Dutch, Frankish French, and English as well as the modern Germans. This (inconvenient?) fact is sometimes forgotten.

108. Weinbrot (1980) 70.

109. Weinbrot (1992).

110. Cf. J. Clive "Gibbon's Humor" in Bowersock, Clive, and Graubard (1977) 183–191.

111. I 54 (Bury edition).

112. M. W. Brownley "Appearance and Reality in Gibbon's History" *Journal of the History of Ideas* 38 (1977) 651–666.

113. I 213 (Bury edition).

114. G. Giarrizzo "Toward the *Decline and Fall*: Gibbon's Other Historical Interests" in Bowersock, Clive, and Braubard (1977) 237.

115. Quinn (1984) 56.
116. Gay (1974) 22–23. Gibbon's onetime (and only) beloved, Susanne Curchod—later Mme. Neckar, the mother of Mme. de Stael—called Tacitus the model and perhaps the source of much of the *Decline and Fall*. Mme. Neckar *Miscellaneous Works* II 176–180.
117. G. W. Bowersock "Gibbon on Civil War and Rebellion in the Decline of the Roman Empire" in Bowersock, Clive, and Graubard (1977) 27ff.
118. On the theatricality, cf. R. Porter *Edward Gibbon: Making History* (London, 1988) 88f.
119. Von Stackelberg (1960) 149–158; Schellhase (1976) 166.
120. S. Caramella "Vico, Tacitus and Reason of State" in Tagliacozza, G. and White, H. (eds.) *Giambattista Vico* (Baltimore, 1969) 29.
121. Kelley (1992).
122. Voltaire was particularly offended by the *Germania*, but he elsewhere says of the account of Nero and Agrippina: "I was tempted to believe none of it" (*Le Pyrrhonisme de l'Histoire* chapter 13). Cf. Von Stackelberg (1960) 224–226.
123. *Voltaire's Correspondence* (ed. T. Besterman) vol. 69 (Geneva, 1961) Letter no. 14202.
124. I use the recent translation of Montesquieu by A. Cohler, B. Miller and H. Stone (Cambridge, 1989).
125. Parker (1937) 14ff. points out that Tacitus was read in seven of the ten collèges attended by important revolutionaries.
126. J. Von Stackelberg "Rousseau, D´Alembert et Diderot—traducteurs de Tacite" *Studi Francesi* 6 (1958) 395–407.
127. Momigliano (1990) 127.
128. Volpilhac-Auger (1985) 27–32.
129. *Principes politiques d'un souverain* Nr. 63, cited in Von Stackelberg (1960) 233.
130. Parker (1937) 18f.
131. Tacite en trait de flamme accuse nos Séjans
    Et son nom prononcé fait pâlir les tyrans.
    These lines are by Marie-Joseph Chénier, not his more famous brother André (as Schellhase [1976] 167 and Walker [1960] 282). Cf. Ramorino (1898) 71.
132. Cited in Von Stackelberg (1960) 238: "c'est également le règne des délateurs."
133. Quoted in Von Stackelberg (1960) 236–237; cf. also Parker (1937) 148.
134. Boissier (1906) 159.
135. Parker (1937) 149 points out that the reactionary paper *Actes des*

apôtres also used Tacitus and linked their Jacobin opponents with Tiberius and Nero.

136. Quoted in French in Von Stackelberg (1960) 235.

137. *Tableau historique de l'Etat* (3rd. ed.; 1818) 165 cited in Von Stackelberg (1960) 238.

138. Quoted in Janssens (1946) 311. (my translation)

139. Ramorino (1898) 71f.

140. *Mémoires du Prince de Talleyrand* (Paris, 1891) II 442–446. (my translation)

141. *Mémoires du Prince de Talleyrand* I 442–443. (my translation)

142. Quoted from Napoleon's discussion with J.-B. Suard in Wankenne (1967) 260.

143. Quoted in Von Stackelberg (1960) 243; Ramorino (1898) 71ff. and 107 n. 126.

144. Gummere (1963) 126.

145. M. Reinhold *Classica Americana: The Greek and Roman Heritage in the United States* (Detroit, 1984) 153.

146. Gummere (1963) 192.

147. H. T. Colbourn *The Lamp of Experience* (Chapel Hill, 1965) 26.

148. T. J. Luce "Tacitus" in Luce (1982) 1003.

149. L. J. Cappon *The Adams-Jefferson Letters* (Chapel Hill, 1959) II 291 (January 21, 1812); II 462 (February 2, 1816).

150. Gummere (1963) 179.

151. Janssens (1946) 311–319.

152. "Essay on History" in *The Complete Works of Thomas Babington Macaulay Critical and Historical Essays* (New York, 1910) I 262.

153. "Oration Delivered at Plymouth, December 22, 1802," (Boston, 1802) translates *Agricola* 32: "maiores vestros et posteros cogitate."

154. Henry Adams *The Education of Henry Adams* (Boston, 1974) 92.

155. White (1973) sees nineteenth-century historical writing as "poetic, scientific, and philosophical," behind the mask of "realism."

156. G. Lukács *The Theory of the Novel* (Cambridge, Mass., 1971) 112.

157. Quoted in Schellhase (1976) 171: F. Meinecke "The Year 1848 in German History" *Review of Politics* 10 (1948) 475–492.

158. T. A. Dorey *Tacitus* (London, 1969).

159. Syme (1958) 521: "The lessons that Tacitus is supposed to inculcate are by no means unequivocal."

Epilogue

1. J. Joyce *Finnegans Wake* (New York, 1970) 17.

❖ ———————————————————————— ❖
Editions and Translations

The three volumes of the Oxford Classical Texts are the most easily available Latin editions of Tacitus; the *Annals* and the *History* are edited by C. D. Fisher and the minor works by H. Furneaux. I have cited and translated Tacitus from these Oxford University Press editions.

The Loeb Classical Library, published by the Harvard University Press, prints in five volumes the complete works of Tacitus with Latin and English on facing pages. It is ideal for those whose rusty Latin needs help, or who wish to see the Latin for a particularly striking epigram. One volume contains the *Germania, Agricola,* and *Dialogus* with classic translations expertly revised by leading scholars. The detailed historical and geographical notes to the *Germania* by E. H. Warmington are particularly helpful. Four additional volumes contain the *Histories* and *Annals*, translated respectively by C. H. Moore and John Jackson. These are accurate, if inevitably a bit dated.

The most economical editions (and the easiest to read) now are the paperback translations issued by Penguin Books. Michael Grant's *Annals* is a very enjoyable read, though (alone of the translations here discussed) it does not provide paragraph numbers so that references cannot be easily checked. It has a useful introduction. Kenneth Wellesley's 1964 *Histories* is both accurate and readable, as befits the leading British scholar of this work. H. Mattingly's *Agricola* and *Germania* has an extended introduction.

Other good paperback translations include Donald Dudley's *Annals* (Mentor) and Herbert Benario's *Agricola, Germania and Dialogus* (Bobbs-Merrill)—the only paperback edition of the *Dialogus* now available.

For the more scholarly reader who desires help with a particular passage, Ronald Martin's *Tacitus* (Berkeley, 1981) provides an excellent guide to the range of available editions and commentaries, both in English and German, on all of Tacitus's works.

Bibliography of Works Cited

Allott, T. (1980) "Tacitus and Some Late Plays of Corneille" *Journal of European Studies* 10 pp. 32–47

Anderson, J. G. C. (1938) *Germania* (Oxford)

Auerbach, E. (1953) *Mimesis: The Representation of Reality in Western Literature* (Princeton)

Baldwin, B. (1972) "Women in Tacitus" *Prudentia* 4 pp. 83–101

Barnes, T. D. (1986) "The Significance of Tacitus' *Dialogus de Oratoribus*" *Harvard Studies in Classical Philology* 90 pp. 225–244

Baxter, R. T. S. (1971) "Virgil's Influence on Tacitus in Book 3 of the *Histories*" *Classical Philology* 66 pp. 93ff.

Benario, H. (1975) *An Introduction to Tacitus* (Athens, Ga.)

Benjamin, E. J. (1965) "Bacon and Tacitus" *Classical Philology* 60 pp. 102–110

Boissier, G. (1906) *Tacitus, and other Roman Studies* (London)

Bolgar, R. R. (1976) *Classical Influences in European Culture AD 1500–1700* (Cambridge)

Borchardt, F. L. (1971) *German Antiquity in Renaissance Myth* (Baltimore)

Borzsak, I. (1970) "Zum Verständnis der Darstellungskunst des Tacitus: Die Veränderungen des Germanicus-Bildes" *Acta Antiqua Academiae Scientiarum Hungaricae* 18 pp. 272–292

Bowersock, G. W., Clive, J., and Graubard, S. R. (1977) *Edward Gibbon and the Decline and Fall of the Roman Empire* (Cambridge, Mass.)

Bowersock, G. W. (1992) "Tacitus and the Province of Asia" in Luce, T. J. and Woodman, A. J. (eds.) *Tacitus and the Tacitean Tradition* (Princeton) forthcoming

Breissmann, A. (1955) *Tacitus und das flavische Geschichtsbild* (Wiesbaden)

Burke, P. (1966) "A Survey of the Popularity of Ancient Historians 1450–1700" *History and Theory* 5 pp. 135–152

Burke, P. (1969) "Tacitism" in Dorey, T. A. (ed.) *Tacitus* (London) 149–171

Butler, P. (1959) *Classicism et Baroque dans l'oeuvre de Racine* (Paris)

Classen, C.–J. (1988) "Tacitus—Historian between Republic and Principate" *Mnemosyne* 41 pp. 93–116

Cook, A. (1988) *History/Writing* (Cambridge)

Costa, C. D. N. (1969) "The *Dialogus*" in Dorey, T. A. (ed.) *Tacitus* (London) 19–33

Croll, M. (1966) *Style, Rhetoric and Rhythm* (Princeton)

Daitz, S. (1960) "Tacitus' Technique of Character Portrayal" *American Journal of Philology* 81 pp. 30–52

Dauge, Y. A. (1981) *Le Barbare: Recherches sur la conception romaine de la barbarie et de la civilisation* (Brussels) *Collection Latomus* vol. 176

Dorey, T. A. (1969) "'Agricola' and 'Germania'" in Dorey, T. A. (ed.) *Tacitus* (London) 1–18

Etter, E.–L. (1966) *Tacitus in der Geistesgeschichte des 16. und 17. Jahrhunderts* (Basel)

Ferrero, L. (1962) *Rerum Scriptor: Saggi sulla storiografia romana* (Trieste)

Fornara, C. (1983) *The Nature of History in Ancient Greece and Rome* (Berkeley)

Gay, P. (1974) *Style in History* (New York)

Gibbon, Edward *The History of the Decline and Fall of the Roman Empire* ed. J. B. Bury (London, 1897–1900) 7 volumes.

Gill, C. (1983) "The Question of Character-Development: Plutarch and Tacitus" *Classical Quarterly* 33 pp. 469–487

Ginsburg, J. (1981) *Tradition and Theme in the Annals of Tacitus* (Salem)

Ginsburg, J. (1992) "*In maiores certamina:* Past and Present in Tacitus' *Annals*" in Luce, T. J. and Woodman, A. J. (eds.) *Tacitus and the Tacitean Tradition* (Princeton) forthcoming

Goodyear, F. R. D. (1970a) *Tacitus* Greece and Rome, New Surveys in the Classics 4 (Oxford)

Goodyear, F. R. D. (1970b) "Cyclic Development in History: A Note on Tacitus *Ann.* 3.55.5" *Bulletin of the Institute of Classical Studies* 17 pp. 101–106

Goodyear, F. R. D. (1972; 1981) *The Annals of Tacitus: Books 1–6* (Cambridge) volumes I and II

Grant, M. (1970) *The Ancient Historians* (New York)

Gummere, R. M. (1963) *The American Colonial Mind and the Classical Tradition* (Cambridge, Mass.)

Güngerich, R. (1980) *Kommentar zum Dialogus des Tacitus* (Göttingen)

Hammond, M. (1963) "Res olim dissociabiles: Principatus ac Libertas" *Harvard Studies in Classical Philology* 67 pp. 93–113

Janssens, E. (1946) "Stendhal et Tacite" *Latomus* 5 pp. 311–319

Keitel, E. (1978) "The Role of Parthia and Armenia in Tacitus *Annals* 11 and 12" *American Journal of Philology* 99 pp. 462–473

Keitel, E. (1981) "Tacitus on the Deaths of Tiberius and Claudius" *Hermes* 109 pp. 206–214

Keitel, E. (1991) "The Structure and Function of Speeches in Tacitus' 'Histories'; I–III" *Aufstieg und Niedergang der römischen Welt* (Berlin) II 33.4 2772–2794

Keitel, E. (1992) "Speech and Narrative in Tacitus *Histories* IV" in Luce, T. J. and Woodman, A. J. (eds.) *Tacitus and the Tacitean Tradition* (Princeton) forthcoming

Kelley, D. (1992) "*Tacitus Noster:* The *Germania* in the Renaissance and Reformation" in Luce, T. J. and Woodman, A. J. (eds.) *Tacitus and the Tacitean Tradition* (Princeton) forthcoming

Kliger, S. (1952) *The Goths in England: A Study in Seventeenth and Eighteenth Century Thought* (Cambridge, Mass.)

Klingner, F. (1961) "Tacitus" in *Römische Geisteswelt* (Munich) pp. 490–513 [= *Die Antike* 8 (1932) pp. 151–169]

Laistner, M. L. W. (1947) *The Greater Roman Historians* (Berkeley)

Laugier, J.-L. (1969) *Tacite* (Paris)

Leeman, A. D. (1963) *Orationis Ratio* (Amsterdam)

Leeman, A. D. (1973) "Structure and Meaning in the Prologues of Tacitus" *Yale Classical Studies* 23 pp. 169–208

Leo, F. (1896) "Tacitus" (Göttingen) reprinted in Pöschl, V. (ed.) (1969) *Tacitus* (Darmstadt) 1–15

Lofstedt, E. (1948) "On the Style of Tacitus" *Journal of Roman Studies* 38 pp. 1–8

Lucas, J. (1974) *Les Obsessions de Tacite* (Leiden)

Luce, T. J. (ed.) (1982) *The Ancient Writers* (New York)

Luce, T. J. (1986) "Tacitus' Conception of Historical Change: The Problem of Discovering the Historian's Opinions" in Moxon, I. S., Smart, J. D., and Woodman, A. J. (eds.) *Past Perspectives* (Cambridge) 143–157

Luce, T. J. (1989) "Ancient Views on the Causes of Bias in Historical Writing" *Classical Philology* 84 pp. 16–31

Luce, T. J. (1991) "Tacitus on 'History's Highest Function': *Praecipuum Munus Annalium* (Ann. 3.65)" *Aufstieg und Niedergang der römischen Welt* (Berlin) II 33.4 2904–2927

Luce, T. J. (1992) "Reading and Response in the *Dialogus* of Tacitus" in Luce, T. J. and Woodman, A. J. (eds.) *Tacitus and the Tacitean Tradition* (Princeton) forthcoming

Luce, T. J. and Woodman, A. J. (eds.) (1992) *Tacitus and the Tacitean Tradition* (Princeton) forthcoming

McCulloch, H. Y. (1991) "The Historical Process and Theories of History in the 'Annals' and 'Histories' of Tacitus" *Aufstieg und Niedergang der römischen Welt* (Berlin) II 33.4 2928–2948

Malissard, A. (1991) "Le décor dans les 'Histoires' et les 'Annales': Du stéréotype à l'intention signifiante" *Aufstieg und Niedergang der romischen Welt* (Berlin) II 33.4 2832–2878

Marañon, G. (1956) *Tiberius* (London)

Marsh, F. B. (1931) *The Reign of Tiberius* (Oxford)

Martin, R. (1981) *Tacitus* (Berkeley and Los Angeles)

Martin, R. and Woodman, A. J. (1989) *Tacitus Annals Book IV* (Cambridge)

Martin, R. (1990) "Structure and Interpretation in the 'Annals' of Tacitus" *Aufstieg und Niedergang der römischen Welt* (Berlin) II 33.2 1500–1581

Mellor, R. (1987) "Roman Historiography and Biography" in M. Grant, and Kitzinger, R. (eds.) *Civilization of the Ancient Mediterranean* (New York) vol. III 1541–1562

Mendell, C. W. (1957) *Tacitus: The Man and His Work* (New Haven)

Michel, A. (1966) *Tacite et le destin de l'Empire* (Paris)

Miller, N. P. (1956) "The Claudian Tablet and Tacitus: A Reconsideration" *Rheinisches Museum* 99 pp. 304ff.

Miller, N. P. (1969) "Style and Content in Tacitus" in Dorey, T. A. (ed.) *Tacitus* (1969) 99–116

Miller, N. P. (1975) "Dramatic Speech in the Roman Historians" *Greece and Rome* 22 pp. 45–57

Miller, N. P. (1978) "Tacitus' Narrative Technique" *Greece and Rome* 25 pp. 13–22

Miller, N. P. (1987) "Talking About Tacitus" *Proceedings of the Classical Association* 84 pp. 7–14

Momigliano, A. (1937) "Tacitismo" in *Enciclopedia Italiana* vol. 33 pp. 172–173

Momigliano, A. (1947) "The First Political Commentary on Tacitus" *Journal of Roman Studies* 37 pp. 91–100 reprinted in *Essays in Ancient and Modern Historiography* (Middletown, 1977)

Momigliano, A. (1962) *Journal of Roman Studies* 52 pp. 282–283 (review of Von Stackelberg)

Momigliano, A. (1966) *Studies in Historiography* (New York)

Momigliano, A. (1990) *The Classical Foundations of Modern Historiography* (Berkeley)

Montesquieu, C. de. *The Spirit of the Laws* edited and translated by Cohler, A., Miller, B., and Stone, H. (Cambridge, 1989)

Morford, M. (1990) "Tacitus' Historical Methods in the Neronian Books of the 'Annals'" *Aufstieg und Niedergang der römischen Welt* (Berlin) II 33.2 1582–1627

Morford, M. (1992) "Tacitean *Prudentia* and the Doctrines of Justus Lipsius" in Luce, T. J. and Woodman, A. J. (eds.) *Tacitus and the Tacitean Tradition* (Princeton) forthcoming

Murphy, J. (1991) "Tacitus on the Education of the Orator" *Aufstieg und Niedergang der römischen Welt* (Berlin) II 33.3 2284–2297

Newbold, R. F. (1976) "The Vulgus in Tacitus" *Rheinische Museum für Philologie* 119 pp. 85–92

Ogilvie, R. M. and Richmond, I. (1967) *Agricola* (Oxford)

Ogilvie, R. M. (1991) "An Interim Report on Tacitus' 'Agricola'" *Aufstieg und Niedergang der römischen Welt* (Berlin) II 33.3 1714–1740

Otis, B. (1967) "The Uniqueness of Latin Literature" *Arion* 6 pp. 185–206

Parker, H. (1937) *The Cult of Antiquity and the French Revolutionaires* (Chicago)

Pelling, C. (1992) "Tacitus and Germanicus" in Luce, T. J. and Woodman, A. J. (eds.) *Tacitus and the Tacitean Tradition* (Princeton) forthcoming

Pippidi, D. M. (1944) *Autour de Tibère* (Bucharest)

Plass, P. (1988) *Wit and the Writing of History: The Rhetoric of Historiography in Imperial Rome* (Madison)

Quinn, K. (1963) *Latin Explorations: Critical Studies in Roman Literature* (London)

Quinn, K. (1979) *Texts and Contexts: The Roman Writers and Their Audience* (London)

Quinn, A. (1984) "'Meditating Tacitus': Gibbon's Adaptation to an Eighteenth Century Audience" *Quarterly Journal of Speech* 70 pp. 53–68

Ramorino, F. (1898) *Cornelio Tacito nella stòria della cultura* (Milan)

Reinhold, M. (1984) *Classica Americana: The Greek and Roman Heritage in the United States* (Detroit)

Ridé, J. (1977) *L'image du Germain dans la pensée et la littérature allemandes de la récouverte de Tacitus à la fin du XVIème siècle* (Lille–Paris) 3 volumes

Roberts, M. (1988) "The Revolt of Boudicca (Tacitus *Annals* 14, 29–39) and the assertion of Libertas in Neronian Rome" *American Journal of Philology* 109 p. 118–132

Ross, D. (1973) "The Tacitean Germanicus" *Yale Classical Studies* 23 pp. 209–227

Rutland, L. (1987) "The Tacitean Germanicus" *Rheinisches Museum* 130 pp. 153–164

Ryberg, I. S. (1942) "Tacitus' Art of Innuendo" *Transactions and Proceedings of the American Philological Association* 73 pp. 383–404

Sage, M. M. (1990) "Tacitus' Historical Works: A Survey and Appraisal" *Aufstieg und Niedergang der römischen Welt* (Berlin) II 33.2 853–1030

Salmon, J. H. M. (1980) "Cicero and Tacitus in Sixteenth Century France" *American Historical Review* 85 pp. 307–333

Schellhase, K. (1976) *Tacitus in Renaissance Political Thought* (Chicago)

Scott, R. T. (1968) *Religion and Philosophy in the Histories of Tacitus* (Rome)

Seager, R. (1972) *Tiberius* (Berkeley)

Segal, C. (1973) "Tacitus and Poetic History: The End of Annals XIII" *Ramus* 2 pp. 107–126

Sinclair, P. (1991) "Rhetorical Generalization in *Annals* 1–6: A Review of the Problem of Innuendo and Tacitus' Integrity" *Aufstieg und Niedergang der römische Welt* (Berlin) 33.4 2795–2831

Storoni-Mazzolani, L. (1976) *Empire Without End* (New York)

Syme, R. (1958) *Tacitus* 2 vol. (Oxford)

Syme, R. (1960) "Roman historians and Renaissance Politics" in *Society and History in the Renaissance* Folger Library (Washington)

Syme, R. (1970) Ten Studies in Tacitus (Oxford)

Syme, R. (1974) "History or Biography. The Case of Tiberius Caesar" *Historia* 23 pp. 481–496 (review of Seager *Tiberius*)

Tanner, R. G. (1991) "The Development of Thought and Style in Tacitus" *Aufstieg und Niedergang der römischen Welt* (Berlin) II 33.4 2689–2751

Tenney, M. F. (1935) "Tacitus Through the Centuries to the Age of Printing," *University of Colorado Studies* 22 pp. 341–363

Tenney, M. F. (1941) "Tacitus in the Politics of Early Stuart England" *Classical Journal* 37 pp. 151–163

Thomas, R. F. (1982) *Lands and Peoples in Roman Poetry: The Ethnographic Tradition* (Cambridge)

Toffanin, G. (1921) *Machiavelli e il tacitismo* (Padua) reprint Naples, 1972

Volpilhac-Auger, C. (1985) *Tacite et Montesquieu* Studies on Voltaire and the Eighteenth Century 232 (Oxford)

Von Fritz, K. (1957) "Tacitus, Agricola, Domitian, and the Problem of the Principate" *Classical Philology* 52 pp. 73–97

Von Stackelberg, J. (1960) *Tacitus in der Romania* (Tübingen)

Walker, B. (1960) *The Annals of Tacitus: a Study in the Writing of History* (Manchester; 2nd ed. reprint of 1952 edition)

Wallace-Hadrill, A. (1982) "Civilis Princeps: Between Citizen and King" *Journal of Roman Studies* 72 pp. 32–48

Wankenne, A. (1967) "Napoleon et Tacite" *Les Etudes Classiques* 35 pp. 260–263

Wardy, B. (1979) "Jewish Religion in Pagan Literature during the Late Republic and Early Empire" *Aufstieg und Niedergang der römische Welt* 19.1 pp. 592–644

Weinbrot, H. (1980) *Augustus Caesar in "Augustan" England* (Princeton)

Weinbrot, H. (1992) "Politics, Taste, and National Identity: Some Uses of Tacitism in Eighteenth-Century Britain" in Luce, T. J. and Woodman, A. J. (eds.) *Tacitus and the Tacitean Tradition* (Princeton) forthcoming

Wellesley, K. (1954) "Can You Trust Tacitus?" *Greece and Rome* 1 pp. 13–33

Wellesley, K. (1969) "Tacitus as a Military Historian" in T. A. Dorey, (ed.) *Tacitus* (London) 63–97

Wellesley, K. (1972) (ed.) *Tacitus The Histories Book III* (Sydney)

White, H. (1973) *Metahistory: The Historical Imagination in Nineteenth-Century Europe* (Baltimore)

Williams, G. (1978) *Change and Decline: Roman Literature in the Early Empire* (Berkeley)

Winterbottom, M. (1970) "Introduction to *Dialogus de Oratoribus*" in *Tacitus* vol. I Loeb Classical Library (Cambridge, Mass.)

Wirszubski, C. (1950) *Libertas as a Political Idea at Rome* (Cambridge)

Wiseman, T. P. (1979) *Clio's Cosmetics* (Leicester)

Woodman, A. J. (1975) "Questions of Date, Genre and Style in Velleius: Some Literary Answers" *Classical Quarterly* 25 pp. 272–306

Woodman, A. J. (1977) *Velleius Paterculus: The Tiberian Narrative* (Cambridge)

Woodman, A. J. (1979) "Self-Imitation and the Substance of History: Tacitus *Annals* 1.61–65 and *Histories* 2.70, 5.14–15" in West, D. and Woodman, A. J. (eds.) *Creative Imitation and Latin Literature* (Cambridge)

Woodman, A. J. (1988) *Rhetoric in Classical Historiography* (London)

Woodman, A. J. (1989) "Tacitus' Obituary of Tiberius" *Classical Quarterly* 39 pp. 197–204

Woodman, A. J. (1992) "Amateur Dramatics at the Court of Nero (*Annals* 15.48–74) in Luce, T. J. and Woodman, A. J. (eds.) *Tacitus and the Tacitean Tradition* (Princeton) forthcoming

Index

Roman names are listed under their most familiar element—sometimes the *nomen* (Julius Caesar) and sometimes the *cognomen* (Cicero)

Index of Passages Translated

Printed in the United Kingdom
by Lightning Source UK Ltd.
‏024UK00001B/241-243/P

9 780415 910026